Enhancing and Capturing More Value from the Caribbean Community's Value Chains

Enhancing and Capturing More Value from the Caribbean Community's Value Chains

By

Don Charles

Cambridge
Scholars
Publishing

Enhancing and Capturing More Value from the Caribbean Community's Value Chains

By Don Charles

This book first published 2019

Cambridge Scholars Publishing

Lady Stephenson Library, Newcastle upon Tyne, NE6 2PA, UK

British Library Cataloguing in Publication Data
A catalogue record for this book is available from the British Library

ISBN (10): 1-5275-2815-4
ISBN (13): 978-1-5275-2815-4

TABLE OF CONTENTS

CHAPTER ONE

GENERAL INTRODUCTION

1.0 Background and Motivation

Globalization has brought significant change to the international trade arena. Improvement in technology and communication has allowed better connections between the private sector, government, and labour actors in all parts of the world. Many companies, in seeking to cut costs to achieve better productive efficiency opt to outsource their most inefficient operations to more efficient producers. This has resulted in a transformation of the production process for goods to the point where currently very few producers actually produce every component of a final product. In fact, each producer produces only one or a few parts of an entire product, giving rise to the concept of the value chain, which is a vast web of production processes spread over various actors, and often over various countries.

A value chain is the set of activities that is required to bring a product or service from conception, to production, to the consumption of the consumer. Production of a final product involves the utilization of several inputs, each of which could have been produced by different actors. The objective of a profit maximizing firm is to minimize costs and maximize revenue. Since costs are not uniformly distributed among all stakeholders in every country, the cost of production is lower among some producers and countries than others. Some firms seeking to capture cost advantages may shift various stages of their production process to low cost areas, and sell their final product in markets where they can maximize their revenue. Thus, the global value chain (GVC) is the network of different actors,[1] and production processes, in various countries involved in producing and delivering a final product to a consumer.

It is noteworthy that while cost advantages may be the main driver of GVCs in some industries and businesses, they are not the sole driver of global value chains. The main drivers include the endowments of natural resources

---

[1] GVCs link firms, workers, governments, regulators, and consumers.

and factors of production, economies of scale, learning and spillovers, varying patterns of capacity utilization, interrelationships and integration, locational factors, and institutional factors.

Nevertheless, GVCs offer opportunities for businesses to source inputs globally, enhance efficiency, improve profitability, and increase their gains from international trade. GVCs allow the specialization and concentration of activities to go to specific actors and locations. For instance, the extraction and intermediate production of raw materials are off-shored to geographic locations richly endowed with the natural resource, the processing of primary products into immediate products could be concentrated at locations which have good access to capital and automation processes, while activities which are heavily reliant upon research could be concentrated at locations with good access to universities with strong research work programmes.

Since the publication of Michael Porter's book, *Competitive Advantage,* global value chain analysis (GVCA) has been applied by many researchers to map the activities involved in production as well as the critical path to move a product from its inception to the hands of the consumer. GVCA allows one to understand how global industries are organized by examining the roles and interrelationships between various stakeholders involved in an industry. GVCA allows a viewer to get a holistic view of an entire industry from both the top-down and bottom-up aspect.

Gereffi and Fernandez-Stark (2016) assert that GVCA is comprised of six basis dimensions: i) an input-output structure; ii) the geographic scope; iii) the governance structure; iv) the prospects for upgrading; v) the local economic and social elements; and vi) the interrelationships between the local industry stakeholders.

The input-output structure is part of the top-down approach which considers the various processes involved in coordinating the transformation of inputs into final products. Secondly, the geographic scope considers in which countries specific segments of the GVC are predominantly located.

The third aspect of the top-down approach is the issue of governance, and which actors control which parts of the GVC. In many cases, GVCs are controlled by large multinational firms. They situate various stages of their production at locations which would provide an advantage, then they export and sell their final product in various markets. Small micro enterprises (SMES) also form part of the larger GVC. While they do not control the overall GVC, they are often large in number, and occupy a very small part of the overall value chain, focusing on producing inputs, providing support services, distributing, or selling the final product to the consumer.

The bottom-up approach includes the latter three dimensions. The prospect for upgrading refers to the extent to which local producers can innovate and improve their production processes, and/or participate in more segments of the GVC. Upgrading would be affected by local and social elements, which in turn are determined by the local factor conditions, the interrelation between local stakeholders, and the enabling environment provided by the government.

GVCs have implications for countries' investment, production, and trade, which in turn affect their economic activity and economic prosperity. GVCA can be used to analyse a country's industrial performance, assess its constraints, and inform recommendations and strategies to help improve its industry and trade performance. In fact, GVCA would be an excellent tool to be applied to the industrial performance of small developing economies that are faced with a range of supply side constraints that limit the extent in which they actually achieve economic benefits from international trade.

The countries in the Caribbean region are one such group of countries that grapple with supply side constraints. They are small in size (in terms of land size, population size, and economy (national output)), but heterogeneous in structure. Historically, agriculture was the main economic activity in all the islands. However, the gradual erosion of trade preferences in the export of agricultural commodities to the European market motivated the governments of some of the Caribbean Community (CARICOM) member states to diversify into new industries.

Currently, production and export in the CARICOM region are concentrated among a few industries. Agriculture based exports remain important in some economies, but it continues to be threatened by weather-related natural disasters. Some of the member states have managed to diversify their production structures towards services.

Also notable is the general energy insecurity of the region. With the exception of Trinidad and Tobago (T&T), as recent as 2018, all of the member states were net importers of hydrocarbon products for energy production and consumption. T&T has commercial hydrocarbon reserves and currently produces and exports crude oil and natural gas. Guyana also has commercial hydrocarbon reserves, and is set to become a major producer and exporter post 2020.

The region is also characterized by a high degree of trade openness. There is a large number of small and micro enterprises (SMEs) in each member state, but presently, they do not actively participate in cross border interregional trade. The policy makers drafting and signing the Revised Treaty of Chaguaramas establishing the Caribbean Community, including the CARICOM Single Market and Economy (CSME), recognized the importance of SMEs to the international trade within the region. This is reflected in the Preamble of the Revised Treaty which asserts

> *Recognising also the potential of micro, small and medium enterprise development to contribute to the expansion and viability of national economies of the Caribbean Community and the importance of large enterprises for achieving economies of scale in the production process.* (CARICOM Secretariat 2001, 1)

Yet the SMEs still lack the correct enabling framework to help leverage their productive capacities and increase their participation in international trade.

1.1 Objective

There is a high demand for resources to address a wide range of developmental challenges, but the resources of the Governments of the CARICOM member states are finite. Given the opportunity costs associated with such a central economic problem, the industrial policy of the Governments of the CARICOM member states should focus on picking winners rather than supporting losers. It is against this backdrop that a global value chain analysis framework should be used, to identify potential "winning industries" which require better policies and an enabling environment to facilitate success and economic prosperity. Furthermore, a global value chain analysis framework is needed to properly determine how CARICOM's producers may upgrade and capture more value from the global value chain.

This book presents various case studies which analyse some of the prevalent constraints experienced in industries in the CARICOM member states. However, the main objective of this book is to identify practical policy recommendations which can be used to address such challenges, and allow the member states to capture more value from their industries' global value chains. Thus, this book is industry- and trade policy-oriented since its recommendations can help member states realize better gains from trade.

1.2 Book Outline

This book is structured as follows. The first case study is provided in Chapter Two. It undertakes a GVCA of the Agriculture Industry in T&T. T&T historically was a producer and exporter of a variety of agricultural products. In fact, in 1985, T&T's agriculture sector contributed approximately 3.02 per cent of the country's GDP. From the 1990s to the 2000s, the gradual erosion of preferences in agricultural exports to the European Union (EU) market, as well as declining agricultural productivity led to a significant contraction in the country's agricultural output and its contribution to GDP.

When the International Revealed Comparative Advantage (IRCA) index is applied to T&T agricultural export data over the 2000 to 2015 period, it reveals that the only products in the agriculture value chain in which T&T ever had any comparative advantage were Sugar/sugar prep/honey (SITC 06), Miscellaneous food products (SITC 06), Beverages (SITC 11), Tobacco/manufactures (SITC 12), Crude fertilizer/minerals (SITC 27), and Manufactured fertilizers (SITC 56). The data suggest that sugar is the only primary agricultural product in which the country ever had a comparative advantage, but it was lost after the year 2005.

The Government of the Republic of Trinidad and Tobago (GORTT) would face two dilemmas in the agriculture industry. On one hand, the dependence on the remaining farmers on agriculture, as well as the need to safeguard some amount of domestic production to partially satisfy domestic consumption needs, presents an argument for government policy to try to encourage primary agricultural production. On the other hand, the present comparative advantages lie in fertilizers and agro-processing rather than primary production. Therefore, as the government would have finite resources, it would be rational to focus government policy on enhancing areas where the country is strong, and can perform well in international trade.

Regardless of whether the GORTT decides to provide some policy support to uncompetitive primary agriculture, and the competitive fertilizer and agro-processing segments of the agriculture value chain, this chapter explores the constraints experienced in each segment, and the prospects for upgrading.

Thc second case study in this book is presented in Chapter Three, and undertakes a global value chain analysis of the maritime industry in T&T. The country's maritime sector is comprised of port operations, ship repair, leisure marine (yachting) and marine services. In 2018, the GORTT announced plans to develop a ship repair facility in La Brea in Trinidad. This move is a bold step in the right direction, as it has potential to create significant commerce through a multiplier effect. However, all of the segments of T&T's maritime sector are interrelated and affect each other. For instance, the efficiency of customs and immigration affects the import of goods, and the immigration and length of stay of leisure marine tourists. Since many of the intermediate products for the ship repair works must be imported, the efficiency of the ports affects the supply of the products for ship repair. T&T's international trade, the bunkering and transshipment occurring in the Gulf of Paria, and the inflow of leisure marine tourists all influence the amount of work available for ship repair stakeholders. Therefore, in order to maximize the value that can be captured from any segment of T&T's maritime value chain, the challenges in the entire value chain must be addressed.

This chapter examines the competitiveness factors for T&T's maritime sector and the challenges and supply side bottlenecks that act to restrict the development of the maritime sector, and considers some potential strategies to address the challenges. Moreover, attention is also placed on how T&T may upgrade along the maritime value chain.

Chapter Four extends the global value chain analysis to the banana industry in Dominica. In 2017, the Commonwealth of Dominica was hit by Hurricane Maria. The hurricane did significant damage to the country's infrastructure, and completely wiped out its banana crop. The occurrence of the hurricanes, the gradual erosion of trade preferences to the EU market, and the persistence of diseases (especially the Black Sigatoka disease) continue to threaten Dominica's banana industry.

Dominica participates only in the primary production segment of the banana global value chain. Its producers are small-scale farmers, who are also price takers. The banana global value chain is currently dominated by large vertically integrated producers, large-scale retailers, and large supermarket chains purchasing the product. The small-scale producers have no choice but to accept whatever is given to them.

In moving forward, the Government of Dominica is committed to building climate resilience within its country's banana industry. The government announced plans to create a new state-owned organization, the Climate Resilient Execution Agency for Dominica (CREAD), which will lead the country's recovery and execute projects within a climate resilient national plan over a four-year period. Technological projects such as the installation of early warning systems, as well as ecosystem-based projects such as ecological restoration and better soil management practices are good initiatives which can be adopted to help build the country's climate resilience.

More value added can be extracted from bananas through the agro-processing of bananas. Therefore, it would be sensible for the country to seek partnerships to help develop new capacity in the agro-processing of bananas and its by-products into processed foods, medical products, and consumer goods.

From Chapter Five, this book starts considering case studies involving more than one country in the CARICOM region. As previously mentioned, both T&T and Guyana have commercial reserves of hydrocarbons. Currently, there are multinationals producing and exporting the hydrocarbons in T&T. The multinational in Guyana is set to commence its hydrocarbon export from 2020. The multinationals operating in both countries will make supernormal profits from the hydrocarbon exports. However, in the absence of an adequate correct policy framework to allow the benefits of the hydrocarbon industry to spill over to the local population, the locals will be mere spectators of their hydrocarbon industry rather than true actors.

A comprehensive local content policy (LCP) that includes local content requirements (LCRs) is needed for both countries to correct this deficiency. There is scope to use an LCP and LCRs to strengthen the backward and forward linkages between the hydrocarbon and non-hydrocarbon sectors in both economies.

It is noteworthy that LCRs are contrary to the WTO's non-discriminatory principles established in its Trade Related Investment Measures (TRIMs) agreement. But there is a double standard in this non-discriminatory principle. In fact, the United States (US), which was very eager to raise a dispute at the WTO against India for its "Make in India" and "Digital India" programmes, has many LCRs providing preferential treatment to its locals in several of its states. International trade rules should not be restrictive for developing countries and supportive for developed countries. It is the responsibility of governments in developing countries to implement policies which can develop their people. And a comprehensive LCP can help the governments of T&T, and Guyana achieve this.

Chapter Six addresses the energy insecurity challenge in the CARICOM region. With the exception of T&T, the islands in the region are net importers of hydrocarbon energy resources, resulting in a high energy import bill. Contrastingly, all of the CARICOM member states experience a good supply of solar energy. Thus, there is an untapped potential in solar energy.

The solar photovoltaic panel global value chain is comprised of segments for the production of silicon crystals, ingots, wafers, cells, and modules, and the installation of the final product. Presently, there is limited participation of stakeholders in the installation segment in the solar photovoltaic panel value chain in CARICOM.

The region has a number of factors that favour increase participation along the solar photovoltaic value chain. Given that strong research capacity is required for the production of high efficiency photovoltaic crystals, ingots, and wafers it is unlikely that any CARICOM firm can emerge as a significant global player in these segments on their own. The main components of a solar system that CARICOM member states may consider manufacturing domestically are the solar cells, solar modules, inverters, trackers, mounting structures and general electrical components. Moreover, CARICOM firms can consider developing partnerships with more experienced international producers to help develop their local competencies. Furthermore, the governments of the region have a key role to play in using policy to provide an enabling environment to encourage the development of the solar energy industry in the region.

Chapter Seven considers a strategy for strengthening the CARICOM region's intra-regional trade. The CSME was created to establish a common market and encourage significant intra-regional trade. In practice the intra-regional trade is weak relative to its inter-regional trade with its extra-regional trading partners. Moreover, the intra-regional trade is dominated by T&T and its large-scale producers.

While the governments in each member state tend to be significant employers, they cannot employ every person. An alternative would be for people to seek employment opportunities in the private sector. Unfortunately, the multinationals and the foreign direct investment (FDI) are attracted to the mineral-rich countries. Additionally, the multinationals tend to employ a small percentage of the labour force, even in the hydrocarbon-rich economies. Therefore, some people have no choice but to become entrepreneurs in order to earn a living. Given that many of the people who become entrepreneurs do not have a vast amount of physical or financial capital to engage in business, they are likely to become SMEs. These SMEs tend to service the domestic populations with their supply of goods and services, and do not actively engage in cross-border trade.

The size of operations may limit traditional international trade. Indeed, in traditional sea-based cargo, trade importers may request their suppliers to provide at least a container of their exports on a weekly basis. SMEs may not have the capacity to fill a container on such a frequent basis. However, technology has revolutionized international trade. The internet and electronic commerce (e-commerce) have made it viable for smaller scale suppliers to ship small quantities of products to consumers in different geographic locations. The SMEs in the developed countries are already reaping the benefits of international trade through e-commerce, while some developing countries are lagging behind.

Indeed, it is time for the governments of the CARICOM member states to unlock the e-commerce highway for their SMEs. This chapter assesses the readiness of Barbados, Jamaica, and Trinidad and Tobago, three CARICOM member states, to enable their SMEs to engage in cross-border e-commerce. Cross-border e-commerce is advocated as a strategy to promote SME value chains in the region. This chapter also places emphasis on identifying the correct policy framework to facilitate cross-border e-commerce.

1.3 Summary Insight

Globalization has allowed firms to shift different parts of the production process to various geographic locations which may generate an advantage. As a result, the production of goods and services is very fragmented. Due to this fragmentation there is a need for appropriate policy in countries to try and capture more engagement and value in global value chains. In order to better inform such policy, the global value chain analysis framework can be used to determine countries' current level of participation in global value chains, critically examine the bottlenecks that constrain production, and assess the prospects for upgrading. Certainly, the global value chain analysis framework can be a useful tool to analyse the industries in the CARICOM region, and inform policy to improve their gains from international trade.

Indeed, the industries in the CARICOM member states continue to be confronted by a series of challenges which in turn curb their gains from trade. The economies historically relied on agriculture as a means to earn export earnings and finance their consumption of imported products. But the WTO ushered in a new era of trade liberalization that gradually eroded the member states' preferential treatment. The remaining farmers in the primary agriculture industry continue to be confronted by a multitude of challenges, which can range from adverse weather conditions, to pests and diseases. In order for the remaining farmers to survive in the primary agriculture industry, they need climate resilient agriculture strategies. While the small-scale farmers have a comparative disadvantage in primary agriculture relative to large-scale producers in Latin America, it is still important to encourage some amount of domestic production to partially satisfy domestic consumption needs.

The hydrocarbon-rich economies are fortunate to have the option of using their hydrocarbon endowments to diversify away from agriculture. Certainly, a hydrocarbon exporting facility will generate more revenue than a 2-acre farm cultivating legal crops. But how much of the total value produced in the hydrocarbon carbon economies will be captured by the locals? Local content policy could be used to ensure that the nationals of an economy can capture their fair share of the total value.

An alternative challenge in the CARICOM member states is the vulnerability generated from high oil prices, and the statistical change in weather patterns caused by increased greenhouse gas (GHG) emissions and the greenhouse effect. Greater investments in solar energy could be used as a strategy to collectively mitigate the effects of climate change, while at the same time generating commerce and employment opportunities.

The economies can also consider the development of the sub-industries in the maritime sector as a means of diversification. Attention should also be placed on improving the enabling environment for SMEs so they can also reap the benefits from international trade.

These case studies explored in this book attempt to examine some of the industries in the CARICOM region. The findings and the recommendations can be used to help inform and improve the trade policy and industrial policy of member states within the region.

References

CARICOM (Caribbean Community) Secretariat. 2001. "Revised Treaty of Chaguaramas Establishing the Caribbean Community including the CARICOM Single Market and Economy." Accessed September 1, 2018. https://caricom.org/documents/4906-revised_treaty-text.pdf.

Gereffi, Garry, and Karina Fernandez-Stark. 2016. *Global Value Chain Analysis: A Primer. 2nd Edition.* Durham, NC: Center on Globalization, Governance & Competitiveness (CGGC), Duke University.

CHAPTER TWO

GLOBAL VALUE CHAIN ANALYSIS OF THE AGRICULTURE INDUSTRY IN T&T

Abstract

Trinidad and Tobago (T&T), a twin island state in the Caribbean region, has historically been a producer of a variety of agricultural products. From the 1990s to the present, T&T's production and export of agricultural primary products have been drastically reduced. However, an agro-processing industry has emerged in the country over the associated period. Crafting policy to encourage agricultural production and agro-processing in T&T requires an understanding of how the country participates in the global value chain. This study takes an in-depth look at the agriculture/agro-processing industry in T&T. Moreover, this study reviews T&T's position in the global value chain for agriculture and agro-processing, and considers policy action to facilitate upgrading.

2.1 Introduction

For many countries, increasing integration into the global economy provides an opportunity to assess a wider range of goods and services and increase their economic incomes, and economic wellbeing. Notably, preferential trade agreements tend to increase export market assessment opportunities for agro-industry products. This presents opportunities for developing countries, which often produce various agro-industry commodities.

While increased market access offers many opportunities for the economic growth of exporting countries, developing countries are often daunted by a number of challenges. Among these challenges are bottlenecks in production and distribution, intense competition, and high-quality standards imposed by international consumers. Hence, there is a need for a comprehensive approach to value chain management in order for developing countries to capture the benefits from international trade.

Global value chains (GVCs), as defined by Gereffi and Fernandez-Stark (2011), is a full range of activities that firms and workers perform in order to bring a product from its conception to its end use. The main activities in a value chain include the sourcing of inputs, production, marketing and distribution of the product to the consumer. As opposed to focusing only on production, value chain analysis focuses on the creation of value at every stage, thereby treating production as just one stage in a larger value-adding chain. The fact that the value-adding activities are increasing, spread across several countries, makes the value chain "global" (Greenville et al. 2017).

A value chain in agriculture is the set of activities performed by various actors which brings an agricultural good from the field to final consumption, while adding value to each stage of the production process (WTO and OECD 2013). The development of agro-industry value chains can be beneficial to economies as it presents an opportunity to capture more value added from domestically produced agricultural products, offer more sustainable employment for farmers, and create business opportunities for small and medium enterprises (SMEs). Furthermore, it can also enhance food security by reducing post-harvest losses and by extending the shelf life of agricultural products (UNIDCO 2009).

Trinidad and Tobago (T&T), a small twin island state in the Caribbean, confronts numerous internal development challenges as it aspires to transition from an energy-dependent to a diversified economy. In fact, apart from energy and energy-related products, the twin island state has demonstrated relative competitiveness in producing agro-industry products for export in several markets. Indeed, global value chain analysis of the agro-processing industry would be of use for the policy makers of the country as it could provide a greater understanding on how to deepen the productive base of the economy, generate more employment and income-earning economic activity, and facilitate sustainable economic growth. By the examination of the country's strengths and weaknesses, value chain analysis may help policy makers to identify corrective measures, investment priorities, and development opportunities.

The main objectives of this chapter are to i) determine T&T's position in the agro-processing global value chain; ii) map the agro-processing value chain to provide insight into the activities, key actors, and relationships involved in the value chain; and iii) identify a strategy for upgrading along the value chain.

This chapter is structured as follows. Section 2.2 provides an overview of the global agro-processing industry. Section 2.3 assesses Trinidad and Tobago's position in the agro-processing industry's global value chain. Section 2.4 applies the diamond competitiveness model to examine T&T's agro-processing industry. Section 2.5 focuses on the challenges experienced in T&T's cluster. Section 2.6 considers policy measures which can be used to facilitate upgrading in the value chain. Section 2.7 concludes the chapter.

2.2 Global Agriculture Industry

The agriculture industry encompasses the cultivation of products for food. It includes the harvesting of crops and plants, the rearing of livestock, and the processing of intermediate food production into final products. The agriculture industry also includes florists, greenhouses, aquaculture, and nurseries. However, for the purposes of this report, the agriculture industry will refer to the production of food products, both intermediated, and processed final goods. Thus, the agriculture or agro-food industry refers to the production, processing, promotion, and distribution of agricultural products.

The agriculture industry is essential for the economic prosperity of countries. Directly, the agriculture sector provides the foods that people need for nutrition. Thus, it can afford food security to nations. However, the agriculture industry has extended benefits as it may act as a source of income. In fact, both small-scale producers and large-scale enterprises can generate income, although of varying proportions. Agriculture's income generation role for small-scale producers is of significance as it can be used to address poverty, one of the Sustainable Development Goals.

At a macroeconomic level, some countries may specialize in agricultural production, earning a significant share of their total export revenue. Other countries may opt for the net import of agricultural output. For the importing countries, increasing their production of domestic agricultural output may reduce their agricultural import dependence, and improve their balance of trade. Moreover, given that foreign exchange is required to purchase agro-industry imports, the production of agricultural products domestically can reduce foreign exchange consumption pressures.

Agriculture GVCs are complex, expanding with the use of biotechnology and information systems, and are under pressure to increase output and quality. As there are multiple agricultural products, each product can fit within its own GVC, resulting in multiple GVCs for the agriculture industry (Ahmed and Hamrick 2015). For simplicity, assume there is one main agriculture value chain comprised of multiple segments. Figure 2.1 provides an overview of the agriculture industry value chain.

Figure 2.1: Agriculture Industry Global Value Chain

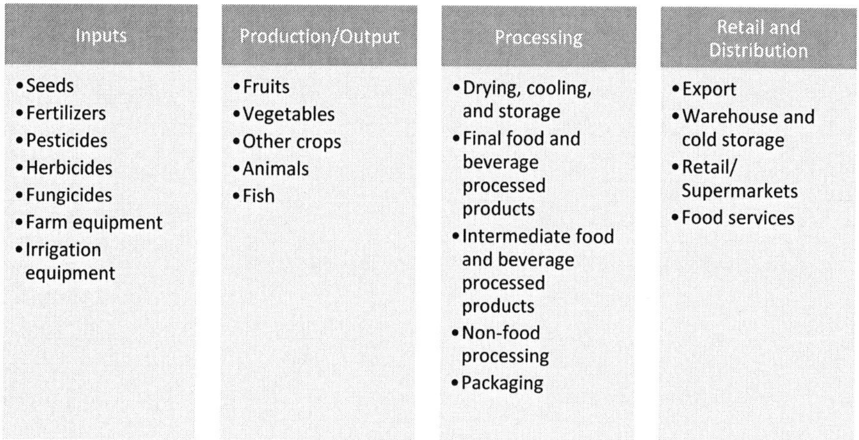

As can be seen in Figure 2.1, the first column in the chain, "Inputs," refers to the main intermediate products that are necessary for producing agricultural output. It includes the seeds for crops, fertilizers, herbicides, and pesticides as well as the tools and equipment necessary for production. The agricultural input segment to a large extent determines the output of the following production segment.

Within the past forty years, the agricultural seed industry has transformed from one that was primarily composed of small, family-owned farms/businesses, into an industry dominated by a small number of transnational pharmaceutical/chemical corporations (Howard 2009). In the United States (US) many farmers purchase their seeds rather than using seeds saved from previous harvests. The seed business has evolved to one that integrates plant breeding to improve agricultural output. In fact, seeds are also exported globally, to the extent that small-scale farmers can purchase imported seeds to cultivate their crops.

As can be seen in Table 2.1, the global seed export industry was a US$70 billion industry in 2016. The US is the top exporter of seeds worldwide, with their 35% market share of total world seed exports. With regard to other major regions, Latin America and the Caribbean (LAC) ranks number 2 in global seed exports, followed by the EU-27 region.

Table 2.1: Top Seed Exporters (countries/regions)

	2000	2010	2015	2016	2000	2010	2015	2016
Export Share					Export Value US$1,000			
United States	0.41	0.35	0.29	0.35	$5,763,369	$19,782,449	$20,770,560	$24,757,528
China	0.03	0.01	0.01	0.01	$416,675	$707,202	$1,017,145	$975,117
Japan	0.00	0.00	0.00	0.00	$726	$2,399	$6,049	$9,515
EU-27	0.11	0.12	0.10	0.10	$1,579,669	$6,574,841	$7,219,119	$7,235,241
Sub-Saharan Africa	0.02	0.03	0.02	0.00	$323,217	$1,580,017	$1,092,071	$310,490
Latin America- Caribbean	0.26	0.34	0.40	0.37	$3,741,884	$19,073,600	$29,027,855	$26,157,727
All countries					$14,209,790	$56,208,848	$72,041,139	$70,617,300

Source: WITS (2017a)

With regard to individual companies, the top firms in the global seed-producing industry are displayed in Table 2.2.

Table 2.2: Top Seed-producing Firms Globally

Company – 2007	Seed sales (US$ millions)	% of global proprietary seed market
Monsanto (US)	$4,964 m	23%
DuPont (US)	$3,300 m	15%
Syngenta (Switzerland)	$2,018 m	9%
Groupe Limagrain (France)	$1,226 m	6%
Land O' Lakes (US)	$917 m	4%
KWS AG (Germany)	$702 m	3%
Bayer Crop Science (Germany)	$524 m	2%
Sakata (Japan)	$396 m	<2%
DLF-Trifolium (Denmark)	$391 m	<2%
Takii (Japan)	$347 m	<2%
Top 10 Total	$14,785 m	67% [of the global proprietary seed market]

Source: GM Watch (2009)

Monsanto, a US-based firm, captured 23% of the global proprietary seed industry in 2007. It was closely followed by DuPoint, another US-based firm, then by Syngenta, a Switzerland based firm. Collectively, the top three companies accounted for 47% of the global proprietary seed industry.

The top firms in the seed industry achieve and maintain their dominant status by conducting scientific research and genetic modification of seeds, which in turn produce high yielding agricultural products. Moreover, the Gene Giants have used intellectual property laws to secure their oligopolistic power over the industry (Fernandez-Cornejo 2004; GM Watch 2009; Howard 2009, 2015).[2]

[2] Seeds were previously a common resource that was not controlled by governments or firms. Subsequently, innovations could benefit anyone. However, in the US, the right to save and replant seeds has been increasingly restricted. There was a granting of full patent protections on transgenic seeds, to legally prevent the saving of seeds

The agro-chemical industry is comprised of the fertilizer, pesticide, herbicide and fungicide industries. Fertilizer, which refers to any material of natural or synthetic origin that is used as nutrients for crops, is used to increase agricultural output, especially in monoculture farming. Pesticides and herbicides are complementary to fertilizers since monoculture fields are highly attractive to certain weeds and insect pests. Additionally, the ability for crop diseases to wipe out the entire agricultural output where monoculture farming is practised provides justification for fungicides.

The three main macronutrients of fertilizers are Nitrogen, Phosphorus, and Potassium. Ammonia is a compound of nitrogen and hydrogen, and is also used as the main ingredient for fertilizer. Urea, which is comprised of carbon, nitrogen, and oxygen, is also used for the production of fertilizer. The secondary macronutrients of fertilizers are sulphur, magnesium, and calcium. Out of the aforementioned macronutrients, nitrogen is most important for higher crop yields (Yara 2014).[3]

As can be seen from Table 2.3, the top exporters of ammonia in 2015 were T&T, with its 21% market share; Russia, with its 18% market share, Saudi Arabia with its 16% market share; then followed by Canada with its 10% market share. Collectively, the top four ammonia exporting countries represent 65.1% of total ammonia exports in 2015. Such dominance in the ammonia industry stems from the aforementioned countries' factor endowments in natural gas.

However, when considering the top fertilizer exporters for 2015, China emerges as the number one exporter with its 19% market share, followed by Russia and Canada with shares of 16% and 11% respectively. It is notable that when the entire fertilizer industry is considered, T&T only has approximately 1% of total exports, in contrast to its dominance in the ammonia industry. Globally, the top ammonia producing firms are Yara, CF Industries, the DF Group, and PotashCorp.

---

from produced crops. Furthermore, the US seed industry also became more oligopolistic due to the mergers and acquisitions of multiple small firms into larger ones from the 1970s to the present (Howard 2015).

[3] Note: nitrogen fertilizers can also be linked to the natural gas industry's global value chain. However, for simplicity, only the agriculture value chain is considered in this chapter.

Table 2.3: Top Ammonia Exporters (SITC rev 3. 52261)

	2000	2010	2015	2016	2000	2010	2015	2016
Export Value (US$1,000)					Export share			
T&T	359878	1376692	1640193	n.d.	20%	25%	21%	n.d.
Russia	286960	746515	1356205	828540	16%	13%	18%	27%
Saudi Arabia	n.d.	n.d.	1245060	n.d.	n.d.	n.d.	16%	0%
Canada	203810	462054	728138	641067	11%	8%	10%	21%
Indonesia	135816	373257	434208	330946	7%	7%	6%	11%
Ukraine	193524	372026	252105		10%	7%	3%	0%
Australia	93	146352	215678	98426	0%	3%	3%	3%
Malaysia	7598	154110	131677	133785	0%	3%	2%	4%
US	5420	20879	59711	59030	0%	0%	1%	2%
China	180	1844	20064	5215	0%	0%	0%	0%
Egypt	12225	229620	15708	18763	1%	4%	0%	1%
India	253	7328	3534	4125	0%	0%	0%	0%
All	1845306	5530426	7632853	3094384				

Source: WITS (2017)

Table 2.4: Top Fertilizer Exporters (SITC rev 3. 562)

	2000	2010	2015	2016	2000	2010	2015	2016
Export Value (US$1,000)					Export share			
China	$313,391	$5,385,815	$10,843,375	$6,512,953	3%	11%	19%	16%
Russia	$1,579,547	$7,365,879	$8,849,691	$6,633,693	13%	14%	16%	16%
Canada	$2,122,376	$5,967,075	$6,102,969	$4,210,261	17%	12%	11%	10%
US		$3,724,993	$3,566,249	$2,970,138	0%	7%	6%	7%
Saudi Arabia	$243,598	$1,248,274	$1,067,923		2%	2%	2%	0%
Egypt	$77,250	$1,151,786	$421,768	$847,766	1%	2%	1%	2%
Indonesia	$209,436	$356,888	$297,320	$349,972	2%	1%	1%	1%
Malaysia	$134,913	$427,205	$480,972	$360,640	1%	1%	1%	1%
T&T	$61,008	$218,440	$504,598		0%	0%	1%	0%
Ukraine	$413,723	$935,546	$533,725		3%	2%	1%	0%
Australia	$42,884	$300,766	$272,804	$275,441	0%	1%	0%	1%
India	$5,770	$38,638	$86,922	$77,335	0%	0%	0%	0%
All countries	$12,262,885	$51,012,299	$56,585,844	$41,531,685				

Source: WITS (2017)

With regard to consumer markets, Asia is the largest fertilizer market. Moreover, China and India are the two largest consumers of fertilizers. Figure 2.2 displays the import of fertilizer by country.

Figure 2.2: Fertilizer Consumption in the Top Five Countries, 1961-2011

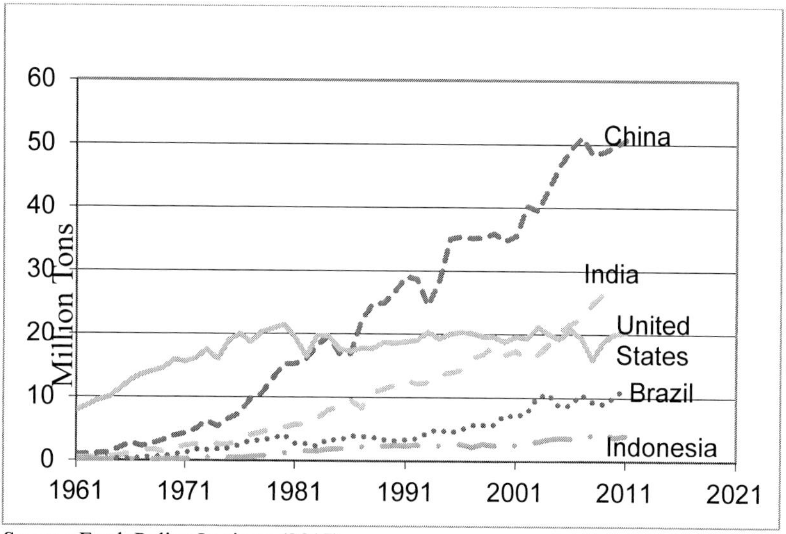

Source: Earth Policy Institute (2017)

In the agro-chemical industry (SITC revision 3. 591), the top exporters in 2016 were Germany, with its 14% market share, followed by China with its 12% market share, then France and the US, both with an 11% market share. See Table 2.5.

The world's "Big Six" agricultural chemical companies are BASF and Bayer, from Germany; Dow Chemical, DuPont, and Monsanto from the US; and Syngenta from Switzerland. The factors favouring the aforementioned companies dominating the industry, include: 1) their vertical and horizontal integration (they operate at multiple segments in the agriculture input industry value chain); 2) mergers and acquisitions; 3) a protective environment; and 4) their continuous research (MacDonald 2017).

In the agricultural equipment industry, the EU-27 region and North America are the top exporting regions. See Table 2.6.

Table 2.5: Top Agro-chemical Exporters (SITC rev 3. 591)

	2000	2010	2015	2016	2000	2010	2015	2016
Export Value (US$1,000)					Export share			
Germany	$1,751,655	$2,982,991	$3,970,632	$4,030,078	17%	13%	13%	14%
China	$462,953	$1,769,684	$3,545,441	$3,707,765	4%	8%	11%	12%
France	$1,493,881	$2,752,830	$3,922,239	$3,353,773	14%	12%	12%	11%
US	$1,411,484	$2,442,678	$3,402,069	$3,273,368	14%	11%	11%	11%
India	$240,839	$1,140,234	$1,931,128	$2,064,095	2%	5%	6%	7%
Belgium	$358,634	$1,524,530	$1,756,830	$1,833,492	3%	7%	6%	6%
UK	$1,072,381	$1,291,828	$1,384,006	$1,268,006	10%	6%	4%	4%
Spain	$249,050	$752,429	$1,153,624	$1,117,272	2%	3%	4%	4%
Israel	$143,013	$682,579	$1,015,214	$943,581	3%	3%	2%	2%
Italy	$307,734	$658,121	$703,392	$730,726	3%	3%	2%	2%
All	$10,445,034	$22,659,200	$31,488,142	$29,688,810				

Source: WITS (2017)

Table 2.6: Agricultural Machinery Exporters (SITC rev 3. 721+722)

	2000	2010	2015	2016	2000	2010	2015	2016
	Export Value (US$1,000)				Export share			
EU27	$11,319,808	$26,429,137	$30,344,820	$28,753,074	62%	59%	59%	60%
North America	$4,063,444	$8,042,981	$8,563,052	$7,369,890	22%	18%	17%	15%
Asia Pacific	$1,274,774	$2,349,915	$2,050,057	$2,012,135	7%	5%	4%	4%
S America	$210,769	$1,447,831	$931,641	$826,353	1%	3%	2%	2%
Sub-Saharan Africa	$30,328	$153,628	$177,622	$158,915	0%	0%	0%	0%
C America	$7,721	$10,731	$14,044	$11,410	0%	0%	0%	0%
All	$18,264,592	$45,104,747	$51,565,577	$47,568,508				

Source: WITS (2017)

The top manufacturing firms in the industry are John Deere, CNH, AGCO, CLAAS, Same Deutz-Fahr, and Kubota. The lead firms in the industry achieve their dominance by excelling in technological research, which has the effect of enhancing the operational efficiency and productivity of the agricultural machines (Research and Markets 2015).

The second column of Figure 2.1, "Production/Output", is another segment of the agriculture value chain. Here it refers to agricultural, livestock, and fish output. It includes both primary products that will be used for food consumption and non-food products. At the Standard International Trade Classification (SITC) revision 3 (rev 3) double-digit level, there are twelve product groups of agricultural commodities: live animals except fish (SITC 00); meat and preparations (SITC 01); dairy products and eggs (SITC 02); fish and shellfish (SITC 03); cereals and cereal preparations (SITC 04); vegetables and fruit (SITC 05); sugar, sugar prep and honey (SITC 06); coffee, tea, cocoa, and spices (SITC 7); animal feed (SITC 08); miscellaneous edible products and preparations (SITC 09); beverages (SITC 11); and tobacco (SITC 12).

Within each product group, there are several commodities. Some countries may produce all commodities within a product group. While other countries may specialise in the production and export of one or a few commodities from a larger product group. For simplicity, the product groups are aggregated at the single digit level into SITC 0 (Food and Live Animals), and SITC 1 (Beverages and Tobacco).[4]

The top exporters of SITC 0 and 1 are displayed in Tables 2.7 and 2.8.

As can be seen in Table 2.7, over the 2000 to 2016 period, the US was the top exporter of SITC 0 (Food and Live Animals). In as recent as 2016, the US held a 10% share of the total food and live animals export market. In 2015, it was followed by the Netherlands with its 6% market share, then Germany with its 6% export share.

---

[4] It is important to note that SITC 2 (Crude materials, inedible, except fuels) can also be considered as part of the agriculture industry. However, this sector was not considered in this chapter.

Table 2.7: Export of SITC 0 (Food and Live Animals)

	Export Value (US$1,000)			Export share			
	2000	2015	2016	2000	2010	2015	2016
United States	$38,721,566	$97,898,093	$96,058,983	12%	10%	10%	10%
Netherlands	$21,293,393	$62,611,692	$65,200,956	7%	6%	6%	7%
Germany	$18,430,864	$59,402,497	$59,782,738	6%	6%	6%	6%
China	$12,281,714	$58,154,356	$61,077,120	4%	5%	6%	7%
Brazil	$9,230,345	$45,956,368	$45,035,947	3%	5%	5%	5%
France	$23,124,470	$43,948,613	$41,830,071	7%	5%	4%	5%
Canada	$14,809,560	$36,388,848	$34,897,270	5%	3%	4%	4%
Spain	$12,620,048	$36,378,328	$38,363,343	4%	4%	4%	4%
Belgium	$14,490,565	$32,472,043	$33,995,404	4%	4%	3%	4%
Italy	$10,397,269	$27,912,900	$28,598,657	3%	3%	3%	3%
Australia	$10,966,888	$26,807,056	$24,308,074	3%	2%	3%	3%
Thailand	$9,666,639	$26,686,454		3%	3%	3%	0%
India	$4,764,604	$26,330,455	$25,536,548	1%	2%	3%	3%
Argentina	$8,497,132	$23,579,681	$26,264,193	2%	2%	2%	3%
Mexico	$6,353,904	$21,558,855	$23,587,897	2%	2%	2%	3%
Poland	$2,295,002	$20,825,906	$21,261,745	1%	2%	2%	2%
Vietnam	$3,536,062	$20,108,218		2%	2%	2%	2%
New Zealand	$5,583,836	$18,323,747	$18,240,785	2%	2%	2%	2%

United Kingdom	$8,985,638	$17,937,977	$17,831,994	3%	2%	2%	2%
Denmark	$8,943,514	$15,471,121	$15,880,558	3%	2%	2%	2%
All	$325,966,830	$1,002,060,721	$929,557,059				

Source: WITS (2017)

Table 2.8: Export of SITC 1 (Beverages and Tobacco)

	Export Value (US$1,000)			Export share			
	2000	2015	2016	2000	2010	2015	2016
France	$8,285,561	$16,158,202	$16,384,919	15%	13%	12%	13%
Germany	$3,281,281	$10,304,556	$10,664,282	6%	9%	8%	9%
United Kingdom	$6,363,689	$10,039,472	$9,538,944	12%	8%	8%	8%
Italy	$3,214,729	$8,312,851	$8,722,583	6%	6%	6%	7%
United States	$6,697,120	$6,744,136	$6,485,253	12%	5%	5%	5%
Netherlands	$4,408,095	$6,728,924	$6,640,499	8%	7%	5%	5%
Spain	$1,640,167	$4,477,746	$4,490,776	3%	3%	3%	4%
Belgium	$1,492,599	$4,435,019	$4,481,550	3%	3%	3%	4%
Mexico	$1,613,748	$4,414,574	$4,711,849	3%	3%	3%	4%
China	$744,835	$3,309,290	$3,538,643	1%	2%	3%	3%
Poland	$115,528	$3,209,396	$2,928,772	0%	2%	2%	2%
Brazil	$911,577	$2,328,589	$2,256,291	2%	2%	1%	2%
Australia	$1,022,932	$1,899,347	$1,998,900	2%	2%	1%	2%
Thailand	$172,121	$1,489,854		0%	1%	1%	0%

New Zealand	$156,798	$1,284,093	$1,319,136	0%	1%	1%	1%
India	$194,121	$1,152,797	$1,224,179	0%	1%	1%	1%
Argentina	$339,784	$1,136,945	$1,307,944	1%	1%	1%	1%
Denmark	$544,037	$1,128,132	$1,141,368	1%	1%	1%	1%
Canada	$1,045,142	$968,837	$996,598	2%	1%	1%	1%
Vietnam	$17,815	$568,386		0%	0%	0%	0%
All	$54,045,947	$130,838,296	$125,333,010				

Source: WITS (2017)

As can be seen in Table 2.8, France dominated the export of SITC 1 (Beverages and Tobacco) over the 2000 to 2016 period. In 2015, France held a 12% export share in the world beverages and tobacco market. It was followed by Germany, then the United Kingdom (UK) which both held 8% market shares.[5]

The "Processing" segment of the Agriculture Value Chain processes raw materials and intermediate products derived from the agriculture sector into more final products. The processing segment adds value to the primary and intermediate agricultural products. The activities in the processing segment range from simple preservation (such as sun drying), to using capital-intensive methods to produce final products (such as chocolates, textiles, pulp, and paper).

The agro-processing sector entails both food industries and non-food industries. The food industries are much more homogeneous than the non-food industries, as the former produces products for the same end use: human nutrition. Most preservation techniques for food tend to be similar over a whole range of perishable food products, regardless of whether they are fruit, vegetables, milk, meat or fish. In fact, the need/demand for food preservation is a significant reason why the more perishable food products are processed (FAO 1997).

The non-food industries are more heterogeneous than the food industry as they have a wide variety of end uses. For example, cotton can be used to produce textiles, which in turn would be used to produce clothing; wood, on the other hand, can be used to produce furniture, tools, houses, souvenirs, etc. Almost all non-food agricultural products must undergo a high degree of processing in order to produce a final product.

The agro-processing sector may also be classified into upstream and downstream sub-industries. Upstream sub-industries engage in the initial processing of agricultural commodities to produce intermediate products. Examples of upstream processing include rice and flour milling, saw-milling, leather tanning, cotton ginning, and fish canning. Downstream sub-industries process intermediate products made from agricultural materials into finished products. Examples of downstream processing include bread and cake making, paper production, clothing and footwear manufacturing (FAO 1997).

---

[5] The top exporting firms are not presented due to the aggregation of multiple agricultural products creating an aggregation bias.

The final segment of the agriculture value chain is "Retail and Distribution." This involves the transportation of products, the export of products to international markets, warehousing, retail, and the distribution of products to the final consumer.

The purpose of retail and distribution is to efficiently get the products in good condition to a location where it is convenient for the consumer to purchase them. Intermediaries, such as wholesalers and retailers, tend to add efficiency to the distribution system as they can perform specialized tasks better than the consumer or the manufacturer. The retail and supermarket distribution channels allow a consumer to buy one item at a time at a convenient location rather than travelling to a factory, which may not be in the consumer's country, to purchase the item.

Distributors add efficiency by disaggregating the bulk quantity of items. The consumer often wants to buy small quantities at a time. However, in order to benefit from economies of scale, producers (farmers and processers) may generate large quantities of the product. By including wholesalers and retailers in the value chain, large quantities are gradually disaggregated, allowing the consumer to purchase individual quantities.[6] Figure 2.3 provides an illustration of the distribution network.

As the objective of the wholesaler and retailers is to earn a profit, by disaggregating, they charge a markup on products producing a gross profit margin.[7]

In some developed countries, such as the countries of the European Union (EU) and the US, regulators inspect food products to ensure that they are in compliance with their standards (EC 2010). The US Department of Agriculture (USDA) has quality standards for agricultural products such as

[6] For example, if a consumer wanted to buy flour directly from the farmer/processor, they may be required to purchase at least one hundred bags. This amount may be greater than the consumer's ability to consume or store the item, resulting in wastage. If the consumer was to buy directly from a wholesaler, the minimum requirement may be ten bags. But if the consumer was to buy from the retail supermarket, they would be able to purchase one bag.

[7] The gross profit margin is the difference between the total revenue and total costs, expressed as a percentage of total revenue. The net profit margin is the difference between gross profit and operational costs, expressed as a percentage of total revenue.

Figure 2.3: Agriculture Industry Distribution Network

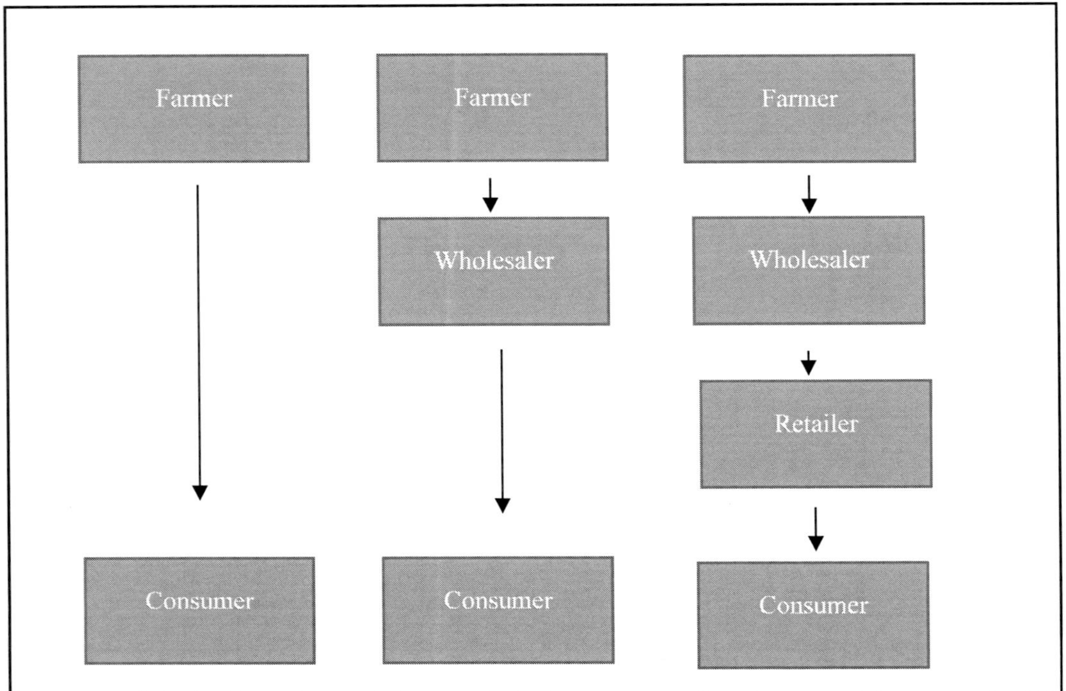

cotton, dairy, fruits and vegetables, livestock, poultry, grains, and processed foods. Exporters of agricultural products into the US market must employ equivalent sanitary and health measures to US standards in their production of agricultural products, to ensure that US consumers are extended the same level of protection achieved domestically. Furthermore, the US has a number of institutions such as the Food and Drug Administration (FDA), and the Food Safety and Inspection Service (FSIS) to ensure that agricultural and food products have been inspected and meet US food standards[8] before distribution in the US market (EP 2015).

The EU food and agriculture requirements are classified as follows:

- Food safety and plant and animal health regulations. These regulations are designed to guarantee a high level of protection of consumers from consuming food in the EU market.[9] For example, in food production, it sets maximum limits for microbial and chemical contamination. The law also facilitates the trade of safe food and feed manufactured in the EU.
- Labelling regulations. The food law establishes that consumers in the EU are entitled to information regarding the content, composition, and origin of food products. This is to allow consumers to make an informed decision when purchasing food products. Mandatory requirements are for safety and quality, the nature of ingredients, storage conditions, and shelf life. Voluntary information which may be provided by the producer includes: trademark, brand, product positioning claim, logo, and other marketing information. Furthermore, there should be no misinformation provided to the consumer concerning the characteristics (composition, quantity, storage life, origin, etc.) of the food product.

---

[8] The US Department of Health and Human Services' (HHS') FDA has responsibility for protecting US consumers' interests for 80% of food (except for meat and poultry products). The FDA ensures the safety of foods for humans, including dietary supplements; ensures the safety of animal feed and the safety and effectiveness of animal drugs; sets standards for preventing foodborne illness; ensures compliance with the established standards; and ensures that food labels contain accurate information regarding the product's ingredients, processing, and origin (EP 2015). The USDA's FSIS inspects and ensures that meat, poultry and processed egg supply for distribution in the US is wholesome, safe and properly labelled.

[9] In 2002, the European Parliament adopted Regulation (EC) No. 178/2002, establishing the general food law (EC 2017a).

- Environmental regulations. This is where farmers operating in the EU are encouraged to engage in sustainable agricultural practices. Their farming methods should ensure the conservation of species, avert biodiversity loss, preserve soil and the quality of the water supply.[10]
- Processing methods. This is the requirement for organic processed products to be produced via processing methods which guarantee that the organic integrity of the product is maintained. This requirement also indicates the types of ingredients which may be included in foods.[11]
- Marketing standards. This mechanism promotes product quality by applying general marketing standards to agricultural products.[12] The marketing standards were also implemented to protect EU consumers from deception and unacceptable practices. For example, a maximum limit on the proportion of water added to poultry meat is set in a marketing standard.
- Regulations for organic products. This establishes the rules of organic production and how organic products are to be labelled (EC 2010).

Apart from the standards in the EU, the Agreement on the application of Sanitary and Phytosanitary (SPS) measures adopted in the 1994 Uruguay Round of the General Agreement on Tariffs and Trade (GATT)[13] agreement makes provisions for countries to take safety precautions to protect their consumers from diseases, and contaminants. Countries can adopt sanitary (relating to animals) and phytosanitary (relating to plants) measures that provide a higher level of protection than international standards, provided that there is a good scientific justification to do so (EC 2010).

---

[10] Note: Farmers operating outside of the EU are not directly affected by EU environmental regulations.

[11] Article 21 of Council Regulation (EC) 834/2008, specifies the types of ingredients which may be used. In summary, additives, processing aids, flavourings, water, salt, preparations of micro-organisms and enzymes, minerals, trace elements, vitamins, as well as amino acids, may be used as ingredients in processed organic food (EC 2017b).

[12] National authorities in the EU can exempt products that are labelled "products intended for processing" or "for animal feed" from specific marketing standards (EC 2017c).

[13] The Uruguay round sought to multilaterally reduce barriers (tariffs, quotas, export subsidies, SPS measures) to trade in agricultural and food products (Henson and Loader 2001).

Many developing countries, including the Caribbean, enjoy preferential access to the EU market for most of their agricultural products. However, the high standards that the EU enforces limit the market penetration of many small farmers, especially those that lack the resources to comply with the standards (Henson and Loader 2001; EC 2010).

SPS measures on trade can be grouped into three categories: 1) they reduce trade by imposing an import ban; 2) they divert trade from one partner to another; and 3) they increase the overall costs for all potential suppliers (Henson and Loader 2001). SPS measures have been blamed as an impediment to the export of fish (Josupeit 1997; Cato 1998); spices (UNCTAD/Commonwealth Secretariat 1996); oilseeds, oils, and fats (FAO 1998); livestock products (Colby 1997); and horticultural products (Giles 1997).

2.3.0 Overview of the Agriculture Industry in Trinidad and Tobago

In 1985, T&T's agriculture sector contributed approximately 3.02 per cent of GDP. This share gradually decreased, dropping below one per cent of GDP in 2003. Although over the 2014 to 2016 period, there have been marginal increases in the share of agriculture's contribution to GDP, this was driven by the contraction in the GDP of T&T. In fact, the output of agriculture declined over the associated period. See Table 2.9.

Table 2.9: Agricultural Contribution to T&T's GDP

	GDP at Market Prices (TT$ Mn)	GDP at Market Prices Agriculture (TT$ Mn)	
1985	18,049	545.1	3.02%
1990	21,539	564.3	2.62%
2000	50,962	718.6	1.41%
2003	71,108	696.9	0.98%
2007	136,952	509	0.37%
2008	175,287	640.7	0.37%
2009	121,281	721.8	0.60%
2010	141,268	734.8	0.52%
2011	163,008	744.2	0.46%

2012	165,203	770.1	0.47%
2013	170,318	795.7	0.47%
2014	167,764	768.9	0.46%
2015	150,247	761	0.51%
2016	145,911	750.5	0.51%

Source: CBTT (2017); World Bank (2017a)[14]

The sharp decline in T&T's agricultural output is directly linked to the history of the agriculture sector in the country. The next section provides a review.

2.3.1 History of T&T's Agriculture Industry

The agriculture industry in T&T has been shaped by the country's colonial history. Under colonial rule, T&T specialized in the production and export of sugar, cocoa, coffee, and citrus fruit to the United Kingdom (UK). Sugar was the primary cash crop.

During the 1880s, there were more than three hundred sugar plantations in Trinidad. The country's agriculture model was comprised of large plantations for the cultivation of crops for export; and multiple small farms, on plots less than 5 acres, which produced agricultural output for families, and the domestic market.[15]

After the country achieved independence in 1962, sugar continued to be the most important cash crop. Later in 1970, the government acquired a 51 per cent equity stake of Tate and Lyle, a multinational sugar producing firm. By 1975, the enterprise was fully government owned, and renamed Caroni (1975) Limited. Caroni (1975) Limited operated on approximately 77,000 acres of land and directly employed 9,200 workers. The company also produced additional products, such as rice, citrus fruits, and rum. Outside of Caroni 1975 Ltd, there were approximately 6,000 independent sugar cane farmers in Trinidad (Allard 2012).

---

[14] Data from 1985 to 2003 were derived from the World Bank. The Trinidad and Tobago Dollar (TTD) was computed by multiplying the exchange rate to achieve the United States Dollar (USD) amount.

[15] Up to 2012, 87 per cent of the agricultural holdings in T&T are on plots of land of 5 acres or less (Allard 2012).

Sugar export was only profitable for T&T due to unreciprocated preferential access to the EU market. Preferential access was granted from the European Economic Community (EEC) to the Africa Caribbean and Pacific (ACP) countries under the Lomé (1975) agreement. The EEC committed to buying 1.33 million tons of raw sugar at prices, typically in excess of world market prices (Richardson 2013). Under successive Lomé renegotiations, the collective power of the ACP countries was gradually weakened. However, the formation of the WTO in 1995 signalled the eventual end of non-reciprocal preferential trade agreements. Then in 1997, the WTO Dispute Settlement Body ruled against the EU's agriculture commodity import regime with the ACP countries, declaring it in conflict with the WTO's principle of non-discrimination and granting countries permission to apply sanctions against the EU as a penalty. Although, the sugar protocol continued into the 2000 Contonou Agreement, both the EU and the ACP countries were alerted that preferential trade agreements would need to be WTO-compatible (Richardson 2013).

Given the gradual erosion of preferences in the international trade industry, as well as productivity challenges domestically, the Government of Trinidad and Tobago (GORTT) took the decision to shut down Caroni (1975) Limited in 2003. The closure of the sugar company directly caused the retrenchment of 9,200 workers. Moreover, the closure resulted in the decline in the production of sugar, as well as the other crops formerly produced by the company (Allard 2012). Thus, from 2003 to 2016 the agricultural output in T&T declined.

2.3.2 T&T's Main Agricultural Exports

As previously indicated, T&T's main agricultural export was sugar. However, in 2015, T&T's top agro-industry export was beverages. It was followed by the export of cereals and cereal preparations, then tobacco. In fact, as can be seen from Table 2.10, sugar was T&T's 8th top export in 2015.

Table 2.10: Top Agricultural Exports of Trinidad and Tobago

Export in $1,000 USD	2015
11 -- Beverages	$145,218.60
04 -- Cereals/cereal preparations	$73,912.02
12 -- Tobacco/manufactures	$47,303.20

05 -- Vegetables and fruit	\$31,839.74
09 -- Misc food products	\$30,164.35
07 -- Coffee/tea/cocoa/spices	\$13,473.28
03 -- Fish/shellfish/etc.	\$9,783.365
06 -- Sugar/sugar prep/honey	\$8,255.298
01 -- Meat and preparations	\$6,504.365
02 -- Dairy products and eggs	\$6,339.907
08 -- Animal feed ex unml cer.	\$930.356
00 -- Live animals except fish	\$25.304

Source: WITS (2017)

To assess T&T's relative export strength, the International Revealed Comparative Advantage (IRCA) index is used. The IRCA index compares a given country's export structure to the world export structure (Pitigala 2005). The IRCA index is given by:

$$IRCA = \frac{(X_{ij}/X_{wj})}{(\Sigma X_i/\Sigma X_w)} \quad (2.01)$$

where $IRCA_{ij}$ is the index of revealed comparative advantage of country i in commodity j; X_{ij} is country i's export of commodity j; X_{wj} is world exports of commodity j; ΣX_i is total exports of country i; and ΣX_w is total world exports.

Note: $$\frac{(X_{ij}/X_{wj})}{(\Sigma X_i/\Sigma X_w)} = \frac{(X_{ij}/\Sigma X_i)}{(X_{wj}/\Sigma X_w)} \quad (2.02)$$

The IRCA is used rather than the Balassa (1965) RCA index, as the IRCA can be used to compare a country's strength in exporting a product relative to the rest of the world, whereas the Balassa (*ibid*) index is more appropriate for assessing bilateral trade. In other words, the IRCA is a measure of export competitiveness between a country and the rest of the world, while the Balassa (*ibid*) index assesses country i's competitiveness into country k's market.

The theoretical range of the IRCA is from 0 to $+\infty$. Like the RCA, values less than 1 imply that the exporting country has a weakness in the production and export of a particular commodity. An RCA greater than 1 reveals comparative advantage and strength in the production and export of a particular commodity.

The IRCA is computed for all T&T export products using SITC rev 3 double-digit data. The results revealed that T&T had international competitiveness in the production and export of only 12 product groups out of 62 in at least 1 year over the 2000 to 2015 period. The results are displayed in Table 2.11.

Table 2.11: T&T IRCA

Year	Product	IRCA
2000	06 -- Sugar/sugar prep/honey	**4.4**
2005	06 -- Sugar/sugar prep/honey	**1.3**
2010	06 -- Sugar/sugar prep/honey	0.1
2015	06 -- Sugar/sugar prep/honey	0.3
2000	09 -- Misc food products	**1.2**
2005	09 -- Misc food products	0.5
2010	09 -- Misc food products	0.4
2015	09 -- Misc food products	0.6
2000	11 -- Beverages	**3.2**
2005	11 -- Beverages	**1.9**
2010	11 -- Beverages	**1.7**
2015	11 -- Beverages	**2.5**
2000	12 -- Tobacco/manufactures	0.6
2005	12 -- Tobacco/manufactures	**1.0**
2010	12 -- Tobacco/manufactures	**1.0**
2015	12 -- Tobacco/manufactures	**2.1**
2000	27 -- Crude fertilizer/mineral	0.1
2005	27 -- Crude fertilizer/mineral	0.4
2010	27 -- Crude fertilizer/mineral	0.2
2015	27 -- Crude fertilizer/mineral	**3.5**
2000	28 -- Metal ores/metal scrap	0.1
2005	28 -- Metal ores/metal scrap	0.2
2010	28 -- Metal ores/metal scrap	0.1
2015	28 -- Metal ores/metal scrap	**1.8**
2000	33 -- Petroleum and products	**6.2**
2005	33 -- Petroleum and products	**4.4**
2010	33 -- Petroleum and products	**3.8**

2015	33 -- Petroleum and products	**2.0**
2000	34 -- Gas natural/manufactured	**9.3**
2005	34 -- Gas natural/manufactured	**14.0**
2010	34 -- Gas natural/manufactured	**9.3**
2015	34 -- Gas natural/manufactured	**18.4**
2000	51 -- Organic chemicals	**2.9**
2005	51 -- Organic chemicals	**3.0**
2010	51 -- Organic chemicals	**2.8**
2015	51 -- Organic chemicals	**5.9**
2000	52 -- Inorganic chemicals	**15.5**
2005	52 -- Inorganic chemicals	**16.8**
2010	52 -- Inorganic chemicals	**23.6**
2015	52 -- Inorganic chemicals	**31.2**
2000	56 -- Manufactured fertilizers	**4.4**
2005	56 -- Manufactured fertilizers	**1.3**
2010	56 -- Manufactured fertilizers	0.1
2015	56 -- Manufactured fertilizers	0.3
2000	67 -- Iron and steel	**1.2**
2005	67 -- Iron and steel	0.5
2010	67 -- Iron and steel	0.4
2015	67 -- Iron and steel	0.6

Source: Computed

As can be seen from Table 2.11, the only agro-industry products in which T&T had an international comparative advantage were Sugar/sugar prep/honey (SITC 06), Misc food products (SITC 06), Beverages (SITC 11), Tobacco/manufactures (SITC 12), Crude fertilizer/mineral (SITC 27), and Manufactured fertilizers (SITC 56).

It is noteworthy that sugar was the only primary agricultural product in which T&T ever had a comparative advantage. However, as previously mentioned, sugar was only viable due to the preferential treatment it received in its export to the UK. With the erosion of trade preferences, sugar was no longer viable in T&T. It should thus be no surprise that the statistics reveal a loss in the country's comparative advantage in sugar shortly after the closure of Caroni (1975) Limited, the state-owned sugar company.

The next section examines the segments in the agriculture value chain in which T&T operates.

2.3.3 Segments in the Agriculture Global Value Chain in which T&T Operates

T&T operates in multiple segments in the agriculture industry global value chain. In the inputs segment, T&T has a minor role. The country does not commercially produce and export seeds, pesticides, herbicides, fungicides, farm equipment, or irrigation equipment. All of the aforementioned products are imported for domestic use. Some seeds produced by local crops are used for cultivation by families, or distributed in the domestic market.

The fertilizer industry is an exception as an area where T&T has competitiveness. Due to the country's endowment of natural gas, it produces ammonia, and urea, the macronutrients of fertilizers. Based on a feasibility study commissioned for the GORTT in 1975, the government decided to enter the ammonia and urea business. Subsequently, in 1977, the GORTT entered a joint venture agreement with W. R. Grace, to form Tringen I. In 1978, the GORTT and W. R. Grace commissioned Tringen II. In that same year, the GORTT and Amoco formed a joint venture to establish the Fertilizers of Trinidad and Tobago Limited (Fertrin).[16] The Amoco International Sales Company (AISC), a subsidiary of Amoco, was created in 1979 with the mandate to market and transport Fertrin's ammonia outside the Caribbean Community (CARICOM) market (Boopsingh and McGuire 2014).

For Amoco, given that the GORTT was not open to the idea of directly exporting liquefied natural gas in the 1970s, ammonia was viewed as an alternative means to export natural gas, through some form of primary processing.[17] Point Lisas was selected as the location for the ammonia plant. For urea, after Amoco decided to pass on the project, the GORTT ventured into the industry alone with its 100 per cent equity in the Trinidad and Tobago Urea Company (TTUC) (Boopsingh and McGuire 2014).

Despite significant revenue at their inception, the profitability of both Tringen and Fertrin plummeted in the 1980s, as ammonia prices followed international oil and natural gas prices. The government changed in 1986, leading to a review of public policy, and the restructuring and privatization of loss-making state-owned organizations.

---

[16] Fertrin was in the ammonia export business.

[17] Natural gas (i.e., methane) is converted into hydrogen in a process called steam reforming. Then nitrogen is added to hydrogen to produce ammonia.

Presently in 2017, there are eleven ammonia plants, and two urea plants in T&T. Table 2.12 provides an overview of the plants and their operators.

Table 2.12: Ammonia and Urea Plants in T&T

Ammonia Plants in T&T		
Plant	**Start-up Year**	**Annual Capacity (MT)**
Yara Trinidad Limited	1959	285,000
Tringen I	1977	500,000
PCS 01	1981	445,000
PCS 02	1981	445,000
Tringen II	1988	495,000
PCS 03	1996	250,000
PCS 04	1998	650,000
Point Lisas Nitrogen Limited (PLNL)	1998	650,000
Caribbean Nitrogen Company (CNC)	2002	650,000
Nitrogen 2000 (N2K)	2004	650,000
AUM Ammonia	2009	650,000
Urea Plants in T&T		
Plant	Start-up Year	Daily Capacity metric tonnes (MT)/day
PCS Nitrogen Trinidad Limited	1983	2023
A-U-M Complex	2010	2100

Source: GORTT MEEI (2017)

In the output segment of the value chain, at the double-digit SITC level, T&T produces all products from SITC 00 to 12. T&T agricultural exports at the triple-digit level are displayed in Table 2.13.

Table 2.13: Total Agricultural Exports for T&T in 2015

111 -- Beverage non-alcohol n.e.s.	90,101
048 – Cereal, etc., flour/starch	71,082
112 -- Alcoholic beverages	55,118
122 -- Tobacco, manufactured	47,303
098 -- Edible products n.e.s.	21,957
073 -- Chocolate/cocoa preps	9,659
034 -- Fish, live/fresh/chilled/frozen	8,808
091 -- Margarine/shortening	8,207
062 -- Sugar confectionery	7,299
022 -- Milk products exc butter/cheese	6,274
017 -- Meat/offal preserved n.e.s	4,703
046 -- Flour/meal wheat/meslin	2,772
075 -- Spices	1,850
072 -- Cocoa	1,745
012 -- Meat n.e.s., fresh/chilled/frozen	1,553
061 -- Sugar/molasses/honey	957
081 -- Animal feed excl unmilled cereals	930
036 -- Crustaceans molluscs, etc.	493
035 -- Fish, dried/salted/smoked	470
016 -- Meat/offal preserved	205
071 -- Coffee/coffee substitute	187
025 -- Eggs, albumen	47
011 -- Beef, fresh/chilled/frozen	43
042 -- Rice	35
074 -- Tea and mate	32
001 -- Live animals except fish	25
037 -- Fish/shellfish, prepared/preserved	13
047 -- Cereal meal/flour n.e.s	13
024 -- Cheese and curd	12
044 -- Maize except sweetcorn	9
023 -- Butter and cheese	6
045 -- Cereal grains n.e.s.	1
041 -- Wheat/meslin	0
043 -- Barley grain	0
121 -- Tobacco, raw and wastes	0

Source: WITS (2017)

The total value of the agricultural exports in 2015 was US$341,910,000. The top four exports: Beverage non-alcohol n.e.s. (SITC 111); Cereal, etc., flour/starch (SITC 048); Alcoholic beverages (SITC 112); and Tobacco, manufactured (SITC 122) accounted for 77 per cent of T&T's total agricultural (SITC 0 and 1) exports. However, the top exported agricultural products are not pure primary products. In fact, they should be considered as agro-processed products as they have all undergone some form of processing. The primary non-processed products[18] accounted for approximately 6.5 per cent of T&T's total exported agricultural products.

In the beverage industry, the top producers are House of Angostura,[19] Carib Brewery,[20] the Solo Beverage Company,[21] and SM Jaleel & Co. Ltd.[22] It is important to note that several multinational firms maintain an agro-processing presence in T&T, as a hub for the distribution of regional exports. Some of these multinationals include: Nestle, Pepsi, and Coca-Cola.[23]

In the manufactured tobacco (cigarettes) industry, the West Indian Tobacco Company (WITCO) is the leading manufacturer in the entire Caribbean region. Its products include Dunhill, du Maurier, Broadway, and Mt d'or. Although the company was founded in 1904, it is currently still a subsidiary of British American Tobacco (Investments) Limited.

---

[18] These primary agriculture products include: Milk products excl butter/cheese (SITC 022); Meat/offal preserved n.e.s (SITC 017); Flour/meal wheat/meslin (SITC 046); Spices (SITC 075); Cocoa (SITC 072); Meat n.e.s., fresh/chilled/frozen (SITC 012); Sugar/molasses/honey (SITC 061); Animal feed excl unmilled cereals (SITC 081); Crustaceans molluscs, etc. (SITC 036); Fish, dried/salted/smoked (SITC 035); Meat/offal preserved (SITC 016); Coffee/coffee substitute (SITC 071); Eggs, albumen (SITC 025); Beef, fresh/chilled/frozen (SITC 011); Rice (SITC 042); Tea and mate (SITC 074); Live animals except fish (SITC 001); and Fish/shellfish, prepared/preserved (SITC 037).

[19] Angostura produces both alcoholic and non-alcoholic beverages. Angostura uses Trinidad Distillers Limited (TDL) to distil all of its products.

[20] Carib Brewery produces both alcoholic and non-alcoholic beverages. Some of their products include: Malta, Carib beer, Shandy Carib, and Stag.

[21] The Solo Beverage Company produces non-alcoholic beverages.

[22] SM Jaleel & Co. Ltd. is the largest manufacturer of juices and other non-alcoholic beverages in T&T. Some of their products include: Chubby, Fruita, Busta, Island Fusion, Trinidad Juices, Caribbean Cool, Viva flavoured water, Oasis purified water, and Cole Cold soft drinks.

[23] Nestle, Pepsi, and Coca-Cola all produce non-alcoholic beverages.

Other top producers in T&T's agro-processing industry include: the Bermudez Group;[24] KC Confectionery,[25] Associated Brands,[26] Chief Brand Products,[27] and Flavorite Ice Cream. Indeed, the agro-processing industry in T&T is oligopolistic, and dominated by a few large players. The top firms in the industry achieve and maintain their dominance either by practising product differentiation, or acquisitions of smaller firms in the industry.

It is noteworthy that small-scale producers of processed products do exist in T&T. They produce a range of products such as chows, peppers, pastries, juices and punches, alcoholic beverages, doubles, poulorie, cooked nuts, and home-cooked dishes. These small-scale producers are typically organised to obtain a food badge from the public health inspectorate from the regional borough corporations in order to sell their products to the general public. They opt to sell their products directly to members of the general public at markets, malls, schools, work, or home cafeterias, and via street vending. The output of the small-scale entrepreneurs is minuscule relative to that of the larger players in the industry.

In the retail and distribution segment of the agriculture value chain most follow the monopolistic competition structure. There are several supermarkets in almost every community in T&T. A few of the larger ones, with multiple branches include: Budget Foods; JTA; Massy (formerly Hi-Lo) supermarket;[28] Price Mart; Tru Valu; and Xtra Foods. There are multiple small/micro mini-marts, which are family businesses that provide services to rural communities.

The retail and distribution segment in T&T also includes a restaurant and fast food sub-segment. This includes a number of domestic businesses, small catering services, as well as international franchises.[29]

---

[24] The Bermudez Group produces cookies, biscuits, and snacks. They are also the owners of the Kiss Baking Co., and Holiday Snacks.

[25] KC Confectionary produces sweets and sugar related snacks.

[26] Associated Banks produces biscuits and other snacks. They are also the owners of Sunshine Snacks, Charles Candy, Devon Biscuits and Sunshine and Universal Cereals.

[27] Chief Brand Products is the largest producer and exporter of processed and packaged spices in T&T.

[28] Massy supermarket has the most branches in T&T.

[29] Prestige Holdings has the licence for several international franchises in T&T. They are Kentucky Fried Chicken (KFC), TGI Fridays, Subway, Pizza Hut, and Starbucks.

2.3.4 Main Export Markets

The top three main export markets for T&T's output in the agriculture value chain[30] are CARICOM, the US, and South America. See Table 2.14.

Table 2.14: T&T's Agricultural Export Destinations

	2000	2005	2010	2015	Export Share
CARICOM	$153,322	$203,552	$199,397	$292,741	56%
US	$58,509	$115,569	$110,146	$117,818	23%
South America	$42,037	$73,552	$89,216	$105,917	20%
EU-27	$47,720	$42,673	$14,109	$29,307	6%
Canada	$5,383	$17,451	$4,090	$11,813	2%
UK	$30,833	$28,491	$4,621	$4,821	1%
Asia Pacific	$2,276	$2,583	$3,706	$4,129	1%
World	$299,036	$437,499	$418,774	$522,200	

Source: WITS (2017)

Agricultural exports to CARICOM represent 56 per cent of T&T's total agricultural exports in 2015. It was followed by agricultural exports to the US, with a 23 per cent export share, then to South America with a 20 per cent export share. The European Union (EU-27) region comprised only 6 per cent of T&T's total agricultural exports. The UK, T&T's former main trading partner in sugar, accounted for approximately 1 per cent of T&T's total agricultural exports.

2.4.0 Application of the Diamond Competitiveness Model

Porter's diamond of competitiveness model identified the attributes of the national environment, which influence the competitive advantage of firms. The factor conditions, demand conditions, related and supporting industries, and firm strategy, structure, and rivalry, work together as a system to facilitate or inhibit the creation of competitive advantage for firms within a nation. Furthermore, there are two additional determinants, the government,

[30] This output in the agriculture value chain is comprised of Food and Live Animals (SITC 0); Beverages and Tobacco (SITC 1); Ammonia nitrate fertilizer (SITC 56211); and Urea (SITC 56216).

and chance, which indirectly affects the business environment. Figure 4 presents an illustration.

Figure 2.4: The Diamond Competitiveness Model

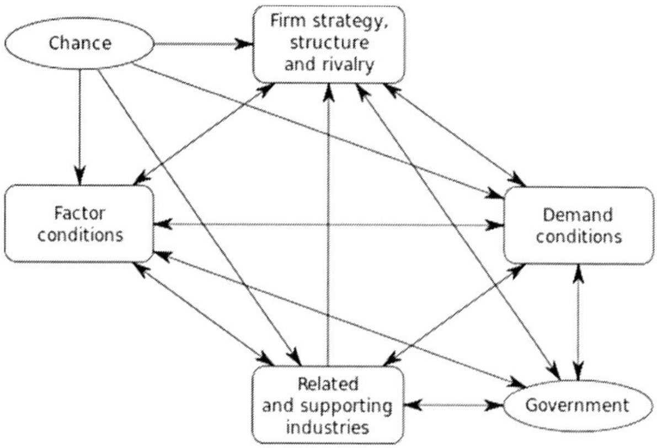

Source: Porter (1990)

2.4.1 Factor Conditions

The factor conditions refer to the factors that are necessary for production. Porter (1990) categorized the factor conditions into: i) human resources; ii) physical resources; iii) knowledge resources; iv) capital resources; and v) infrastructure. Accessing the factor conditions at a low cost, and deploying them in a productively efficient manner should contribute to the competitive advantage of firms.

Porter (ibid.) also classified the factors into primary factors and advanced factors. Primary factors include: natural resources, climate, geographical position, and labour (moderately skilled and unskilled). Such primary factors can be provided in all countries but in different proportions. Advanced factors include: modern information infrastructure, highly-skilled labour, and university research institutes. The advanced factors can be created in time with the correct investment. However, the advanced factors are often built upon the primary factors.

Factors may also be categorized into general factors (such as the transportation and communications system) which may be used in several industries, or specialized factors (such as highly specialized skilled labour) which could only be effectively used in a few industries. The specialized factors are rare; however, they are critical to creating and sustaining competitive advantage.

In T&T, physical resources (land), capital resources (machinery), and human resources are used to produce primary (unprocessed) agricultural crops. The total land area of T&T covers approximately 513,000 hectares (5,128 km^2) (Meditz and Hanratty 1987; Lowitt et al. 2015), of which less than one-third is arable. In the 1970s, over 1,000 km^2 of land were devoted to agriculture. As can be seen in Figure 2.5, there has been a steady decline in agricultural land use from the 1980s to 2014. In fact, from 2006 to 2014, only 540 km^2 (54,000 hectares) of land was used in agriculture.

Figure 2.5: Land Area Devoted to Agriculture in T&T

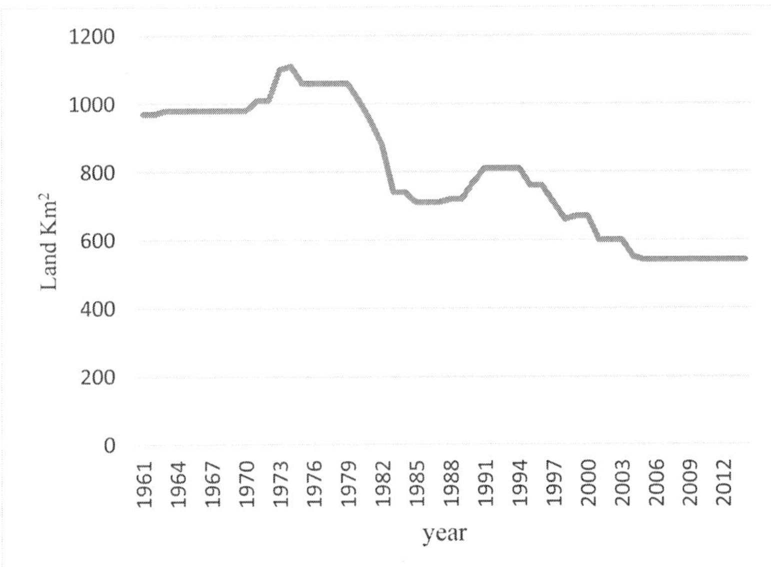

Source: World Bank (2017b)

Data from the World Bank (2017c) also indicate that in 2012, only 9.25% of total agricultural land was irrigated. With regard to fertilizer, it is also used in agricultural cultivation, although its application has been declining over time. Figure 2.6 displays T&T's fertilizer consumption.

Figure 2.6: Fertilizer Consumption (kilograms per hectare of arable land) in T&T

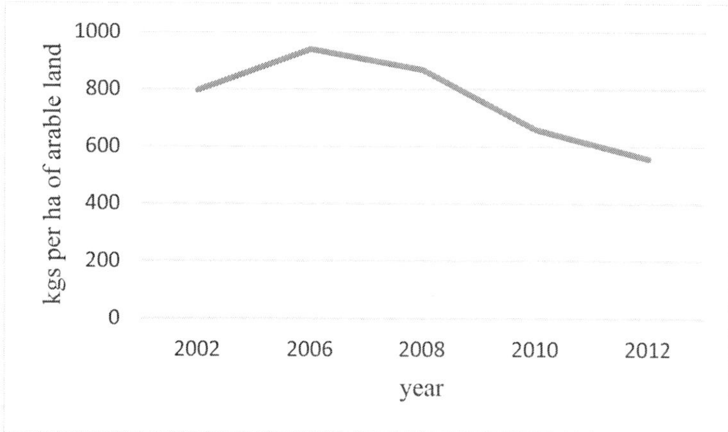

Source: World Bank (2017d)

Agricultural equipment such as tractors is also used for primary crop production. The number of tractors available for agricultural use has steadily increased from 1800 in 1961 to 5129 in 2004. All machinery used in the agriculture industry in T&T is imported since the country does not engage in heavy or specialized machinery manufacturing. See Figure 2.7.

Figure 2.7: Amount of Agricultural Machinery (Tractors) in T&T

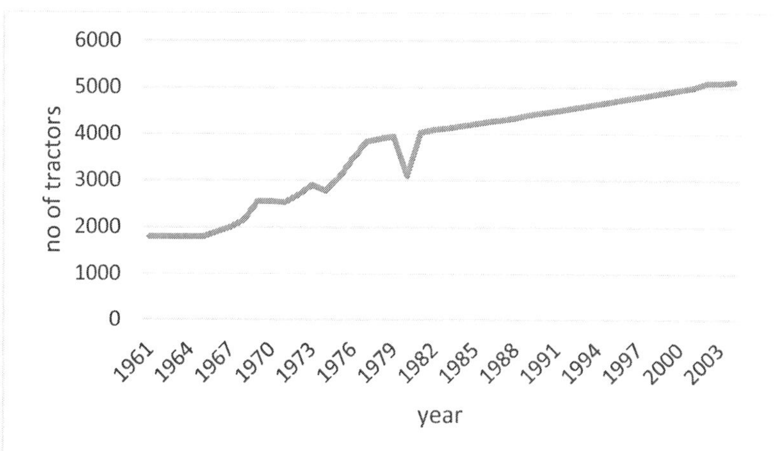

Source: World Bank (2017e)

With regard to research, some is done at the Caribbean Agriculture Research and Development Institute (CARDI) on hot peppers, sweet potato, cassava, small ruminants and organic agriculture (CARDI 2017). Some research is also done at the University of the West Indies (UWI), the University of Trinidad and Tobago (UTT), and the Caribbean Industrial Research Institute (CARIRI) to improve agricultural production methods. However, cutting-edge research in biotechnology and genetics is not done in the country.

With regard to labour, there has been a decline in employment in agriculture. See Figure 2.8.

Figure 2.8: Agriculture share of Total Employment

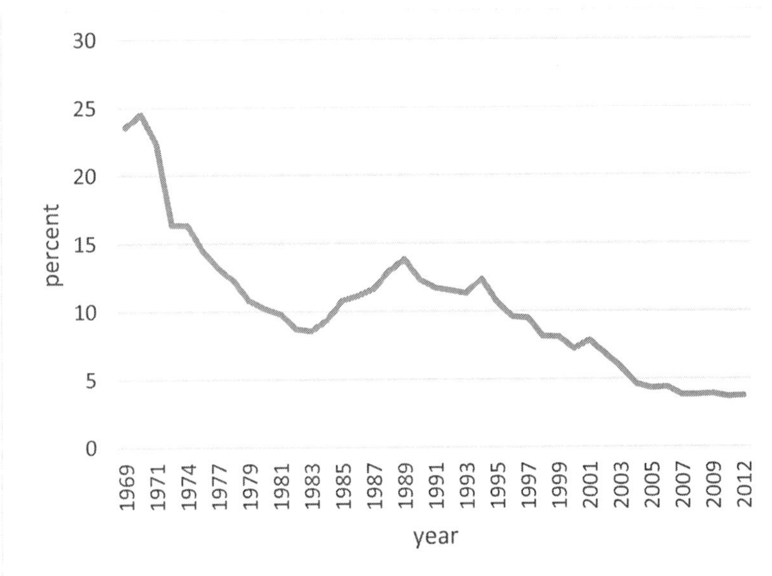

Source: World Bank (2017f)

In 1970, the agriculture sector contributed 24.56 per cent of employment. By 1980, this share had declined to 10.21 per cent. There was a modest improvement in agricultural employment, peaking at 13.89 per cent in 1989, however, from the 1990s onwards, there was a continuous decline in agricultural employment, reaching 3.73 per cent by 2012.

The sharply declining interest in farming is attributed to a number of challenges, including crop loss from diseases, floods, and larceny, the multiplier effect from the shutdown of Caroni (1975) Limited, and the country's increased focus on the energy sector (Lowitt et al. 2015).

It is noteworthy that tertiary education is free in T&T. In the undergraduate and postgraduate degrees in Agricultural Science offered by UWI, students cover courses in General Genetics; Microbiology; Biochemistry; Plant Anatomy and Physiology; Crop Science and Production; Post-harvest Technology; Animal Nutrition; Soil Fertility and Fertilizer Technology; Ruminant Production Systems; Parasitology, Animal Health and Diseases; Tropical Crop Protection; Non-Ruminant Production Systems; Statistics; and Soil and Water Management (UWI 2017). Subsequently, the country produces skilled labour for agriculture.

T&T's agro-processing industry, as previously indicated, follows the oligopoly market structure. The dominant entrepreneurs in the industry have access to financial capital to fund their investments. They import the required machinery, and hire the required labour to facilitate their production. Furthermore, through the process of mergers and acquisitions, they have managed to increase their market share.

2.4.2 Demand Conditions

Porter (1990) highlighted that three attributes of demand in the home country were essential to building competitive advantage. The first attribute is the size of the home demand relative to world demand. Obviously, if the home country is large and its domestic demand represents a significant share of world demand, its demand characteristics can influence what will be supplied. Furthermore, if a domestic firm can build competitiveness in the home market, it increases its likelihood of building competitiveness in the world market.

The second characteristic is the sophistication of the buyers. As buyers become more sophisticated, they may demand a better quality of product on the domestic market. This can force domestic firms to innovate in order to reach the domestic standards.

The third factor is the internationalization of home demand. Firms can gain competitive advantage where domestic markets provide an accurate outlook of emerging buyer demand.

There is a demand for both unprocessed and processed agricultural products in T&T. In fact, the country imported approximately US$1 billion of food products[31] in 2015. See Figure 2.9.

Figure 2.9: Food Product Imports in T&T

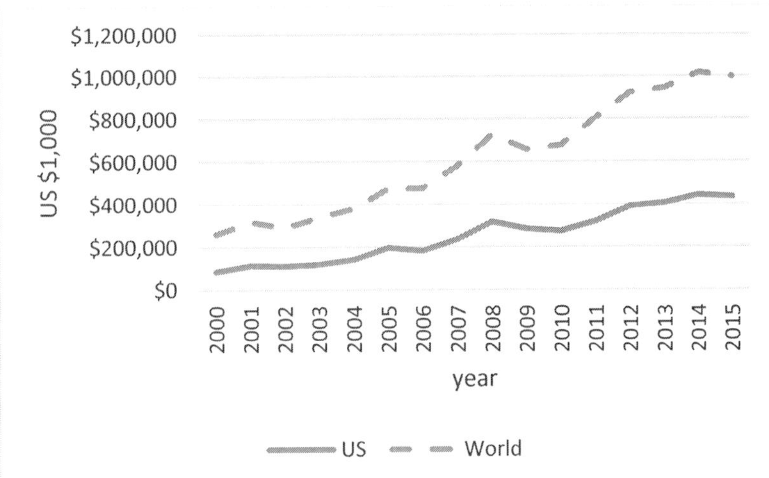

Source: WITS (2017)

As can be seen in Figure 2.9, the imports of food products continuously increased over the 2000 to 2015 period. This reflects an increasing demand for food products in T&T. Indeed, increasing the amount of processed and unprocessed products domestically can reduce T&T's food import bill. Furthermore, increased specialization in agro-processing can allow manufacturers to capture more value added.

T&T's total import of food products is very small relative to the world total imports of food products. In fact, T&T's import of food products is less than 1 per cent of world total food imports. Thus, it cannot influence the world demand for food products. Furthermore, the buyers in the T&T market are not sophisticated enough to demand higher quality standards for any food products.

Nevertheless, there is sufficient demand in the domestic market to allow entrepreneurs (both foreign and local) to earn a profit. Moreover, demand preferences have allowed the restaurant and fast food industry to flourish

[31] Here the "food products" were comprised of SITC 0 and SITC 1.

domestically. In fact, the country's unique culture[32] complements the beverages industry, the restaurant industry, and the fast food industry.

2.4.3 Firm Structure and Rivalry

While there has been a decline in the number of persons engaged in the production of primary (raw/unprocessed) agricultural products, there has been a proliferation of agro-processed food products in T&T. There is competition between the top producers in the agro-processing industry in T&T. The competition has encouraged product differentiation, sales promotions, and different marketing strategies.

However, competition can be strongly seen in the restaurant and fast food industry. Small-scale entrepreneurs often compete with large-scale businesses in the supply of fast food. In fact, small-scale entrepreneurs may set up a small food cart on the outside of the large-scale businesses, and manage to obtain sales.[33]

2.4.4 Related and Supporting Industries

Apart from ammonia and urea, T&T has weak participation in the inputs segment of the agriculture global value chain. Subsequently, there are few support industries. Seeds, agro-chemicals, and agricultural equipment are often imported, and sold at hardware stores to facilitate cultivation. Some farmers may reuse seeds from domestically produced crops, however, there is almost no domestic trade in such seeds.

Given the declining and limited amount of primary agricultural output produced domestically, large-scale firms in the agro-processing industry and the fast food and restaurant industry often resort to importing primary agricultural products to use as inputs.

---

[32] During the February to March period, T&T celebrates carnival. During this period, there are several events and parties, all of which are accompanied by high alcoholic and non-alcoholic consumption. Additionally, there is high demand for purchased food by the participants of the events.

[33] It is important to note, that the sales of the small-scale businesses tend to be significantly smaller than those of the large-scale businesses. For instance, on any random night, a small-scale food cart business may earn a few hundreds to a few thousand dollars. A small-scale food cart would typically earn less than TT $10,000 on the average night. However, the large-scale businesses, such as KFC, could earn hundreds of thousands of dollars on a given night.

However, the GORTT, through its Ministry of Agriculture and several of its agencies, tries to provide support for farmers and agricultural exporters. For instance, the Ministry of Agriculture through its Farmers Incentive Programme provides a wide range of subsidies to partially offset the cost of farming (GORTT 2017).[34]

The National Agriculture Marketing and Development Corporation (NAMDEVCO) provides marketing assistance to farmers.[35] In fact, NAMDEVCO's farmer's market provides the infrastructure and a framework to directly connect farmers with consumers, allowing such consumers to access primary agricultural goods at wholesale prices. Furthermore, NAMDEVCO collects retail and wholesale price data from the retail and distribution facilities in T&T. The data are fed into NAMDEVCO's National Agricultural Market Information System (NAMISTT), an online database, to provide real-time access to information to the agriculture industry stakeholders, to facilitate decision-making.

ExporTT provides technical training to all exporters seeking to implement a food safety management system.[36] ExporTT also provides training to current and potential exporters in: Market Access; Trade Agreements; Certificate of Origin; Market Research; Export Pricing; Rules of Origin; International Marketing; Packaging and Labelling for Exports; and Export Planning.

The Trinidad and Tobago Agri-business Association (TTABA) was created as a "For Development Company" by private sector agri-business stakeholders to facilitate the planning and development of the local agri-business sector. TTABA implements the GOTT-funded National Agri-business Development Programme (NADP), which has development and commercial components. The developmental aspects are focused on supporting farmers' associations. The commercial components involve establishing new agro-processing facilities, and the marketing of new value-

---

[34] The GORTT provides rebates on: vehicles used for agriculture, the cost of irrigation, land preparation, soil conservation, waste management, and pest management (GORTT 2017).

[35] NAMDEVCO identifies potential local and international buyers; provides farmers with contacts for freight, financing and credit insurance; and helps farmers to gain access to packing houses.

[36] ExporTT also collaborates with the Ministry of Trade and Industry to gain market access to new foreign markets for current and potential exporters.

added food, feed, and non-food products from agricultural produce (Persad et al. 2009).

The Agricultural Development Bank (ADB) provides development financing for the agriculture sector. Its financial packages (of credit, and amortized lending, with low interest rates) are uniquely tailored to meet the diverse needs of farmers and other agri-entrepreneurs.

The Export Import Bank of Trinidad and Tobago Limited (EXIM Bank) provides loan finance to exporters in T&T. The EXIM Bank scope is not limited to any one sector. Thus, any exporter, even primary agriculture, agro-processing, or agricultural fertilizer producers may approach the EXIM Bank for loan finance to help develop their productive capacity and engage in international trade.

2.5.0 Challenges Experienced in T&T's Cluster

T&T's agriculture industry faces a wide range of challenges. There are production constraints due to pests and diseases, adverse weather conditions, poor irrigation, praedial larceny, and labour shortages (Arnold Babwah & Associates 2015). The ammonia and urea industries, which are downstream natural gas industries, also face supply side constraints.

2.5.1 Pest and Diseases

Crops produced in T&T have been affected by several diseases. For cocoa, the crops tend to be affected by two main diseases: Black Pod Disease, and Witches' Broom. For Black Pod Disease, the discolouring of pods is the main symptom. The disease tends to flourish where there is excessive moisture in the field. Continuous rainfall, poor drainage, and impeded air circulation create conditions which facilitate the spread of the disease (CRC 2017).[37]

Witches' Broom, which is caused by a mushroom-like fungus (Moniliophthora perniciosa), results in flower distortion, pod infection, and destruction of the cocoa beans (Aime and Phillips-Mora 2005; CRC 2017). Although the

[37] Preventing moisture retention in the field, the regular removal of infected pods from trees, as well as regular spraying with fungicide help to reduce the incidence of black pod (CRC 2017).

spores of this fungus are spread by the wind, it must receive water in order to germinate. As a consequence, it mainly spreads during rainy periods.[38]

In the years that Caroi (1975) operated, sugar cane cultivation in T&T was negatively affected by the Froghopper (Monecphora saccharina) (MOALMR 1995; Sinha 2011). The insect sucks the leaf sugar cane, eventually drying up and killing the plant. The insect also tends to abound in hot, humid conditions. Like most insects, froghopper numbers can be controlled with insecticides.

In citrus, the crop yields have been negatively affected by the Citrus Tristeza Virus (CTV). Some of the common symptoms of the virus include the yellowing of mature leaves, the rotting of roots, and even plant death. The disease is often spread via the black citrus aphid (Toxoptera citricidus Kirk). Long-distance transmission of CTV also occurs by the movement of infected plant material or plant material infested with CTV-infected aphids (Dawson et al. 2013).[39]

Table 2.15: Major Pests and Diseases affecting T&T's Agriculture

Pest/Disease	Crop
Black pod disease	Cocoa
Froghopper	Sugar cane
Citrus tristeza virus, Asian Citrus Psyllid	Citrus
Black sigatoka	Plantain/Banana
Thrips, whitefly, bacterial wilt and anthracnose	Vegetables
Cassava bacterial blight and Megastes grandalis	Root crops
Tephritid fruit fly	Tropical fruits

Source: Adapted from MOALMR (1995); Sinha (2011)

In vegetables, T&T has experienced problems with thrips (MOALMR 1995). Thrips suck the juices of plants, and scrape their leaves, flowers, and

[38] Witches' broom may be addressed by removing brooms and diseased pods before the rainy season; applying fungicide; and growing disease resistant crops (CRC 2017).

[39] The transmission of CTV is controlled via the quarantine of infected trees, and by spraying nursery plants and young trees with insecticide to control aphids (Dawson et al. 2013).

fruits, eventually causing the plant to die.[40] Table 2.15 provides a summary of the common major pests and diseases to have negatively affected crop yields in T&T.

2.5.2 Adverse Weather Conditions

Almost on an annual basis, floods destroy the agricultural output of some farmers in T&T. Some areas such as Caroni, Chaguanuas, Debe, and low-lying areas close to the Oropouche River, are prone to flooding in Trinidad. In fact, as recent as 2017, after Tropical Storm Bret, a number of farmers in Trinidad complained about floods destroying their crops (Santoo 2017).

Ironically, in good weather conditions, a lot of farms suffer from poor irrigation (Persad et al. 2009).

2.5.3 Praedial Larceny

Farmers operating in T&T, often have to deal with the theft of their crops and/or livestock. One report notes

> *Praedial larceny proliferation is primarily driven by the increased demand for supplies in the domestic fresh food chains, where there are many opportunities for praedial activities to become a profitable business with its own set of dynamics in agriculture food distribution.*
>
> *Small and petty thieves, who have organized systems for theft and disposal of food, have become a part of what now appears to be a national system. Not to mention the loss of employment and production as farmers reduce output or leave the sector altogether due to the strain that this crime, combined with other agricultural challenges, puts on their incomes and consequently profits and livelihood. As such, what was once considered a petty crime, committed to put food on the table, has now become a major offence, impacting entire communities*. (Intra-ACP APP 2016, 2).

One study notes that in 2010, T&T experienced a loss of US$11.3 million over a six-month period due to praedial larceny (Graham 2010). Indeed, if farmers become discouraged due to their threat, it would reduce the number of people employed in the primary agriculture industry, as well as reduce agricultural output.

[40] Thrips may be addressed by insecticide, or organically by introducing the minute pirate bugs, which feeds on the thrip eggs (Higgins 1992).

2.5.4 Challenges with the Caroni (1975) "2-acre" Farms

After the closure of Caroni (1975) Limited, the GORTT allocated 2-acre land parcels to approximately 7,800 applicants (Persad et al. 2009).[41] This policy was a key agricultural diversification policy initiative of the GORTT (Persad et al. 2009). Farmers who received the lands encountered numerous predicaments in cultivating the land. One study notes

> *Farmers who attempted to cultivate assigned plots were confronted by a range of technical and socio-economic constraints. Technical constraints included inadequate land clearing and development, impoverished acid soils, rudimentary access roads, inadequate infield drainage for heavy clay soils, and an absence of irrigation facilities. Socio-economic constraints included lack of technical support, uneconomic farm size, limited agricultural knowledge, and distance of plots from farmer residences.* (Persad et al. 2009, 108).

Persad et al. (2009) note that approximately 67 per cent of the land suffered from poor drainage; 88 per cent endured inadequate irrigation facilities; 57 per cent experienced high soil acidity with the pH less than 4.5. Furthermore, these lands were noted to possess low levels of plant nutrients. Table 2.16 provides a summary of the findings from the Persad et al. (2009) study.

Table 2.16: Land Quality Limitations of the Caroni (1975) "2-acre" Farms

Restriction	Acreage	%	Main Sections
Indequate Drainage	4,950	67	Caroni, Waterloo, Exchange, Edinburgh, Felicity
Irrigation (Absence)	6,500	88	All Sections
Soil Acidity, pH <4.5	4,200	57	Jerningham, Exchange, Waterloo, Felicity
Erosion >50% topsoil loss	1,480	20	La Gloria, Cedar Hill, Petit Morne, Picton
Compaction	2,585	35	Jerningham, Caroni, Edinburgh
Low Nutrient Availability	5,620	76	North and Central Sections

[41] The 2015 budget speech noted that the lease issuance exercise was for more than 8,800 former employees of Caroni (1975) Limited, however by September 2014, only approximately 1,700 leases had been distributed (GORTT 2014).

Land Clearing, levelling	6,950	94	All Sections
Adverse Soil Physical Properties	5,320	72	Central and South Sections

Source: Persad et al (2009)

The study goes on to note that

> *The '2-acre' farm model as proposed is not feasible as a production unit and has minimal impact on national food production and food security.* (Persad et al. 2009, 107).

There also appears to be a lack of communication between the government ministries and agencies with regard to land use. One example can be seen in April 2011 when the Housing and Development Corporation (HDC) bulldozed about 25 acres of cultivated land in order to make space for residences, at the request of the Ministry of Housing. Another example can be seen with an incident which occurred in 2011, where the National Gas Company (NGC) bulldozed about 30 acres of cultivated agricultural plots allocated to former Caroni (1975) Limited workers, in order to make room for a natural gas pipeline (Allard 2012).

Furthermore, in the 2015 budget speech, the then Minister of Finance and the Economy, announced that the ex-workers receiving the 2-acre land parcels' agricultural leases were now free to sell the land (GORTT 2014). Such a move would undermine efforts to revive T&T's primary agriculture sector, as flat agricultural lands would be sold and used for non-agricultural purposes.

2.5.5 Labour Limitations

The agriculture sector suffers from shortages of labour. Both the primary agricultural output and the agro-processing segments of the global value chain suffer from labour shortages in T&T. Farmers are discouraged from farming due to pests, bad weather, and praedial larceny issues. However, employed labour has little interest in working in agricultural fields.

The loss of interest in the primary agriculture and agro-processing sectors has been influenced by changing labour dynamics in T&T. As can be seen from Table 18, in 2001, the total employment in Community Social and Personal (CSP) services was 154,400 persons. Make-work programmes, which are included in this sector, increased by 16 per cent to 179,500 persons by 2008. Over the same period, the amount of labour employed in the agriculture sector decreased from 40,080 persons to 23,000 persons, a 43 per cent contraction. Employment in the manufacturing sector increased marginally by 3 per cent, from 53,858 persons to 56,000 persons between 2001 and 2008. These patterns indicate that there was some degree of labour reallocation between the sectors in favour of the CSP services sector. Over the 2008 to 2015 period, employment in CSP increased from 182,500 persons to 201,000 persons, alongside a further decline in agricultural employment from 22,900 to 21,300.

Table 2.17: Employment in Various Sectors of T&T's Economy

	Total Employed Labour Force	Employment in Community social and personal employment (CSP)	Agriculture	Manufacturing
2001	514,126	154,400	40,080	53,858
2002	525,081	158,100	36,115	56,568
2003	534,153	163,200	31,402	55,806
2004	562,378	175,300	26,003	60,296
2005	574,025	176,500	25,030	56,599
2006	586,205	181,100	25,749	56,185
2007	587,892	178,600	22,413	55,379
2008	597,700	179,500	23,000	56,000
2009	588,300	182,500	22,900	53,100
2010	582,100	192,300	21,500	52,100
2011	583,500	192,800	21,738	48,700
2012	614,100	198,400	22,900	48,713
2013	626,300	199,900	22,000	51,000
2014	636,800	205,000	22,900	50,400
2015	623,300	201,000	21,300	51,200

Source: Primary data collected from the Central Statistical Office (CSO)

In 2002, the GORTT government instituted the Community-based Environment Protection and Enhancement Programme (CEPEP), with the objective to provide employment opportunities for the vulnerable nationals of T&T. By 2015, CEPEP realized a cumulative expenditure of TT $4.687 billion. It is noteworthy that during this period the unemployment level tumbled from 61,200 to 24,200, consequently the unemployment rate also tumbled from 10.4 per cent to 3.6 per cent. See Table 2.18.

Table 2.18: Cumulative Expenditure on CEPEP

Fiscal Year	CEPEP	Cumulative CEPEP (TT $mn)	Unemployment (000s)	Unemployment Rate %
May to September 2002	$75	75	61.2	10.4
2003	$155	230	62.4	10.5
2004	$225	455	51.2	8.4
2005	$244	699	49.7	8
2006	$423	1122	39	6.2
2007	$350	1472	34.5	5.5
2008	$328	1800	29	4.6
2009	$330	2130	32.6	5.3
2010	$319	2449	36.7	5.9
2011	$320	2769	31.1	5.1
2012	$320	3089	31.1	4.9
2013	$468	3557	23.9	3.7
2014	$536	4093	21.8	3.3
2015	$594	4687	24.1	3.6

Source: CBTT (2017)

CEPEP and the Unemployment Relief Programme (URP), another type of make-work programme, collectively employs approximately 25,000 people.[42] "Make work programmes" in general can help relatively unskilled workers to obtain work, when the job market may be tight. Of concern is the possibility of "make work programmes" to cheat the private sector out of sufficient supplies of the labour market (Levin-Waldman 1995). Moreover, "make work programmes" by artificially lowering the unemployment rate can mask the urgency of the need for important labour market reform. "Make work programmes" arguably encourage workers to be less diligent in their search for alternative jobs, especially those with more work hours, but the overall "same end of week salary".

[42] It is important to note that CEPEP and URP are not the only make-work programmes to historically be applied in T&T. There has also been: i) the Prime Minister's Special Work Programme in the 1950s; ii) the Developmental Environmental Works Division (DEWD) in the 1960s; and iii) the Labour Intensive Development Programme (LIDP) in 1988.

There has also been some evidence of the Baumol Disease[43] occurring in the agriculture sector in T&T, as employers have to pay higher wages in order to attract workers.

> *Food Production Minister Senator Devant Maharaj ... said one farmer paid $400 a day per worker to harvest peppers but those workers quit as soon as the dry season set in, refusing to work in warm outdoor conditions. They would rather work in KFC or URP for $67.50 a day.* (Trinidad and Tobago Guardian 2015, 1).

2.5.5.1 Age of Farmers

T&T has an aging farming population. In 2004, 63 per cent of the farmers in T&T were over 45 years. Only 2 per cent of the farmers were in the under 25 age group. See Table 2.19. The weak interest by young people in farming is a cause for concern, as it signals that the supply of farmers is not being sufficiently renewed in T&T.

Table 2.19: Private Holders of Agricultural Land in Trinidad and Tobago by Age in 2004

Age Group	No. of holders
Under 25 years	437
25-34 years	1974
35-44 years	4621
45-54 years	5157
55-64 years	3872
65 and over	2958
Not stated	36
Total	19055

Source: Allard (2012)

2.5.6 Small Scale Constraints

Of the 19,143 total holders in T&T in 2004, 96.6 per cent (18,505) of holders were categorized as Individual/Household/Sole Proprietor (18505

[43] Baumol Disease refers to a situation where workers who have not experienced any increase in productivity end up receiving a rise in their salary due to a rise in the salary of other workers in the economy.

holders). In terms of farm size, 96 per cent of all holdings were less than 10 hectares. The two largest categories of farms were 2 to <5 hectares (34.1%) and under 0.5 hectares (22%). See Figure 2.10. Thus, the data suggest that the majority of T&T farmers are small-scale farmers.

Figure 2.10: Agriculture Holdings in T&T by Size in 2004

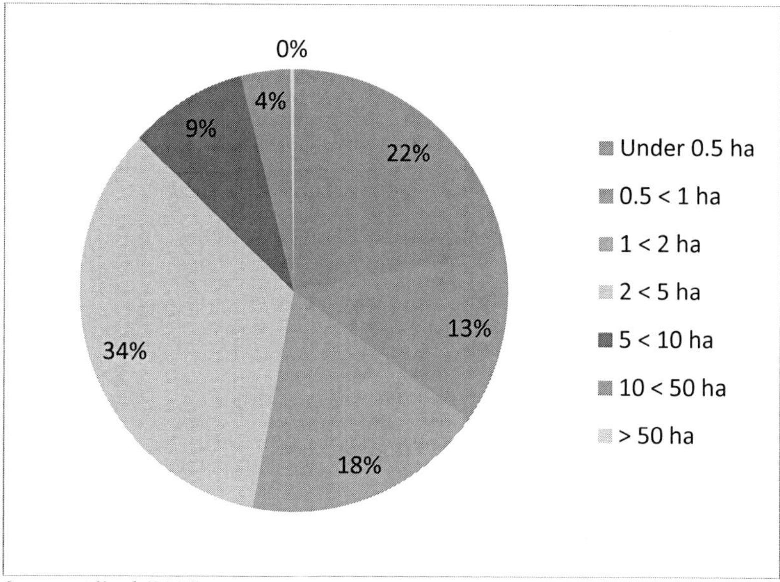

Source: Allard (2012)

Small-scale farmers, with volatile income and limited collateral experience difficulty in gaining access to finance. Banking and financial institutions are often hesitant to lend to farmers given their perceived risk of start-ups and small-scale enterprises.[44]

Ever since independence in 1962, the Government of Trinidad and Tobago has distributed land for agricultural use. However, the land is often

[44] It is important to note that the ADB provides microloans to a large number of farmers in T&T at low interest rates ranging between 3 per cent and 5 per cent. In 2011, the ADB allocated TT $189 million to provide loans to both new and experienced farmers; and TT $20 million to provide loans to address pests and disease. Farmers may also access unsecured loans up to TT $50,000 to purchase seedlings, fertilizers and small tools; TT $200,000 for the purchase of rice combine harvesters; and TT $50,000 to purchase new or used equipment (Allard 2012).

transferred without providing the farmers with complementary support services such as credit, technical assistance, and marketing, resulting in farmers procuring land which they cannot maintain (Allard 2012).

2.5.7 Supply Side Constraints to the Ammonia and Urea Industries

As previously mentioned, T&T produces ammonia and urea due to its endowment with natural gas. Ammonia accounts for approximately 40% of natural gas-based petrochemical production capacity in T&T, while urea accounts for 5%. The ammonia and urea subsectors faced a supply side challenge due to natural gas supply curtailments, resulting in the temporary closure of some of the ammonia plants.[45]

It is noteworthy that when an ammonia plant is running at full capacity, it operates at a stable state. However, the variable gas supply causes producers to stop and restart plants, exposing the equipment to cycles in pressure and temperature, accelerating wear and tear, and also increasing the plant operating costs due to unproductive gas consumed during start and stop sequences.

Part of the reason for the natural gas curtailments experienced over the 2010 to 2014 period was due to the extensive work undertaken by the major upstream producers (BPTT and BG) to upgrade gas infrastructure (Brooks 2014). Most of these corresponding maintenance projects were completed by 2014 (OPMRTT 2017). Therefore, the curtailments experienced from 2014 to mid-2017 were due to a pause in investment by the upstream producers due to uncertainty in T&T's energy economics environment. Factors such as the expectation of an oversupply of natural gas due to the cancellation of downstream projects (Khan 2017a), more specifically, the cancellation of the proposed aluminum smelter project at La Brea, in Trinidad, as well as delays in the negotiation of new natural gas prices, volumes, and contracts between the GORTT, NGC, and producers in the upstream and downstream industries, contributed to the delays in the natural gas investments (OPMRTT 2017).

Another challenge is the nature of the contractual relationships between the upstream producers and the downstream producers in the natural gas

[45] Three ammonia producers shut down their plants in 2011 (ICIS News 2011), and the Caribbean Nitrogen Company's (CNC) ammonia plant was shut down in 2017 (Sookraj 2018).

industry. Currently the upstream producers directly sell natural gas to Atlantic LNG (ALNG) for the export of natural gas. The National Gas Company (NGC) operates at the midstream where it purchases natural gas from the upstream producers, and sells the gas to downstream producers, including the ammonia and urea producers. NGC has a contractual obligation to supply natural gas to its downstream clients regardless of how much gas it receives from its upstream suppliers. In fact, the estimated supply of available volumes to NGC stood at 1,250 million cubic feet per day (MMcfd) by year end 2017, as against the consumption requirements of 1,960 MMcfd.[46] The inability of NGC to supply its contracted volumes to its downstream stakeholders is problematic, often leading to legal claims. In fact, over the period 2011 to 2015, NGC paid TT$4.5345 billion in legal claims to downstream producers. Indeed, the gas curtailment erodes the profitability of NGC, and the economic rent captured by the GORTT.

2.5.8 Other Challenges

T&T's agriculture sector is also negatively affected by general productivity constraints affecting the country. These include: badly and infrequently maintained roads; inefficient administration from government offices; inefficient ports; and a growing crime rate.

2.6.0 Policy to Facilitate Upgrading

Upgrading is the process of firms moving from low value-added segments/activities to higher value-added activities. According to Humphrey and Schmitz (2002) upgrading is comprised of: i) process upgrading (this is where production methods improve efficiency); ii) product upgrading (this is where production is moved into more sophisticated product lines, measured by e.g., increased unit values); iii) functional upgrading (this is where new functions are acquired, or even new products may be produced); and iv) inter-sectoral upgrading (this is where new productive activities are entered into by clusters of firms).

[46] Over the 2015 to mid-2017 period, T&T was producing just over 3 billion cubic feet (Bcf) of natural gas per day. In November 2017, its total natural gas production was 3.8 Bcfd. However, the country's natural gas demand is approximately 4 Bcfd (GORTT MEEI 2018).

2.6.1 Increasing Primary Agricultural Output (Process and Product Upgrading)

As previously established in Table 2.13, primary agriculture only accounted for 6.5% of T&T's total agricultural product exports in 2015. Furthermore, the reveal comparative advantage statistics reveal that none of T&T's primary agricultural products are competitive. The intuition is that for any export programme to be successful and sustainable, it should of necessity be predicated on comparative advantage and competitiveness. In the absence of such comparative advantage, it may be logical for a government to avoid pursing a primary agriculture-based exporting strategy.

However, there is political motivation for the government to try to encourage primary agricultural production to safeguard some amount of domestic production to partially satisfy domestic consumption needs. This is also justified by the need to attempt to reduce the country's food import bill, which stood at approximately TT$1.7 billion in 2017. Additionally, the government may also be motivated to encourage some amount of primary agricultural production in order to allow the remaining farmers that are still actively engaged in the agriculture industry to earn a sustainable income. Such arguments provide a justification for the government to provide policy support to encourage process upgrading in the primary segment of the agriculture value chain.

As previously indicated, the inputs required for primary agriculture are land, labour, agro-chemicals, and machinery. It is impossible to increase the total land area in T&T beyond 513,000 hectares (5,128 km^2). However, the GORTT planned to allocate 2-acre land parcels to approximately 8,800 of the former Caroni (1975) Limited workers (GORTT 2014).

Given that recipients of plots are neither technically nor financially equipped to cultivate the heavy clay soils with their limited agricultural infrastructure, Persad et al. (2009) recommended the consolidation of 2-acre plots into technical and economic management units. These land units could be managed by the TTABA as it has the technical capacity to address the technical limitations of the land, as well as assist in the processing and marketing of the agricultural output.

Production can be enhanced through crop zoning, and scheduling. Persad's (*ibid*) study recommends

> *The schedule proposes cultivating 5,668 hectares with a contingency allocation of 20% of land allocated for infrastructure development and*

environmental protection. The projected allocation is tropical fruits and tree crops (50%); herbs and spices (0.3%); staples-root crops and vegetables (26%); livestock and aquaculture (20%). (Persad et al. 299, 111).

Table 2.20 illustrates the recommended land use matrix.

Given that not all of the Caroni 2-acre farms have been allocated, and given that potential farmers would lack the resources to cultivate the land an alternative option would be for the government to first implement a land rehabilitation programme before distribution. Such a programme could entail the installation of proper drainage and irrigation infrastructure; the soil acidity being addressed; and the land being treated with fertilizer and pesticides prior to its allocation.

Given that this land rehabilitation programme would incur upfront sunk costs, rather than distributing the land for free, the government can form a national agriculture company. The national agriculture company could retain ownership of the land but would be charged with the mandate to market agricultural produce. It could purchase primary agricultural produce from the farmers, engage in some agro-processing, and then sell the finished product in the domestic or international markets. Such a national agriculture company should operate with the objective to maximise profits, and its economic model should be monitored and evaluated every three years by an agriculture economics board, comprised of experts from the regional universities, as well as policy officials from the Ministry of Agriculture.

It is important to note, the national agriculture company should not hire farmers on a permanent, or "contract of service" basis. It should pay farmers only for the amount of output produced on a "contract for service" basis.[47] To prevent productive inefficiency from arising, there should be no price floor or guaranteed fixed prices for farmers.

---

[47] A person working on a "contract of service" basis is an employee of an organization. In a "contract for service", the person is paid for the services that they provide, but they are not an employee of the organization.

Table 2.20: Land Use Recommendation for Caroni 2-acre farms

Crops	C	OG	JJ	Ed	F	W	EX	M	R/W	PM	LaF	LaG	GH	Total
Sweet Potato	50		200	300	150	150	200				200		100	1350
Cassava						150	200	100	200	100	200		100	1050
Plantain/banana			60			50	50		50			100		310
Corn														0
Vegetables	200	100		150	50	50	50			100	100		100	900
Small Ruminants				100	60			100	100	50	50	50	150	660
Coconut						50	50	100	50	50	50	50	50	450
Pommecythere				100	100	100	100	70	50	100	50		100	770
Fruit							200			150	150	140		640
Dry Legumes	60			50			100		150		50			410
Aquaculture					100	100								200
Other Root Crops					150					100	100			350
Allocated (Acres)	310	100	260	700	610	650	950	370	600	650	950	340	600	7090

C – Caroni
OG – Orange Grove
JJ – Jerningham Junction
ED – Edinburgh
F – Felicity
W – Waterloo
EX – Exchange
M – Montserrat
R/W – Reform/ Williamsville
PM – Petite Morne
LaF – La Fortune
LaG – La Gloria
CH – Cedar Hill

Source: Persad et al. (2012)

Perhaps, farmers could be mandated to first pursue free courses in agricultural production and quality,[48] and obtain certification before being allowed to sell their agricultural produce to the national agriculture company. This strategy would address the land fertility problem, the access to finance problem, and potential SPS barriers, all of which are difficulties currently facing small-scale farmers.

An alternative option would be for the GORTT to collaborate with the ADB and the TTABA, to develop a programme that would train the farmers on how to address the technical challenges of the agricultural lands, as well as provide financing to facilitate cultivation. It is important to note, the Extension, Training and Information Services (ETIS) Division of the Ministry of Agriculture already provides free short-term training (for one month) in various primary agriculture, and small-scale processing. However, an additional required step may be the synchronizing of training, with financing within a programme.

Currently, the GORTT provides subsidies in agriculture by reimbursing the cost borne by farmers. The problem with this strategy is that farmers need to have the money upfront to make the financial transaction before they can be reimbursed. Perhaps, the GORTT could consider amending its subsidy system, whereby grants are provided up front. The downside of this recommendation is the tendency for people to use the agriculture grant for non-agriculture related purposes.

To address the issue of praedial larceny, in 2011 the Ministry of Agriculture established the Praedial Larceny Squad. The Ministry also provides a subsidy whereby farmers can be reimbursed up to TT $30,000 for the installation of security systems.

To address labour challenges, a tempting option would be for the government to directly use employees of CEPEP in primary agriculture cultivation. However, given the past inefficiency of Caroni (1975) Limited, such direct employment should be avoided. Given the length of time CEPEP has been

---

[48] This can be done in collaboration with the TTABA, ExporTT, the UWI/UTT, and the Ministry of Agriculture. Currently ExporTT provides free training to exporters so that they may earn a Preventive Controls Qualified Individual (PCQI) certification. This certification is a requirement by the US Food Safety Preventive Controls Alliance (FSPCA) in order to export food and beverage products to the US. The requirement is to ensure the safe preparation of food products for human consumption in the US.

in operation, it is highly unlikely that the GORTT would downscale CEPEP, as this will cause the unemployment rate to rise above 5%.

Perhaps, the GORTT can consider sourcing labour from other CARICOM member states. Immigrants from other CARICOM member states have already displayed a willingness to work in T&T. If the GORTT implements the consolidated Caroni plots plan (which would be managed with technical assistance from the TTABA), it could use immigrants from the CARICOM member states as labour. However, the focus of this venture should be to earn a profit. If the average variable costs of production are not recoverable in the short run, the business venture should be shut down and re-evaluated.

2.6.2 Increasing Inputs (Ammonia and Urea production) and Product Upgrading

In the ammonia and urea industries, output can be increased by increasing the amount of natural gas allocated towards ammonia and urea production.

Negotiation for increased natural gas production from the Juniper platform was ongoing from 2009. British Petroleum Trinidad and Tobago (BPTT) and the GORTT have engaged in negotiations since the increased rate of natural gas consumption in the country, and the slower rate to natural reserves replacement suggested that a natural gas shortage may develop. The Prime Minister of Trinidad and Tobago notes that a shortage was observed by the GORTT in 2011 (OPMRTT 2017). Although the negotiations for the Juniper platform were completed in 2013 (ORMRTT 2017), the platform fabrication project did not commence until 2015 due to delays in the GORTT renegotiating prices, volume, and supply contracts with the upstream stakeholders.[49]

The Juniper natural gas offshore platform project, resulted in the increase in the country's gas supply by 590 MMcfd[50] in 2017 (Williams 2017).[51] When the BPTT begins producing from the Angeline natural gas platform in 2019, it is expected to add an extra 600 MMcfd to T&T's total natural gas production (Offshore Technology 2018). Furthermore, if cross-border

---

[49] The Juniper topside was fabricated at the TOFCO fabrication yard in La Brea, Trinidad, while the jacket and piles were fabricated at Gulf Marine Fabricators in Aransas Pass, Texas.

[50] 1,000 MMcf = 1 Bcf.

[51] Natural gas production from the Juniper field commenced in August 2017 (BP 2017; Williams 2017).

natural gas with Venezuela as well as potential natural gas from Venezuela's Dragon field are utilized, T&T can significantly increase its natural gas production (Khan 2017b).[52] Some of this natural gas would undoubtedly be allocated to ammonia and urea to increase their production.

It is noteworthy that the Natural Gas Master Plan report of Poten and Partners (2015) revealed that in 2014, LNG realized a netback price of US$3.32 per MMBtu, while the netback to the wellhead for ammonia was approximately US$6.00 per MMBtu. Thus, the export of ammonia is more profitable for the GORTT than the export of LNG. Given that T&T's current gas utilization is 60% LNG export, and 40% domestic consumption, it is sensible for the GORTT to revise the country's gas utilization rates in favour of greater petrochemical production upon the expiry of the ALNG contracts.

The GORTT was in a fortunate position as several of its natural gas supply contracts were due to expire between 2013 and 2018. The GORTT is aware that it is competing with several other countries for investment dollars in its upstream industry. While the GORTT continues to lose approximately US$1.5 billion due to transfer pricing in natural gas annually, and the multinational upstream producers continue to make high returns on investments in Trinidad relative to other energy exporting jurisdictions,[53] it is the position of the upstream companies that

> *they maintain that they share a disproportionate share of the rewards for the level of risk they take. In their view the maturity of T&T as a hydrocarbon province has been occasioned by greater sub-surface and geological risks without the commensurate reward. In their opinion NGC and the downstream companies have benefitted disproportionately in the returns accruing to the sector.... In the final analysis, their position is that unless*

---

[52] The GORTT and the Government of Venezuela have entered a Framework Treaty relating to the Unitization of Hydrocarbon Reservoirs. The Framework Treaty provides a legal framework whereby any hydrocarbon reserves that extend across the maritime boundary of the countries are to be developed as a unit. The known cross-border discoveries between the two countries are the Kapok-Dorado field, the Manakin-Coquina field, and the Loran-Manatee field. However, the governments have only executed a framework treaty for cross-border unitization for the Loran-Manatee field. Approximately 27 per cent of the 7.5 trillion cubic feet (TCF) of the reserves in the Loran-Manatee Field have been allocated to T&T under the agreement (Beckles 2015).

[53] The other jurisdictions are Colombia, Ghana, Brazil, Norway and Nigeria (GORTT MEEI 2018).

the reward matches the risk, there will be reduced investments in the upstream and consequently less gas. (GORTT MEEI 2018, 10).

In lieu of the aforementioned loss of value captured from natural gas, the GORTT has expressed its intention to review its taxation legislation and review its natural gas allocation policy.

2.6.3 Increasing Agro-Processing through Process, Product and Functional Upgrading

In the agro-processing industry, exports of processed food, beverages, and tobacco can be increased if there is an increased supply of inputs. Presently, the firms in T&T's agro-processing industry import primary agricultural products for inputs, as domestic supplies are often insufficient. From the perspective of domestic farmers, this presents an opportunity to increase the domestic supply of primary agricultural output. Moreover, there is the ambit for strengthening the backward linkages between the primary agriculture farmers and the agro-processers in T&T. This can be achieved by using the TTABA to help strengthen the productive capacity of the farmers. The agro-processers in turn can be encouraged to purchase supplies of good quality primary produce from the farmers on a spot market basis.[54]

It would be excellent for primary agriculture producers in T&T to upgrade to agro-processing. It would also be equally admirable for small and micro entrepreneurs (SMEs) to engage in agro-processing and export their final products to different markets.

Bamber and Fernandez-Stark (2012) note that four factors are required for the inclusion of small- and medium-sized producers in global value chains: i) access to markets; ii) access to training; iii) coordination and collaboration building; and iv) access to finance.

For international market access, as a member of CARICOM, and the CSME, T&T has duty-free and quota-free (DFQF) access to the markets of all CARICOM member states. As a member of CARICOM, T&T has signed multiple preferential trading agreements (PTAs) with various regions and

[54] A spot market is where a market participant pays for an asset which has immediate delivery. This is in contrast to a forward market in which the market participant pays for the asset in the present but the delivery date is in the future. A spot market rather than a forward market is recommended since small-scale primary agriculture producers may have difficulty in meeting long-term contractual obligations when there are adverse weather conditions or unforeseen negative circumstances.

countries. The PTAs include: the CARICOM–Venezuela Agreement on Trade and Investment (1992); the CARICOM–Colombia Trade, Economic, and Technical Cooperation Agreement (1994); the CARICOM–Dominican Republic Free Trade Agreement (1998); the CARICOM–Cuba Trade and Economic Cooperation Agreement (2000); the CARICOM–Costa Rica Free Trade Agreement (2004); the CARIFORUM–European Union Economic Partnership Agreement (2008); and the Trinidad and Tobago–Panama Partial Scope Trade Agreement (2013) (GORTT MTI 2016).

Additionally, T&T is also granted preferential access to the US market under the Caribbean Basin Initiative (CBI) (1984), and the Caribbean Basin Trade Partnership Act (CBTPA) (2000). T&T is also granted preferential access to the Canadian market under the Caribbean–Canada Trade Agreement (CARIBCAN) (1986). Food, beverages, and tobacco are afforded DFQF access to the US and Canadian markets under the aforementioned agreements.

The GORTT through its ministry responsible for international trade may encourage the country's small- as well as large-scale agro-processers to take advantage of the increased market access provided by the country's trade agreements. Moreover, ExporTT may work alongside agro-processers to provide them (the agro-processors) with market information and advice about exporting in new markets.

With regard to training, as previously mentioned, the ETIS provides free short-term training to existing and potential farmers, while ExporTT provides training which would be useful in facilitating exports. The UWI and UTT provide degree programmes in agriculture. The Youth Training and Employment Partnership Programme (YTEPP)[55] provides nine months of training in Tilapia Production; Lawn, and Landscape Management; Vegetable Production – the Grow Box System; Grow Box and Plant Propagation; and Agro-Processing.

While the current training programmes offered are commendable, perhaps there is a need to synchronize training with finance. In order to create entrepreneurs, upon the completion of a YTEPP programme, a graduating student should automatically qualify for a grant to start an agro-processing business. Emphasis should be placed on agro-processing, since being vertically integrated into both primary production and processing allows the

[55] YTEPP courses are open to people of all ages, and pay a stipend of TT $60 a day to students. Students are taught theory and given practical training. Additionally, a person can sign up for more than one course.

SME to capture more value added. Such vertical integration is possible for processed fruit juices, peppers, and preserved fruits. Some food products are highly perishable and thus their packaged trade may be out of the reach for an SME. Examples of these products include breads, pastries, and other baked products.

To foster collaboration and coordination, the TTABA could be used to provide technical assistance and help supervise the outcomes of the graduating students. A system can be installed where the TTABA can act as mentor to ensure that graduating students are progressing. Such a programme should be evaluated every two years by independent and external professionals to assess the programme's success rate.

With regard to trade finance, the EXIM Bank can be used to provide loan finance for exporters. Presently, the EXIM Bank provides the following services: export credit insurance, raw material financing, asset financing, and foreign exchange trade.

2.7 Conclusion

The global value chain for agriculture is comprised of inputs, primary agricultural output, processing, and retail and distribution.

In the inputs segment, T&T's endowment of natural gas allows it to be a strong producer of ammonia, and urea, some macronutrients of fertilizer. T&T's comparative advantage in ammonia and urea provides justification for its increased focus on those industries. Furthermore, given that the netback for ammonia and urea is higher than the netback of LNG, it is logical for the GORTT to revise its natural gas utilization strategy in favour of increased petrochemical production. This can be facilitated by increased domestic natural gas production from offshore fields, or by the development of natural gas unitization agreements with Venezuela.

T&T has a comparative advantage in the processing segment of the agriculture value chain. Moreover, there is room to expand capacity in the agro-processing industry, and earn more revenues both domestically and internationally. The retail and distribution segment of the agriculture value chain presents opportunities for both small-scale entrepreneurs, and large-scale firms.

Despite the comparative disadvantage in primary agriculture, the GORTT can extend support to the sector in order to help safeguard some amount of domestic production to partially reduce the country's food import bill, and to strengthen the enabling environment for the remaining farmers to earn sustainable incomes.

Indeed, revitalizing T&T's primary agriculture sector requires policy action. Distribution of the "2-acre plots" which are currently challenged by inadequate drainage and irrigation, high acidity levels, and low nutrition content to people lacking the required technical resources and finance will not improve primary agricultural output. The technical challenges of the land must be addressed, and the TTABA can be used to provide technical support.

T&T has numerous agencies providing training in agriculture. However, there is a need to synchronize the technical training with finance, so that good graduating students would be transformed into successful entrepreneurs. A mentorship programme can be developed with the assistance of the TTABA to ensure that graduating students are developing properly. Furthermore, monitoring and evaluation should be integrated into potential programmes to prevent its integrity from being undermined by corruption.

References

Ahmed, Ghada, and Danny Hamrick. 2015. "Review of Ecuador's Agri-Industries Global Value Chains: Bottlenecks and Roadmap for Implementation." Accessed October 1, 2017. https://gvcc.duke.edu/wp-content/uploads/WorldBank_Ahmed_Hamrick_Review_Ecuador_Agri-Industries_Global_Value_Chains_2015.pdf.

Aime, M.C., and W. Phillips-Mora. 2005. "The causal agents of witches' broom and frosty pod rot of cacao (chocolate, Theobroma cacao) form a new lineage of Marasmiaceae." *Mycologia* 97: 1012-1022.

Allard L., Alia. 2012. "The Contribution of Small Farms and Commercial Large Farms to the Food Security of Trinidad and Tobago." Master of Arts, DePaul University.

Arnold Babwah & Associates. 2015. "Market Study – Trinidad & Tobago, CHF Caribbean Commissioned Report." Accessed October 13, 2017. http://assets.wusc.ca/wuscwebsite/initiatives/propel/market-study-trinidad-and-tobago-january-2015.pdf.

Beckles, Richard. 2015. "Cross Border Unitisation." Accessed December 6, 2016. http://www.tlclaw.org/cross-border-unitisation/.

Boopsingh, Trevor M., and Gregory McGuire, eds. 2014. *From Oil to Gas and Beyond: A Review of the Trinidad and Tobago Model and Analysis of Future Challenges*. New York, United States: University Press of America.

BP (British Petroleum). 2017. "BP Begins Production from Juniper project in Trinidad." Accessed December 6, 2018. https://www.bp.com/en/global/corporate/media/press-releases/bp-begins-production-from-juniper-project-in-trinidad.html.

Brooks, Laura. 2014. "Natural Gas Curtailments in Trinidad and Tobago Due to Lack of Investment: BPTT." *S&P Global* September 14. Accessed December 7, 2018. https://www.spglobal.com/platts/en/market-insights/latest-news/natural-gas/091914-natural-gas-curtailments-in-trinidad-and-tobago-due-to-lack-of-investment-bptt.

CARDI (Caribbean Agriculture Research and Development Institute). 2017. "Trinidad & Tobago: Country Profile." Accessed October 12, 2017. http://www.cardi.org/country-offices/trinidad-tobago/.

Cato, James. 1998. *Economic Issues Associated with Seafood Safety and Implementation of Seafood HACCP Programmes*. Rome: FAO.

CBTT (Central Bank of Trinidad and Tobago). 2017. "Output Annual." Accessed October 7, 2017. https://www.central-bank.org.tt/statistics/data-centre/output-annual.

Colby, Lionel. 1997. *Trade Opportunities for Processed Meat*. Geneva: UNCTAD.

CRC (Cocoa Research Centre). 2017. "Disease Management." Accessed October 13, 2017. https://sta.uwi.edu/cru/diseasemanagement.asp.

Dawson, William, Stephen Garnsey, Satyanarayana Tatineni, Svetlana Folimonova, Scott Harper, and S. Gowda. 2013. "Citrus Tristeza Virus-Host Interactions." *Frontiers in Microbiology* 4: 1-88.

Earth Policy Institute. 2017. "Fertilizer Consumption in Top Five Countries." Accessed October 1, 2017. www.earth-policy.org/datacenter/xls/book_fpep_ch7_14.xlsx.

EC (European Commission). 2010. "Working Document on Standards and Trade of Agricultural Products." Accessed October 6, 2017. https://ec.europa.eu/agriculture/sites/agriculture/files/consultations/advisory-groups/international/2013-01-28/working-document-standards_en.pdf.

—. 2017a. "General Food Law." Accessed October 6, 2017. https://ec.europa.eu/food/safety/general_food_law_en.

—. 2017b. "EU Processed Products." Accessed October 6, 2017. https://ec.europa.eu/agriculture/organic/eu-policy/eu-rules-on-production/processed-products_en.

—. 2017c. "Fruit and Vegetables: Marketing Standards." Accessed October 6, 2017. https://ec.europa.eu/agriculture/fruit-and-vegetables/marketing-standards_en.

EP (European Parliament). 2015. "Food Safety Policy and Regulation in the United States." Accessed October 7, 2017. http://www.europarl.europa.eu/RegData/etudes/STUD/2015/536324/IPOL_STU(2015)536324_EN.pdf.

FAO (Food and Agriculture Organization). 1997. "The State of Food and Agriculture 1997." Accessed October 4, 2017. http://www.fao.org/docrep/017/w5800e/w5800e.pdf.

—. 1998. *Possible Implications of Sanitary and Phytosanitary Measures for Exporters of Oilseed-Based Products to the European Union*. Rome: FAO.

Fernandez-Cornejo, Jorge. 2004. "The Seed Industry in US Agriculture: An Exploration of Data and Information on Crop Seed Markets, Regulation, Industry Structure, and Research and Development." Accessed October 1, 2017. https://www.ers.usda.gov/webdocs/publications/42517/13616_aib786_1_.pdf?v=41055.

Fernandez-Stark, Karina, Penny Bamber, and Gary Gereffi. 2011. "The Fruit and Vegetables Global Value Chain: Economic Upgrading and Workforce Development." Accessed October 18, 2017. https://gvcc.duke.edu/wp-content/uploads/2011-11-10_CGGC_Fruit-and-Vegetables-Global-Value-Chain.pdf.

Gereffi, Gary, and Katherine Fernandez-Stark. 2011. *Global Value Chain Analysis: A Primer*. Durham, NC: Center on Globalization, Governance & Competitiveness (CGGC), Duke University.

Giles, John. 1997. *Trade Opportunities in the International Processed Horticultural Markets*. Geneva: UNCTAD.

GM Watch. 2009. "The world's top 10 seed companies: who owns Nature?" Accessed October 11, 2017. http://www.gmwatch.org/en/gm-firms/10558-the-worlds-top-ten-seed-companies-who-owns-nature.

GORTT (Government of the Republic of Trinidad and Tobago). 2014. "Budget Statement 2015." Accessed September 17, 2017. http://finance.gov.tt/wp-content/uploads/2014/09/Budget-Statement-2015.pdf.

—. 2017. "Incentive Programme." Accessed October 13, 2017. http://www.news.gov.tt/sites/default/files/IncentiveBookletFINAL06July2011_119546169%20%282%29.pdf.

GORTT MEEI (Government of the Republic of Trinidad and Tobago Ministry of Energy and Energy Industries). 2017. "Petrochemicals." Accessed October 11, 2017. http://www.energy.gov.tt/our-business/lng-petrochemicals/petrochemicals/.

—. 2018. "Speech Senator the Honourable Franklin Khan Minister of Energy and Energy Industries Energy Spotlight Our Oil, Our Gas, Our Future." Accessed December 7, 2018. https://www.finance.gov.tt/wp-content/uploads/2018/03/HM-Franklin-Khan-Energy-Spotlight-Speech-Delivered-14_3_18.pdf.

GORTT MTI (Government of the Republic of Trinidad and Tobago Ministry of Trade and Industry). 2016. "Trinidad and Tobago: Bilateral Trade Agreements and Incentive Regime." Accessed October 18, 2017. tradeind.gov.tt/wp-content/.../2016-E-BROCHURE_bilateral-trade-agreements.pdf.

Graham, Barbara. 2010. "Analysis of the State of Praedial Larceny in Member States of CARICOM." Accessed October 11, 2017.

Greenville, Jared, Kentaro Kawasaki and Raphaël Beaujeu. 2017. "How Policies Shape Global Food and Agriculture Value Chains." Accessed September 9, 2017. http://dx.doi.org/10.1787/aaf0763a-en.

Green Cape. 2017. "Agriculture 2017 Market Intelligence Report." Accessed September 24, 2017. https://www.green-cape.co.za/assets/Uploads/GreenCape-Agri-MIR-2017-electronic-FINAL-v1.pdf.

Henson, Spencer, and Rupert Loader. 2001. "Barriers to Agricultural Exports from Developing Countries: The Role of Sanitary and Phytosanitary Requirements." *World Development* 29(1): 85-102.

Higgins, Charlene J. 1992. "Western Flower Thrips (Thysanoptera: Thripidae) in Greenhouses: Population Dynamics, Distribution on Plants, and Associations with Predators." *Journal of Economic Entomology* 85(5): 1891-1903.

Howard, Phillip. 2009. "Visualizing Consolidation in the Global Seed Industry: 1996–2008." *Sustainability* 1: 1266-1287.

—. 2015. "Intellectual Property and Consolidation in the Seed Industry." Accessed October 1, 2017. http://www.apbrebes.org/files/seeds/files/Howard_seed_industry_patents_concentration_2015.pdf.

ICIS News. 2011. "Trinidad Ammonia Plants Shut on Limited Natural Gas from BP." Accessed December 7, 2018.

https://www.icis.com/explore/resources/news/2011/10/20/9501818/trinidad-ammonia-plants-shut-on-limited-natural-gas-from-bp.

Intra-ACP APP (Intra-ACP Agriculture Policy Programme). 2016. "Praedial Larceny: the Domino Effect." Accessed October 15, 2017. http://repositorio.iica.int/bitstream/11324/2708/1/BVE17038762i.pdf.

Josupeit, Helga. 1997. *Trade Opportunities for Processed Fish*. Geneva: UNCTAD.

Khan, Aleem. 2017a. "BpTT: Gas Curtailments due to Pause in Investments." *Trinidad and Tobago Guardian* September 21. Accessed December 7, 2018. http://www.guardian.co.tt/article-6.2.388071.035af82cd8.

—. 2017b. "T&T may get gas from Dragon field by 2019." *Trinidad Express Newspaper*, September 30. Accessed October 16, 2017. http://www.trinidadexpress.com/20170930/business/tt-may-get-gas-from-dragon-field-by-2019.

Levin-Waldman, Oren M. 1995. *Reforming Unemployment Insurance: Towards Greater Employment*. New York, United States: Jerome Levy Economics Institute, Bard College.

Lowitt, Kristen, Gordon M. Hickey, Arlette Saint Ville, Kaywana Raeburn, Theresa Thompson-Colón, Sonia Laszlo, and Leroy E. Phillip. 2015. "Factors Affecting the Innovation Potential of Smallholder Farmers in the Caribbean Community." *Regional Environmental Change* 15(7): 1367-1377.

MacDonald, James M. 2017. "Mergers and Competition in Seed and Agricultural Chemical Markets." Accessed October 2, 2017. https://www.ers.usda.gov/amber-waves/2017/april/mergers-and-competition-in-seed-and-agricultural-chemical-markets/.

MOALMR (Ministry of Agriculture, Land and Marine Resources). 1995. "Trinidad and Tobago: Country's Report to the FAO International Technical Conference on Plant Genetic Resource." Accessed October 13, 2017. http://www.fao.org/fileadmin/templates/agphome/documents/PGR/SoW1/americas/TRINIDAD.pdf.

Meditz, Sandra W., and Dennis M. Hanratty, 1987. *Caribbean Islands: A Country Study*. Washington: GPO for the Library of Congress.

Offshore Technology. 2018. "Angelin Gas Project. Accessed December 6, 2018. https://www.offshore-technology.com/projects/angelin-gas-project/.

OPMRTT (Office of the Prime Minister of the Republic of Trinidad and Tobago). 2017. "Prime Minister Rowley Provides Update on Gas Situation After Visit to Houston." Accessed December 7, 2018.

https://www.opm.gov.tt/pms-statement-on-natural-gas-situation-in-tt-and-visit-to-houston/.

Pitigala, Nihal. 2005. "What Does Regional Trade in South Asia Reveal about Future Trade Liberalization?" World Bank Policy Research Working Paper 3497.

Persad, Seunarine, Ian Rampersad and Ramgopaul Roop. 2009. "Food Crop Production and Land Management for Caroni (1975) Limited's "2 Acre Farms" in Trinidad and Tobago." *Proceedings of the Caribbean Food Crops Society* 45: 138-140.

Porter, Michael E. 1990. "The Competitive Advantage of Nations." *Harvard Business Review* 68(2): 73-93.

Research and Markets. 2015. "Global Top 6 Agriculture Equipment Manufacturers – Strategy Focus & Comparative SWOT Framework Analysis – 2015-2018 – John Deere, CNH, AGCO, CLAAS, Same Deutz-Fahr, Kubota." Accessed October 3, 2017. https://www.researchandmarkets.com/research/25lvk2/global_top_6.

Richardson, Ben. 2013. "Cut loose in the Caribbean: Neoliberalism and the Demise of the Commonwealth Sugar Trade." *Bulletin of Latin American Research,* 0261-3050.

Santoo, Sandhya. 2017. "Floods Claim Crops in Debe ...Farmers Blame Unfinished Highway." *Sunday Express* July 21. Accessed October 15, 2017. http://www.trinidadexpress.com/20170721/news/floods-claim-crops-in-debe.

Sinha, Anil. 2011. "Major Pests and Diseases of Economic Crops in the Caribbean – Belize, Dominica, Grenada, Guyana, Jamaica, Saint Lucia, Trinidad & Tobago." Accessed October 13, 2017. http://www.agriskmanagementforum.org/sites/agriskmanagementforum.org/files/Documents/National_%20Concerns.pdf.

Sookraj, Radhica. 2018. "CNC Urged to Negotiate with NGC." *Trinidad and Tobago Guardian,* January 27. Accessed December 7, 2018. http://www4.guardian.co.tt/news/2018-01-26/cnc-urged-negotiate-ngc.

Trinidad Express Newspapers. 2015. "The Agriculture Challenge for T&T." Accessed October 13, 2017. http://www.trinidadexpress.com/20151222/editorial/the-agriculture-challenge-for-tt.

Trinidad and Tobago Guardian. 2015. "Labour Shortage in Agriculture." Accessed October 15, 2017. https://www.guardian.co.tt/business/2015-06-26/labour-shortage-agriculture.

UNCTAD (United Nations Conference on Trade and Development)/ Commonwealth Secretariat. 1996. *The Global Spice Trade and the*

Uruguay Round Agreements. Geneva, Switzerland: International Trade Centre UNCTAD/WTO.

UNIDCO (United Nations Industrial Development Organization). 2009. "Agro-Value Chain Analysis and Development: The UNIDO Approach." Accessed September 9, 2017. https://www.unido.org/fileadmin/user_media/Publications/Pub_free/Agro_value_chain_analysis_and_development.pdf.

UWI (University of the West Indies). 2017. "BSc (General): Major in Agricultural Science." Accessed October 12, 2017. https://sta.uwi.edu/ffa/foodprod/BScGeneralMajorinAgriculturalScience.asp.

Williams, Curtis. 2017. "BPTT: Juniper starts gas production offshore Trinidad and Tobago." *Oil and Gas Journal* August 14. Accessed December 6, 2018. https://www.ogj.com/articles/2017/08/bptt-juniper-starts-gas-production-offshore-trinidad-and-tobago.html.

WITS (World Integrated Trade Solution). 2017a. "Trade Data (UN Comtrade)." Accessed October 1, 2017. http://wits.worldbank.org/WITS/WITS/AdvanceQuery/RawTradeData/QueryDefinition.aspx?Page=RawTradeData.

World Bank. 2017. "Agriculture, value added (% of GDP)." Accessed October 09, 2017. https://data.worldbank.org/indicator/NV.AGR.TOTL.ZS.

—. 2017b. "Agricultural land (sq. km)." Accessed October 11, 2017. https://data.worldbank.org/indicator/AG.LND.AGRI.K2?locations=TT&view=chart.

—. 2017c. "Agricultural Irrigated Land (% of total agricultural land)." Accessed October 11, 2017. https://data.worldbank.org/indicator/AG.LND.IRIG.AG.ZS?locations=TT&view=chart.

—. 2017d. "Fertilizer Consumption (kilograms per hectare of arable land)." Accessed October 11, 2017. https://data.worldbank.org/indicator/AG.CON.FERT.ZS?locations=TT&view=chart.

—. 2017e. "Agricultural Machinery, Tractors." Accessed October 11, 2017. https://data.worldbank.org/indicator/AG.AGR.TRAC.NO?locations=TT.

—. 2017f. "Employment in agriculture (% of total employment)." Accessed October 12, 2017. https://data.worldbank.org/indicator/SL.AGR.EMPL.ZS.

WTO and OECD (World Trade Organization and Organization for Economic Co-operation and Development). 2013. "Aid for Trade and Value Chains in Agrifood." Accessed September 10, 2017. https://www.wto.org/english/tratop_e/devel_e/a4t_e/global_review13prog_e/agrifood_47.pdf.

Yara. 2014. "Yara Fertilizer Industry Handbook – February 2014." Accessed October 1, 2017. http://yara.com/doc/124128_Fertilizer%20Industry%20Handbook%20with%20notes.pdf.

CHAPTER THREE

A GLOBAL VALUE CHAIN ANALYSIS OF THE MARITIME SECTOR IN TRINIDAD AND TOBAGO

Abstract

Trinidad and Tobago (T&T) is blessed to be richly endowed with commercial reserves of crude oil and natural gas. While the country earns significant revenue from this hydrocarbon export, the oil price crash of 2014 demonstrated the vulnerability of over dependence on a few commodities for economic survival. Thus, it is logical for the Government of the Republic of Trinidad and Tobago (GORTT) to seek industries which can assist in the diversification of the country's revenue base. One excellent industry for the diversification thrust is the maritime industry.

The country's maritime sector is comprised of port operations, ship repair, leisure marine (yachting) and marine services. All of the aforementioned sub-industries are dependent upon each other. Additionally, the aforementioned sub-industries also provide backward linkages which complement the existing energy industry.

The competitiveness factors for T&T's maritime sector include the country's fortunate location between key transshipment routes, and the favourable climate, exchange rate, and political stability. Despite these favourable conditions, labour challenges, port inefficiency, and a limited capacity to achieve economies of scale continue to constrain T&T's maritime sector.

Upgrading and extracting more value in the larger global value chain are attainable through the enhancement of the enabling environment by the government, and through partnerships with technically advanced multinational firms.

3.1 Introduction

Trinidad and Tobago (T&T) is a small island developing state (SIDS) in the Caribbean. The country is endowed with commercial reserves of crude oil and natural gas, and thus is able to derive significant revenue from petroleum and other energy-related exports. However, the unexpected oil price crash of 2014 demonstrated the vulnerability of T&T's economy. Given this macroeconomic threat, it would be rational of the Government of the Republic of Trinidad and Tobago (GORTT) to develop industries which can help diversify revenue inflows. One such industry is the maritime industry.

While it is noteworthy that the horizontal diversification of an economy is no easy feat, the country is fortunate to have developed backward linkages to the maritime sector to support its energy sector. The country's maritime sector, which is comprised of ship repair, ship building, port operations, yachting, and transshipment industries, has tremendous potential to generate economic activity, attract Foreign Direct Investment (FDI), earn foreign exchange, create employment, and accrue government revenue.

The GORTT is also aware that the maritime sector has potential to generate much needed economic growth and revenues. In fact, in 2018 the GORTT announced that it had signed an agreement with the China Harbour Engineering Company (CHEC) to enter a joint venture arrangement to develop a new shipyard/drydock at La Brea, adjacent to the Green-field site which was intended for the Alutrint smelter. What is even more significant in the government's announcement is the fact that the proposed drydock would be large enough to accommodate marine vessels larger than 300 metres poising T&T to capitalize upon the Panama Canal's transshipment traffic.

Indeed, the proposed project would generate positive spillover effects to La Brea, neighbouring communities and the wider economy of T&T. However, an important question arises:

"Will T&T maximize the value that can be captured from the maritime sector?"

This question is of importance since it is possible to develop new industries in developing countries without encouraging the development of strong backward and forward linkages. Subsequently, a lot of value in the global value chain is not captured domestically. Hence, policy makers should be cognizant of the country's current position in the larger global value chain, the opportunities available to current participants in the value chain, and the prospects for upgrading along the value chain.

Thus, this chapter seeks to explore:

i. T&T's current position in the maritime global value chain; and
ii. how T&T may upgrade along the value chain.

This chapter is structured as follows. Section 3.2 provides an overview of the global maritime industry. This is then followed by an overview of T&T's local maritime sector in Section 3.3. Section 3.4 considers the local competitiveness factors in T&T's maritime sector. Section 3.5 evaluates the challenges in T&T's maritime sector. Section 3.6 presents the strategies for upgrading along the value chain. Section 3.7 imparts the recommendations and the conclusion for this chapter.

3.2 The Global Maritime Industry

There are many activities in the maritime industry. In its broadest sense, the maritime industry involves all stakeholders involved in the business of designing, constructing, manufacturing, acquiring, operating, supplying, repairing and/or maintaining vessels, managing and/or operating shipping lines, stevedoring and customs, brokerage services, shipyards, dry docks, marine railways, marine repair shops, shipping and freight forwarding services and similar enterprises (Peretomode 2014).

While there are a vast number of sub-industries within the maritime industry, for the purposes of this chapter, the maritime industry is only considered to include port operations, shipping, ship repair and shipbuilding, and leisure marine.

Each of the sub-industries of the larger maritime industry are interrelated as their activities affect each other. For instance, countries all over the world have port facilities to facilitate the marine transportation of both people and cargo. Marine transportation would not be possible but for the work of ship builders and periodic maintenance undergone at ship repair dry docks.

Many ports in the world act as a transshipment hub. These ports experience significant volumes of cargo on an annual basis. As can be seen in Table 3.1, China leads in port throughput. This is no surprise since China is a significant player in international trade. Other major players include the United States (US), Singapore, and Korea. Table 3.1 highlights the top 10 countries in the world with the highest port throughput.

Table 3.1: World Port Throughput (TEU)

YEAR	2010	2013	2014	2015	2016	2017
China	142,970,010	175,936,351	186,679,051	195,276,751	199,551,751	213,719,925
US	42,058,000	44,427,127	47,849,621	49,527,457	50,181,794	51,425,466
Singapore	29,147,000	33,388,000	34,688,000	31,710,200	32,668,000	33,600,000
Korea	19,456,000	23,711,000	24,818,667	25,354,352	26,152,977	27,427,000
Malaysia	18,141,919	21,376,500	22,645,237	24,259,700	24,570,000	24,719,000
Japan	19,547,865	21,049,617	21,139,091	20,577,013	20,784,617	21,904,443
UAE	15,177,436	18,693,112	20,223,612	21,233,200	20,613,200	21,280,900
China	23,600,000	22,290,000	22,300,000	20,114,000	19,580,000	20,770,000
Germany	14,715,340	19,261,033	20,128,033	19,139,033	19,364,033	19,447,600
Spain	12,558,770	13,897,114	14,213,268	14,271,905	15,267,905	17,065,000
World	560,328,404	656,332,800	687,091,443	695,811,428	710,067,396	752,714,321

UNCTAD (2018)

Shipping is one of the main activities of the maritime industry in almost every country. Shipping is global by nature, and is directly influenced by international trade. In fact, seaborne trade accounts for over 90% of world trade in terms of volume (Mirovic et al. 2018). Since international trade is greatly facilitated through shipping, trade liberalization and globalization have highlighted the need for hub ports within global logistics networks. The physical locations of ports and major shipping routes are based on physical geographic characteristics such as marine currents, winds, depth, tides, etc. Figure 3.1 provides an illustration of the main shipping routes which in turn are actively used by the major actors involved in transshipping to facilitate trade and connect markets.

The desire to improve productive efficiency and reduce costs has pushed the shipping industry to increase the size and capacity of vessels.[56] The expansion in the capacity of marine vessels in turn influences the decision of policy makers to increase the capacity at ports and canals.

For instance, the Panama Canal which provides an all-waterway passage between the Atlantic and the Pacific Oceans – facilitating trade between Asia, Europe, the Caribbean and America, was becoming redundant as it had a total length of nearly 80 kilometres and was limiting the size of ship that could pass through. A Panamax, which refers to the largest size marine vessel which could have passed through the canal prior to the 2015 expansion project, was only 294.1 metres in maximum length, 32.3 metres in beam, and had a draft of 12.04 metres. Subsequently, in 2006, the Government of Panama decided to expand the Canal (Brevik and Melleby 2014).

Before the expansion, a Panamax vessel was only 5,000 twenty-foot equivalent unit (TEU) in 2014 (Brevik and Melleby 2014). After the completion of the expansion project in 2016, the canal allowed the transit of Post-Panamax vessels up to 13,000-14,000 TEU, thus multiplying the capacity by approximately three times (EKNP 2017).

---

[56] The ship owners involved in transshipment would desire vessels with a larger capacity to achieve economies of scale to reduce their shipping costs. Subsequently, the ship owners would request the shipbuilder to manufacture larger ships. Indeed, the shipping industry has strong interrelations as the demands of one set of stakeholders would affect the outcomes of another set of stakeholders.

Figure 3.1: Main Shipping Routes Globally

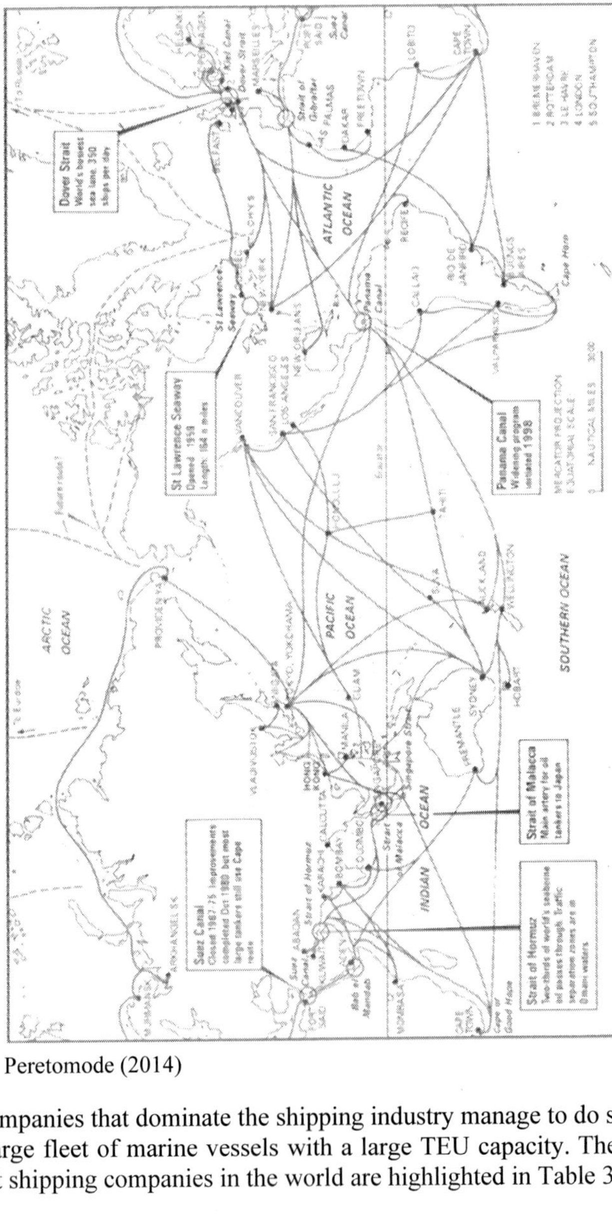

Source: Peretomode (2014)

The companies that dominate the shipping industry manage to do so due to their large fleet of marine vessels with a large TEU capacity. The top ten biggest shipping companies in the world are highlighted in Table 3.2.

Table 3.2: Top Shipping Companies in the World

Rank	Name	Country	Fleet Capacity
1	AP Moller-Maersk Group	Denmark	639 vessels, with a total operating capacity of 4.02 million TEU in 2018.
2	Mediterranean Shipping Company (MSC)	Switzerland	471 vessels with a total operating capacity of 3.2 million TEU in 2018
3	CMA CGM Group	France	494 vessels with capacity ranging from 133 TEU to 18,000 TEU
4	COSCO Shipping Corporation Ltd.	China	1,114 merchant vessels with capacity ranging from 369 TEU to 13,386 TEU.
5	Hapag-Lloyd	Germany	220 marine vessels with a total operating capacity of 1.6 million TEU in 2018
6	Evergreen Marine Corporation	China	150 container ships with a total capacity of 1.15 million TEU in 2018
7	OOCL		57 vessels with capacity ranging from 2,992 TEU to 21,413 TEU
8	Yang Ming Marine Transport Corporation	China	84 container ships with a total capacity of 464,848 TEU in 2018
9	Mitsui O.S.K. Lines, Ltd. (MOL)	Japan	55 marine vessels (40 dry fleet, 15 LNG fleet)
10	Nippon Yūsen Kabushiki Kaisha (NYK Line)	Japan	800 ships, with the maximum container capacity of 14,026 TEU

Source: The Maritime Post (2018)

With regard to shipbuilding and ship repair, traditionally both functions are carried out in the same yards. This is due to the capital and labour requirements for shipbuilding being almost identical to the requirements for ship repair. Although, there are some yards which specialize in ship repair, the similarities in capital, labour and infrastructure requirements have resulted in some of the world leaders in shipbuilding also being leaders in ship repair. Nonetheless, ship repair is a distinct activity from shipbuilding (OECD 2008).

Companies in Europe have historically dominated both the shipbuilding and ship repair industries. However, within the past two decades, new competitors from China, Japan, South Korea, the Philippines and Vietnam have emerged as dominant players (Mickeviciene 2011). In fact, today, commercial shipbuilding is dominated by builders in China, Japan, and South Korea. Table 3.3 highlights the top 10 shipbuilding countries by the end of 2015.

Table 3.3: Top 10 Shipbuilding Countries (2015)

Rank	Country	Gross Tonnage (GT)	Market Share
1	China	25,160	37.2%
2	South Korea	23,272	34.4%
3	Japan	13,005	19.2%
4	Philippines	1,865	2.8%
5	Taiwan	749	1.1%
6	Vietnam	591	0.9%
7	Romania	485	0.7%
8	United States (US)	427	0.6%
9	Germany	384	0.6%
10	Brazil	361	0.5%
	World Total	67,566	

Source: Brun and Frederick (2017)

Commercial shipbuilding is comprised of several vessel categories, however, approximately 80% of total production occurs in three types of vessels: containerships, oil (crude) tankers, and dry bulkers. Containerships, which are designed to carry containers, make up 18% of total annual ship production, crude oil tankers make up 15% of total production, and dry bulkers, which are designed to transport unpackaged bulk cargo (e.g. rice, coal, and ore) make up 48% of total production (Brun and Frederick 2017).

Shipbuilding requires multiple actors to design, construct and maintain a ship. Figure 3.2 provides an illustration of the network of activities involved in the shipbuilding global value chain.

Figure 3.2: Shipbuilding Global Value Chain

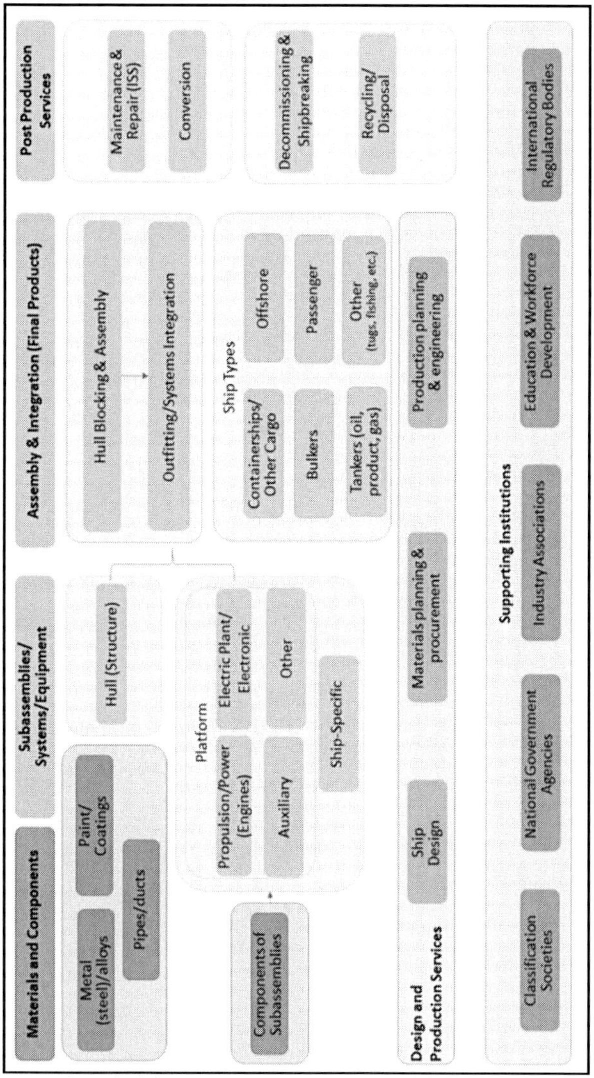

Source: Brun and Frederick (2017)

Figure 3.3: Activities and Phases of the Ship Building and Ship Repair Industry

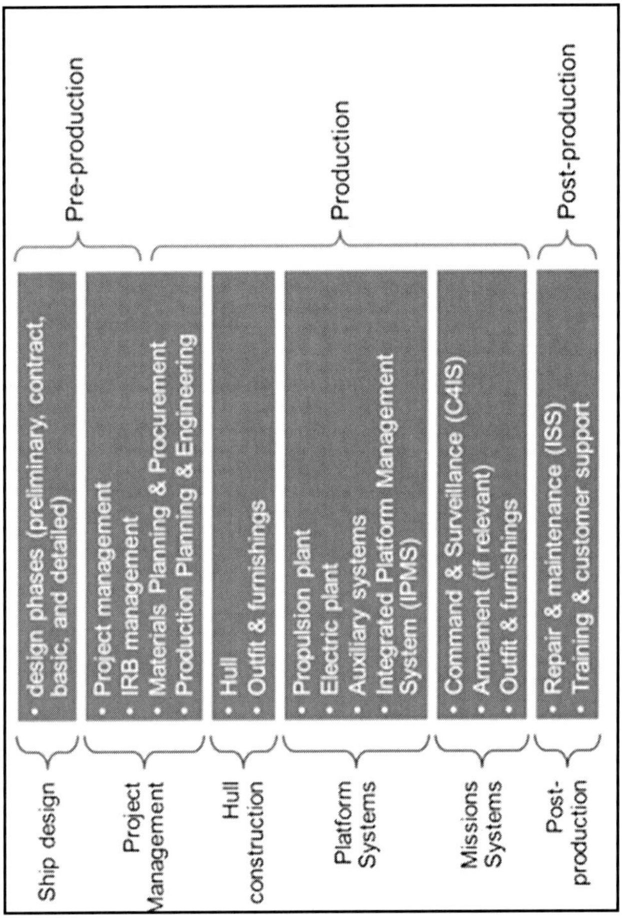

Source: Gereffi et al. (2013)

It is noteworthy that the shipbuilding value chain includes three major phases: pre-production, production, and post-production. In the pre-production phase, ship design and project management activities are undertaken. In the production phase hull construction, platform and mission systems production and integration activities are undertaken. This production stage requires the assembly of a multitude of parts. Subsequently, shipbuilding would be feasible in countries where the parts are manufactured, or in a country where the shipbuilder has easy and cheap access to the relevant parts for production.[57] The post-production stage involves the repair, maintenance, and conversion of marine vessels after their production. Figure 3.3 provides an illustration of the major activities and phases involved in the shipbuilding and ship repair industry.

The leisure marine and yachting is a sub-industry of the wider maritime industry. One author notes

> *The yachting sector can be divided into two (2) distinct segments – recreation and services (Henry 2013). Within the context of recreation, visitors either travel to the region (i) using their own vessels or (ii) renting a vessel within the jurisdiction in order to enjoy the pleasure of the environment. Inherent in this is the need to provide certain goods and services, such as different types of vessels, crew rental, moorings and anchorage and supplies. As it pertains to services, vessels require specific services to ensure proper maintenance. Vessels which generate this need are those which are: rented within the jurisdiction; or sailed in for recreational purposes; or sailed to the region to be serviced.* (Preville 2013, 11).

Yachting is a tourism-based luxury activity. However, specific characteristics of the industry warrant its clear distinction from traditional visitor tourism. Firstly, the yachting tourist may desire to remain in the territory for several months at a time. Secondly, yachting tourists tend to migrate to different marinas, boat yards and anchorages, thus, their location is not static (Preville 2013). Thirdly, stakeholders not engaging in yachting own the vessels as it can be very expensive to purchase and maintain a yacht. As a result, charter and rental of marine recreational vessels have become a core activity within maritime tourism.

Yachting tends to be highly seasonal. For instance, in the Caribbean, the high season for the Bahamas is July to August and for Grenada and Trinidad high season is from May to November.

Globally, the Mediterranean Sea and the Caribbean Sea are the two main yachting destinations in the world (Preville 2013). In the Mediterranean Sea are the coasts of Croatia, France, Greece, Italy, Spain, and Turkey which are popular yachting destinations. The Mediterranean Sea alone attracts

[57] In a country such as T&T where the parts are not manufactured, it is likely that any potential shipbuilder would have to import the required parts. This would place the shipbuilder at a relative disadvantage.

70% of world charters, and the aforementioned countries have a high number of marinas[58] (ECSIP Consortium 2015).[59]

Likewise, popular destinations for yachting in the Caribbean are the Bahamas, the British Virgin Islands (BVI), the Organization of Eastern Caribbean States (OECS) member countries, and T&T.

A marina plays an important role in facilitating a range of other support services. Some of these services are related to the maintenance of the marine vessel, while the remaining proportion of these services is related to the spending of boaters when boating for consumption purposes. Yachting services may include the following:

- rigging and mast services;
- winterization and maintenance;
- sea service assistance;
- engine repairs;
- electric repairs;
- outboard repairs;
- dinghy repairs;
- gpr repairs,
- antifouling and antiosmotic;
- refrigeration and air-conditioning repairs;
- woodwork;
- pump, water system, tanks and water heaters;
- gas system and oven repairs;
- boat cleaning;
- sail maker; and
- yacht transfers (Peretomode 2014).

Indeed, based on the multitude of services that can support the yachting industry, it can be clearly seen that the ship repair and maintenance industry complements the yachting industry.

---

[58] A marina is a docking facility for yachts and other small marine vessels. Marinas typically do not have the capacity to facilitate the docking of bulk cargo vessels.

[59] According to the ECSIP Consortium (2015) the highest number of marinas in Europe can be found in Germany (2,700), Finland (1,770), Sweden (1,500), Poland (1,300), and the Netherlands (1,135).

3.3 Overview of the Maritime Sector in T&T

The GORTT recognizes that the maritime sector is an important contributor to T&T's economy. The Ministry of Trade and Industry (MTI) identified port operations, ship repair, leisure marine (yachting) and marine services[60] as key sub-industries of the country's maritime sector on which it has decided to focus.

3.3.1 Port Operations

With regard to port operations, T&T has two major ports that service container trade: the port of Port of Spain (POS) and the port of Point Lisas. The port of POS is solely owned by the GORTT, and acts as the country's main port to facilitate both domestic trades and regional transshipment (Nathan Associates 2014). The Port Authority of Trinidad and Tobago (PATT), a state-owned organization, manages the operations at the port of POS.

The port of Point Lisas acts mainly as an import terminal mainly for serving shipping lines connecting with the US (mainly Florida). The container terminal in Point Lisas is owned by the Point Lisas Industrial Port Development Corporation (PLIDECO),[61] and it operates more efficiently than the port of Port of Spain.

T&T also has one Liquefied Natural Gas (LNG) terminal, one bauxite transshipment facility, one petrochemical port, and one port for an oil refinery (invesTT 2018). These port facilities facilitate the docking of marine vessels involved in transshipment to and from the country.

T&T's ports facilitate shipping services which are part of those serving the Caribbean Region. Although T&T is fortunate to benefit from hydrocarbon export revenues, its port throughput ranks third in the Caribbean Community (CARICOM) after Jamaica and the Bahamas. See Table 3.4.

---

[60] The MTI asserts marine service operations in the Gulf of Paria including offshore bulk transshipment, bunkering, cold stacking, maritime logistics and open ship registry (GORTT MTI 2016).

[61] PLIDECO is an enterprise which is 51% owned by the National Energy Corporation (NEC), a state-owned agency, and 49% by the private sector.

Table 3.4: T&T's Port Throughput Relative to the Rest of CARICOM (TEU)

Country	2000	2005	2010	2015	2016	2017
Antigua & Barbuda	21,718	26,096	26,366	26,500	31,165	17,311
Bahamas	572,224	1,211,500	1,125,000	1,468,380	1,261,778	920,652
Barbados	68,600	88,763	80,430	86,508	105,326	107,098
Belize	25,537	36,388	31,917	48,141	46,040	44,381
Dominica	10,927	12,826	7,974	7,361	7,361	7,425
Grenada	N.A.	N.A.	N.A.	16,000	19,634	21,914
Guyana	N.A.	N.A.	59,850	52,834	55,168	57,663
Haiti	88,534	91,278	163,456	178,452	176,879	177,141
Jamaica	765,977	1,670,820	1,891,770	1,653,272	1,567,442	1,560,000
St. Kitts & Nevis	N.A.	N.A.	2,424	13,511	13,216	13,767
St. Lucia	41,037	60,725	52,478	41,500	38,383	28,841
St. Vincent & Grenadines	N.A.	12,678	16,967	18,620	19,941	19,191
Suriname	18,000	37,285	59,583	106,014	98,652	112,318
Trinidad & Tobago	347,935	467,712	577,863	520,825	427,427	414,657

Source: ECLAC (2018)

Figure 3.4: T&T Port Throughput

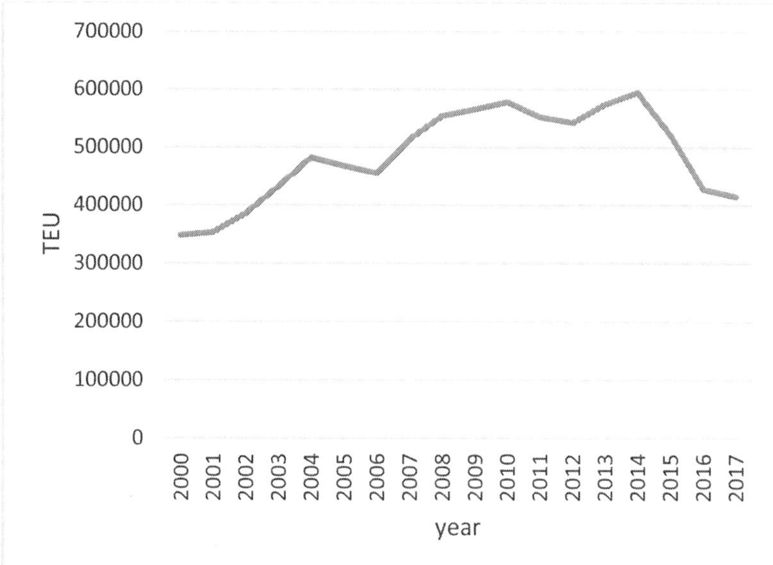

Source: ECLAC (2018)

As can be seen in Table 3.4 and Figure 3.4, T&T's port throughput increased steadily until it reached 577,863 TEU in 2010. The cargo volume remained relatively flat over the 2010 to 2014 period, but declined over the 2015 to 2017 period, the same period in which the country experienced economic decline as a consequence of weak energy prices and economic recession.

3.3.2 Marine Services

As previously mentioned, the marine services which have been acknowledged by the policy makers in T&T are offshore bulk transshipment, bunkering, cold stacking,[62] maritime logistics. However, the MTI in T&T acknowledges Oldendoff Carriers as its greatest success in bulk transshipment.

[62] Cold stacking, also known as mothballing, refers to the process to reduce an oil rig's crew to either zero or just a few key individuals and anchoring the rig in a harbour until the operator is ready to use it. Cold stacking is used as a means to reduce costs.

Since 2012, Oldendorff Carriers has used the Gulf of Paria in T&T's territorial waters as an anchorage and a transshipment harbour for iron ore from the Amazon and Orinoco Rivers to China and the Middle East.

In the bunkering industry, Petrotrin, Aegean Marine Petroleum, and several small-scale operators use double-hulled vessels to provide bunkering services to marine vessels typically operating in the country's offshore energy sector.

With regard to cold stacking, the GORTT earns revenue from multinationals using the Gulf of Paria to store their mothballed rigs. The GORTT charges operators US$200 to US$1000 per day to use the country's territorial waters as an anchorage. Up to as recently as the end of 2017, Trans Ocean Ltd. had 8 vessels anchored in the Gulf of Paria (Ramnarine 2017).

3.3.3 Yachting Industry

The yachting industry in T&T was established in the mid-1990s when foreign cruisers realized that the country's Gulf of Paria is a relatively safe natural harbour that lies outside of the hurricane belt. Prior to the 1990s, the leisure marine industry was dominated more by locally-owned vessels than by foreign-owned vessels. Moreover, a large share of these locally-owned marine vessels was comprised of locally made pirogues which were used for leisure marine and part-time fishing (ECLAC 2002).

Yachting by foreigners was limited to occasional visits, often restricted to the carnival season, however, in 1991 the first yacht haul-out facility was established at Chaguaramas when Powerboats (a company) commissioned a 50-ton travel lift with storage capacity for 45 yachts on land. This was done to capitalize on the new yachting demand that was created when Venezuela imposed a US$50 yacht docking fee. Subsequently, a large cluster of yachts eventually developed at Chaguaramas. However, as yachts would periodically require maintenance, and as the foreigners bring the potential for tourism activities, a cluster of ship repair and maintenance as well as other support services emerged in the Chaguaramas area (ECLAC 2002).

The MTI estimates that there are approximately 180 businesses operating in the yachting industry in T&T, of which the majority are small and micro enterprises (SMEs). Approximately 1,700 persons are employed full-time.

In order for a foreign vessel to dock in T&T's territorial waters, clearance must first be obtained from the immigration division and customs division. Anchorage, the discharge of crew, or the discharge of passenger(s) prior to obtaining such clearance, is a violation of the law and a fineable offence. Until cleared by immigration, foreign vessels must display the quarantine flag (yellow "Q" flag), which is replaced by the national flag upon clearance (Preville 2013).

Navigational fees of TT$50 per month are charged only while the marine vessel is in T&T's waters. Other fees charged to the foreigners include: Customs – Arrival, departure, overtime; (ii) Harbour Master – Navigation dues; (iii) Immigration – Overtimes, extensions (differ by nationality); and (iv) Airport Authority – Departure Tax (Preville 2013).

There are 4 main sub-sectors of yachting in T&T and the wider Caribbean region. At the top there is the mega yacht segment, which is highly seasonal and the clients tend to be high spenders. The second segment consists of the crewed and bare boat charter market, whose expenditure patterns tend to match those of four- or five-star hotel tourists. The third segment includes the cruisers who are characterized by long stays and, often have a more limited budget than the two previous categories. The fourth segment includes the participants of day sailing, yacht racing, diving and the game fishing sub-sector, which are popular with local yachters (GORTT MTI 2017).

The estimated average daily expenditure by yachting tourists is approximately US$35 per day, which is marginally smaller than the US$40 average daily expenditure of the average cruise ship passenger. The average length of stay of the yachting passenger is 98 days which is considerably longer than the average length of stay of the cruise ship passenger. The average daily expenditure does not include expenditure on maintenance works for yachts. The average 40-foot yacht spends approximately US$20,000 (TT$120,000) per annum on repair and maintenance works (Nathan Associates 2014).

Table 3.5: Yacht Arrivals to T&T

	2006	2007	2008	2009	2010	2011
Trinidad	1396	1209	1253	1171	959	1030
Tobago	449	204	229	208	121	202
Total	1845	1413	1482	1379	1080	1232

Source: GORTT MT (2012)

Table 3.5 displays the yacht arrivals at T&T over the 2006 to 2011 period. Given the previously mentioned statistics on expenditure in the yachting industry, approximately US$24,640,000 may have been spent on ship repair and maintenance services for yachts in 2011,[63] and approximately US$4,225,760 in consumption by yachters in 2011.[64] Thus, the yachting industry could have contributed approximately US$28,865,760 (TT$173,194,560) to the economy of T&T in 2011.[65] Note, such estimations do not take into consideration the size of the multiplier effect from any autonomous component of national expenditure.

3.3.3 Ship Repair Industry

T&T currently has a ship repair cluster located at Chaguaramas, in the North Western Peninsula of Trinidad, west of the city's capital Port of Spain. In fact, its relatively close proximity to the country's most active port favours the cluster as it can provide repair and maintenance services to the marine vessels that will require servicing to continue their operation.

There are multiple small ship repair companies in Trinidad, all of which are located in the Chaguaramas area. The well-known ones include: CL Marine Limited (formerly CARIDOC), Maritime Preservation Limited, Austal, Inter Isle Construction and Fabrication Limited, Mariner's Haven Limited, Peakes, and Crews Inn (Nathan Associates 2014). The aforementioned companies tend to rely on the services of many SMEs, some of which are located within the Chaguaramas area, while others are dispersed across the island. The SMEs tend to provide services in welding and fabrication, painting and blasting, chandelling, brokerage, freight forwarding, and marine insurance.

It is notable that each of the major ship repair companies in the Chaguaramas cluster provides services for distinct segments of the marine market. For instance, CL Marine handles large vessels (ocean lines, oil Tankers, etc.), Inter Isle handles medium-sized vessels, some supply vessels and launches, while Peakes and Crews Inn tend to tackle small vessels (e.g. fishing vessels, tugs, and pleasure boats). The major companies need to be

---

63 1232 vessels x US$20,000 = US$24,640,000.

64 1232 vessels x US$35 x 98 days = US$4,225,760.

65 US$24,640,000 for maintenance + US$4,225,760 in consumption = US$28,865,760.

highly competitive as they also compete against regional providers of dry-docking services in the Atlantic region.

3.3.4 Stakeholders in the Maritime Industry

There are several stakeholders in T&T's maritime industry. The main stakeholders include the public agencies (such as the Customs Division, and the MTI), the private sector involved in ship repair activities, the SMEs involved in providing support services, the trade union movement, and the educational institutions.

The Customs Division is an import stakeholder to T&T's maritime industry. In fact, the speed at which the Customs Division clears import and export consignments affects the country's port efficiency and the country's overall ease of doing business.

The MTI is responsible for creating policy and drafting legislation which would create an enabling environment for the country's maritime sector.

The Seamen and Waterfront Workers (SWWTU) trade union is the body responsible for the representation of workers' interests in T&T's maritime industry. The SWWTU is also the recognized majority trade union for workers at the port of POS and the port of Point Lisas. The Public Service Association (PSA) is the recognized majority union for the workers involved in administrative duties in the PATT.

With regard to education, the University of the West Indies (UWI) and the University of Trinidad and Tobago (UTT) provide tertiary education for the citizens of T&T. UTT provides a number of programmes targeting the country's maritime sector, namely

- the Certificate in Applied Maritime Operations;
- the Diploma in Maritime Operations – Engineering;
- the Diploma in Maritime Operations – Navigation;
- the Bachelor of Science Degree in Nautical Science/Maritime Operations; and
- the Master of Science in Operational Maritime Management.

The National Energy Skills Center (NESC) offers short courses in

- Advanced Welding Level 1;
- Advanced Welding Level 2;

- Air Conditioning and Refrigeration – Installation;
- Air Conditioning and Refrigeration – Maintenance;
- Air Conditioning and Refrigeration – Advanced Troubleshooting;
- Building Trade: Carpentry;
- Building Trade: Plumbing;
- Derrickman;
- Electrical Installation – Domestic;
- Electrical Installation – Commercial/Industrial;
- Heavy Equipment Operation (HEO);
- Industrial Mechanical Maintenance – Hydraulic and Pneumatics;
- Industrial Mechanical Maintenance – Hydraulics;
- Shielded Metal Arc Welding – Level 1; and
- Shielded Metal Arc Welding – Level 2.

1-year Craftsman certificates in

- Plumbing; and
- Commercial Electrician

2-year diplomas in

- Welding;
- Electrical; and
- Refrigeration and Air Conditioning.

All of the programmes offered by the NESC provide skills which are very useful for the industries within the maritime sector. The Youth Training and Employment Partnership Programme (YTEPP) also offers courses in welding and fabrication, both of which are useful skills for the ship repair industry.

Other stakeholders in T&T's maritime sector include the Environmental Management Authority (EMA) which enforces environmental protection locally, the Maritime Authority of Trinidad and Tobago (MATT) which regulates matters relating to the maritime industry, and local owners of marine vessels that require the ship repair services, shipping agents, ship brokers, and freight forwarders, and the Shipping Association of Trinidad and Tobago (SATT), which is an association that represents the interests of shipping industry stakeholders.

3.4 Local Competitiveness Factors

Several factors work in favour of T&T's maritime sector. One of T&T's competitiveness factors is its location. The country is located in close proximity to North America, South America, and the Panama Canal in Central America. Thus, it is in an ideal location to encounter vessels from the north–south, and the south–south trade. In fact, over 63 shipping lines utilize ports in the country to facilitate the transshipment of containerized cargo to and from the US, Europe, and the Asia-Pacific region. The completion of the Panama Canal expansion project in 2016 tripled its capacity and registered an increase in tonnage of 23%, and an increase in revenues by 12.5% within the first year after expansion (EKNP 2017). The increase in transshipment volume provides an opportunity for T&T as this increases the number of marine vessels operating in close proximity to T&T that would require maintenance to continue their operations.[66]

T&T's location also provides an advantage as the country is located below the Caribbean's hurricane belt. The Gulf of Paria, located along the western coastline of Trinidad, is one of the largest sheltered deep-water harbours in the world. These two factors provide a secure location where shipping, transshipment, cold stacking, leisure marine, and ship repairs can occur all year round.

The existence of the shipping and leisure marine industry in T&T creates demand for ship repair and maintenance services since the International Maritime Organization (IMO) places mandatory requirements on marine vessels.[67]

Another major competitiveness factor is the presence of a vibrant offshore hydrocarbon exploration and production industry in the country. In fact, the hydrocarbon sector creates local demand for ship repair and a variety of maintenance services. This demand is generated from two general sources. One is export related, as the hydrocarbon sector attracts marine vessels to Trinidad for the purpose of exporting liquefied natural gas (LNG), refined oil, processed asphalt, ammonia, urea, and methanol to markets in the

---

[66] Unfortunately, the public authorities in T&T did nothing to upgrade the capacity of the country's port facilities in anticipation of the completion of the Panama Canal expansion project. Thus, T&T's ports cannot accommodate large marine vessels in excess of 295 metres (Singh 2016).

[67] The Flag State Authority for ship registration enforces compliance with such requirements. These requirements are enforceable when the certificates of marine vessels are renewed.

Caribbean, the United States (US) and Europe (de Gannes and Persad 2010). The second source of demand is generated from the provision of maintenance support to marine vessels involved in bunkering, the transportation of workers, and other marine vessels providing technical support to the country's offshore exploration and production activities.

To some extent, the country's exchange rate, which stood at TTD $6.7993 to USD 1 on August 3, 2018, is relatively stable (RBC 2018). Officially, T&T has floated its exchange rate since 1993 (CBTT 2017). In practice, the exchange rate is a managed float in which the Trinidad and Tobago dollar (TTD) is pegged to the United States dollar (USD). Over the 1997 to 2015 period, the TTD exchange rate with the USD was relatively constant at TTD 6.4 to USD 1. The weakening foreign exchange inflows to T&T in lieu of weak oil prices in the 2014 to 2017 period were accompanied by a minuscule slide of T&T's currency. Indeed, the monetary authorities demonstrated their commitment to defending the T&T exchange rate even in the face of weak revenues from the economic downturn. Such relative financial stability creates an environment that tends to hold investor confidence.

Figure 3.3: TTD–USD exchange rate 1993-2017

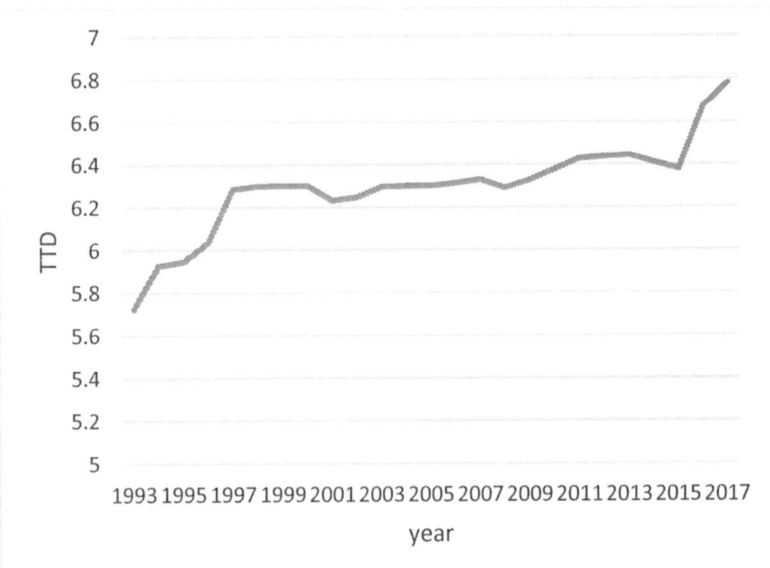

Source: CBTT (2018)

The GORTT education policy is favourable for the country's maritime sector. Under the Government Assistance for Tuition Expenses Programme (GATE), citizens of T&T may access free tertiary education in all disciplines. Thus, citizens of T&T are not constrained by their individual incomes and savings to attain their desired training. By another token, there are a multitude of tertiary institutions operating in T&T which provide training in areas which are beneficial to T&T's maritime sector. Section 3.3.4 provided details of these educational opportunities.

Another policy induced competitive factor is trade facilitation between T&T and several international partners. The GORTT as part of the Caribbean Community (CARICOM) has signed several trade agreements, namely:

- CARICOM–Venezuela (1 July 1991);
- CARICOM–Colombia (July 1994);
- CARICOM–Dominican Republic (22nd August 1998);
- CARICOM–Cuba (5th July 2000);
- CARICOM–Costa Rica (9th March 2004); and
- CARIFORUM (CARICOM and the Dominican Republic)–European Union (EU) – Economic Partnership Agreement (EPA) (29 December 2008).

The trade agreements increase market access for T&T's exporters. Regardless of whether there is an increase in imports or exports, an increase in trade would be accompanied by an increase in shipping, which in turn provides opportunities for the ship repair sector.

The GORTT has also offered a number of incentives for the ship repair industry. They include:

- An incentive introduced in 2016, whereby the GORTT exempts ship repair services from the country's value added tax (VAT).
- A provision where locally registered firms offering ship repair services are allowed duty-free treatment on the import of machinery, equipment and materials required for production.
- An incentive where firms involved in ship repair and shipbuilding activities are allowed a training allowance whereby they may write off 150% of their training expense as an allowance against their taxation liability (GORTT MTI 2016).

T&T's democratic system of government and its stable political climate also create an investor friendly environment, favouring all industries in the country.

3.5 Challenges in the Sub-industries

The maritime sector in T&T is affected by a number of challenges. These challenges do not occur in isolation since problems in one sub-industry may spill over to affect the operational efficiency in other sub-industries. For instance, inefficiency at the port and delays in the clearing of cargos affect the efficiency of shipping companies, and the ease in which ship repair companies can import parts to facilitate their repair and maintenance works.

One of the major challenges to the maritime sector in T&T relates to the operational inefficiency of the Customs Division. Several of the Customs Division administrative functions are paper-based and labour intensive rather than automated. Furthermore, several shipping firms and shipping brokers often express problems with the country's Customs Division with regard to the value of items and the classification of items, both of which affect the amount that must be paid to clear imported goods.

3.5.1 The Ports

The operational performance of the port of POS is not in line with that commonly found in major container terminals. The port's low berth productivity stems from insufficient STS cranes and low crane productivity.

Labour challenges are a notable issue at both container ports, a problem that has persisted for decades. For instance, worker productivity at both container ports has been described as "poor" in important areas related to the organization of work, namely, occupational health and safety, cargo handling techniques, and equipment maintenance. The salaries of the foreign officers employed by Bay Ferries and the Canadian Ferry management and maintenance contract manager at the port of Port of Spain, which can be up to 67% more than the salaries of local counterparts, have been noted by the recognized majority union as a disincentive for work performance. Foreign transshipment firms have been noted for poaching trained stevedores, seamen, linesmen, and crane operators from PLIPDECO (Nathan Associates 2014).

The labour force at the port of POS is also aging as a number of workers are between the ages of 58 and 64 and can no longer work the graveyard shift.

There is a need for simulator equipment training especially in the area of crane operations for new and less experienced crane operators.

The collective bargaining process between the recognized majority union and the employers (the PATT and PLIDECO) is very confrontational. Additionally, there are often delays in the collective bargaining process where the recognized majority union and the employer are negotiating the terms and conditions of employment for workers for a past collective bargaining period. During the negotiations, the unresolved issues typically revolve around compensation for overtime work, flexible and shift hours of work, and the multi-tasking of stevedores and longshoremen (Nathan Associates 2014).

Since 2005, the PATT tugs at the port of POS have been out of service and due for replacement. The NEC subsequently provides towage services.

While the expansion of the Panama Canal increased the volume and size of vessels travelling along its trade route, T&T is unlikely to benefit from the increased Panama Canal traffic since no steps were taken to upgrade T&T's port facilities to accommodate Post-Panamax sized marine vessels.

3.5.2 The Ship Repair Industry

The ship repair industry experiences a number of challenges. Despite the presence of multiple tertiary education institutions, the large firms in the industry face difficulties in retaining competent and qualified personnel (GORTT MTI 2008). This is partially due to the hydrocarbon sector paying higher wages for the same type of work.

Several SMEs in the ship repair industry face difficulties in raising financing. Banks often require a business to have a track record for their business proposal, as well as sufficient cash inflows to cover a loan repayment before providing any loan. Consequently, many SMEs are unable to upgrade as they cannot self-finance initiatives which would increase their productive capacity.

A third major limitation is port inefficiency and tardy government bureaucracy. As T&T has a limited domestic production base, several consumer and intermediate goods must be imported. However, there are often delays in the clearing of containers of imports at the Trinidad port at Port of Spain. In fact, the bureaucracy in public offices in T&T seemingly complements the tardy work performance of many public servants.

Another limitation of the ship repair industry is the inability for T&T's ports to accommodate marine vessels in excess of 295 metres (Singh 2016). Over 63 shipping lines utilize ports in T&T while transporting containerized cargo to and from the US, Europe, and the Asia-Pacific regions (InvesTT 2018). The recent completion of the Panama Canal expansion project in 2016 also allowed the increase in size of marine vessels that could travel through the canal. However, without upgrading the depth of T&T ports in excess of 12.5 metres, T&T will be unable to attract larger sized vessels.

While not a direct limitation, there is a deficiency in research conducted on ship repair and shipbuilding in T&T. Thus, firms in T&T continue to lag behind the dominant producers in Europe and the Asia-Pacific regions.

3.5.3 The Marine Services Industry

The GORTT has been tardy in collecting its anchorage rental fees from international firms using the Gulf of Paria as a harbour to cold stack its marine vessels. Additionally, authorized bunkering has been occurring in T&T's territorial waters as some small-scale operators fill barrels with subsidized diesel and gasoline at gas stations in T&T then resell the fuel to small-scale operators in the Gulf of Paria or in Venezuela.

Piracy, and the trade of illegal items, and the unauthorized transportation of people also occur in the Gulf of Paria.

3.5.4 The Yachting Industry

The yachting industry in T&T has been experiencing decline from the early 2000s to the present in 2018. Some of the deterrents to yacht arrivals at T&T include:

i) piracy in the country's territorial waters;
ii) crime in T&T and the perception by yachting tourists that T&T may be an unsafe country;
iii) the lack of a single entry form to the country's territorial waters;
iv) administrative difficulty for yachting and other leisure marine tourists in gaining extensions to remain in T&T from the Immigration Division;[68] and

[68] Previously an extension could have been obtained at the Immigration and Customs office in Chaguaramas. Presently, yacht visitors have to go to Port of Spain to get the extension.

v) the lack of major marketing events in T&T to attract leisure marine vessels.

The country's poor road network, high traffic congestion especially during working hours, and a high crime rate are general factors which serve as disincentives for all industries in T&T's maritime sector.

3.6 Upgrading strategies

Upgrading strategies should be implemented in order for existing firms and potential new entrants to extract more value from the global value chain. Upgrading provides a wide scope of opportunities to firms that range from increased efficiency to increased penetration of markets. In the global value chain analysis literature, the types of upgrading include: process upgrading, product upgrading, functional upgrading, channel upgrading, and inter-sectoral upgrading.

Process upgrading increases the efficiency of production, product upgrading involves the improvement of product quality, functional upgrading refers to the entry of a firm into a new, higher value-added function, channel upgrading occurs when firms move further down the value chain and enter one or more new end markets in the same basic product, and inter-sectoral upgrading is when a firm can horizontally diversify into a completely new value chain.

3.6.1 The Ports

The GORTT considered a number of initiatives to facilitate the process upgrading of the port. For instance, the government considered the construction of two new perpendicular berths that would replace the present port area and the construction of a new port at the East Sea Lots area (Nathan Associates 2014).

There have been plans to develop port facilities at La Brea. The Brighton International Terminal, the proposed port, would be part of a 196-ha industrial park owned by the NEC.

No plans have been announced by the GORTT to address labour productivity challenges at either of the container ports. However, there is a need for a young, vibrant and competent work force that can continue the critical operations at the port. Moreover, there is scope to implement an effective succession plan where new workers would be trained by mature workers to prevent the loss of skills and institutional knowledge.

3.6.2 Trade Facilitation and Customs

In an attempt to improve the operational efficiency of the Customs Division, the GORTT implemented the UNCTAD Technical assistance project for the implementation of the Automated System for Customs Data – ASYCUDA World (AW). AW is a computerized electronic data interchange (EDI) and management information system (MIS) which modernizes customs procedures. The Customs Act was amended via Customs Act 6 of 2013 to grant the Customs Division the legal basis to use the new AW system.

AW allows 24/7 access, allowing carriers, shipping agents, non-vessel operating common carriers (NVOCCs),[69] freight forwarders, customs brokers, consignee clerks, importers and exporters to electronically lodge trade declarations. It is noteworthy that while AW is currently operational at all major ports of entry in T&T, some unnecessary manual operating procedures continue at the ports.

3.6.3 The Ship Repair Industry

In order for T&T to extract more value and upgrade along the ship repair global value chain various upgrading strategies could be employed. Upgrading occurs when firms or countries move into higher value activities in GVCs in order to increase value added, employment, and profits. It involves strategies to improve the firm or country's position of the global value chain. Government policy, firm strategy, technology and human capital can all lead to successful upgrading. In the global value chain framework four types of upgrading could be applied to the T&T ship repair industry. They include process, product, and functional upgrading.

Process upgrading involves the more efficient transformation of inputs into outputs. This can be achieved by re-organizing various activities by firms in the ship repair industry, the adoption of better technology and a more skilled labour force. In order for the firms in T&T's ship repair industry to attain such process upgrading they can seek partnerships with more efficient international ship repair companies. Alternatively, T&T's ship repair firms

---

[69] An NVOCC is a person or company that organizes shipments for individuals or firms to acquire goods from the manufacturer or supplier.

can procure the services of a change management specialist to help optimize their management efficiency.

Research and continuous improvement in technology conducted at UWI and UTT in ship design areas such as new hull designs, rudder and propeller design, LNG as fuel, ballast water management systems, etc., can be disseminated to T&T's ship repair industry, allowing its firms to upgrade their productive capacities. Such research has allowed South Korea to emerge as a major player in the ship repair industry (Mickeviciene 2011), and it can also propel T&T's ship repair firms.

Product upgrading for the maritime cluster involves serving larger ships. This will require the dredging and upgrading of the capacity of T&T ports to accommodate larger sized vessels. This project would involve high capex costs which T&T is unable to self-finance before 2020. Two options are available to T&T to achieve this upgrade in at least one of its ports. The first option would be to partner a large multinational interested in such a business venture. The second option would be for the GORTT to seek loan financing from a multilateral development bank. Given that T&T's debt to GDP ratio stood at approximately 60% of GDP in 2017, it is not recommended that the GORTT take on a large additional external debt before 2020. Therefore, the better option for the GORTT would be to seek a larger international partner.

Functional upgrading where new functions are added is to increase value captured from the global value chain. T&T currently has companies operating in the ship repair and shipbuilding industries. There is one firm (TOFCO) operating in the offshore construction industry. However, there is scope for more firms to venture into the offshore platform fabrication industry as T&T has a vibrant hydrocarbon industry. Furthermore, given Guyana, a neighbouring CARICOM country, is on the eve of a hydrocarbon boom, there will be many opportunities for offshore platform fabrication. Indeed, offshore platform fabrication is an attractive industry as it will create thousands of jobs per project, and could utilize iron and steel inputs if the domestic iron and steel industry is revived.

3.6.3 The Yachting Industry

The GORTT recognized that the country's yachting industry requires a multi-faceted approach to product development. The government's yachting policy identifies aspirations for product upgrading by sourcing investors to facilitate marina upgrading. The policy also recommended increased marketing of yachting in the country, and the hosting of a major yachting event to attract leisure marine tourists (GORTT MTI 2017).

The GORTT MTI (2017) also proposed a number of upgrading processes, namely

i) the intention to develop the criteria for competency-based qualifications in the yachting industry through the Trinidad and Tobago National Vocational Qualification (TTNVQs) and the Caribbean Vocational Qualification (CVQ);
ii) the implementation of a Single Harmonised Form to facilitate easier clearance for foreigners; and
iii) the development of an electronic Pre-Arrival Notice (ePAN) system to encourage the easier movement of yachting traffic between Trinidad and Tobago.

3.7 Recommendations and Conclusion

The maritime sector is very important to the economy of T&T. Its contribution can be increased, if the constraints facing each of its sub-industries are adequately addressed.

Ports and Customs Division Recommendations

The container ports in T&T, and the Customs Division have labour challenges which contribute to their operational inefficiencies. There is a need for change management in the aforementioned agencies.

In order to help improve labour productivity, labour should be hired and promoted on the basis of qualifications and competence rather than seniority. Furthermore, labour should be compensated based on the achievement of deliverables rather than a fixed monthly salary that is completely detached from productivity. The same principle should apply to port workers as well as management at the port. Additionally, there should also be a comprehensive system to terminate the services of workers and management on the grounds of low productivity if they fail to achieve their agreed deliverables on an annual basis. There should also be tripartite discussions between the GORTT, the PATT, and the recognized majority unions to determine the deliverables to be achieved by each job (for both management and the port's labour) as well as the details to terminate the services of incompetent personnel.

As previously mentioned, importers and ship brokers tend to experience disputes with the Customs Division with regard to the classification and value of items. These two characteristics affect the tax that must be paid in order for the goods to be cleared for legal entry into T&T. In order to address this limitation, the GORTT can simplify the customs clearing process. More specifically, it can restructure the customs system to one that has less classification of items, and charges a lower and more homogenous tariff or customs duty for the clearance of goods.

To facilitate an infrastructure upgrade at the port of POS significant capital injections in the PATT are required. However, the PATT's current inability to address its persistent labour and operational inefficiencies raises doubt about its current ability to manage a large financial injection and achieve improved operational efficiency.

With the exception of the Kingston Container Terminal (KCT), most of the Caribbean port hubs are privately operated. Therefore, it would be rational for the GORTT to continue this trend and privatize the port of POS. It is noteworthy that the privatization of any port will not be a popular move especially in the recognized majority union. This is due to the high likelihood of privatization being accompanied by some form of retrenchment. There were attempts to privatize the port of POS in the past, but they failed due to labour objections. The government will need to decide whether it is willing or not to tolerate the inefficiencies which will continue to compromise the economic growth that can be generated from the maritime sector.

Ship Repair Recommendations

The ship repair industry can be a flagship industry for the diversification of T&T's economy. In order to facilitate the expansion and growth of the ship repair cluster a number of things are needed. One recommendation is for the increase of the pool of skilled labour. This can be achieved by persuading young adults to pursue technical vocational training, rather than academic training which has no significant employment opportunities available in T&T.

A second recommendation for the ship repair industry is to encourage greater cooperation between the SMEs to pool and share their resources and equipment, and collectively enhance their productive capacity. This chapter also highlighted that SMEs face challenges in accessing financing. While it is highly unlikely that T&T's domestic banks would create new provisions to facilitate a capacity upgrade of SMEs in the ship repair industry, the GORTT can create a new financing facility for the SMEs.

A third recommendation for the ship repair industry is for the formation of international partnerships between domestic SMEs, domestic firms, and international ship repair firms to enhance their local productive capacity. Additionally, there is scope for process upgrading via the improvement of workflow processes. Through partnerships with more dominant international firms in the ship repair industry, local firms may gain positive spillover effects, and achieve process upgrading.

Yachting Recommendations

The improvement in the administrative process for the clearing of yachting tourists is likely to improve yachting tourist arrivals in T&T. This can be done by the re-opening of the Customs and Immigration Division Office at Chaguaramas. Moreover, the hosting of marine events in T&T, can also serve to improve yacht tourist arrivals at T&T.

The occurrence of piracy and the trade of illegal goods in the Gulf of Paria are a result of the insecurity of the country's maritime border. The GORTT has announced its intention to purchase new offshore patrol vessels from Austal, an Australian company. When these vessels arrive, they can be utilized for patrols by the Coast Guard to decrease piracy, the trade of illegal goods, and the unauthorized transportation of people in the Gulf of Paria.

Overall Recommendations

There is also scope for the GORTT to increase the efficiency of the public service in order to enhance doing business in T&T.

The formation of partnerships is highly desirable to improve operational efficiency in T&T's maritime sector. Moreover, international partnerships can be used as an excellent strategy to attract the required capital and FDI to facilitate the upgrading of physical infrastructure, and the removal of bottlenecks at T&T's ports.

As previously indicated, trade acts as the instrument to bring marine vessels to T&T, which in turn could serve as clients for the country's ship repair industry. Rather than just increasing market access, the GORTT can put effort into enhancing market penetration to the markets of its partner trading countries. This can increase the volume of trade, and the amount of work available for the country's maritime sector.

References

Brevik, Thomas, and Christoffer Melleby. 2014. "The Expansion of the Panama Canal: A Study of Consequences in the Container Shipping Industry." Master of Science in Economics and Business Administration thesis, Norwegian School of Economics.

Brun, Lukas, and Stacey Frederick. 2017. "Chapter 4: Korea and the Shipbuilding Global Value Chain." Accessed September 20, 2018. https://gvcc.duke.edu/wp-content/uploads/Duke_KIET_Korea_and_the_Shipbuilding_GVC_CH_4.pdf.

CBTT (Central Bank of Trinidad and Tobago). 2017. "Exchange Rate Management." Accessed December 3, 2017. https://www.central-bank.org.tt/about/our-mission/exchange-rate-management.

—. 2018. "Data Centre." Accessed August 4, 2018. https://www.central-bank.org.tt/statistics/data-centre.

de Gannes, Wilfred, and Andre Persad. 2010. "Development of the Shipbuilding and Ship Repair Industry in Trinidad and Tobago." IEM 2010 Conference of Fostering Engineering Networking, Collaboration and Competence, Trinidad and Tobago, 7-8 October, 2010.

ECLAC (Economic Commission for Latin America and the Caribbean). 2002. "Trinidad and Tobago: The Yachting Sector." Accessed September 21, 2018. https://www.cepal.org/publicaciones/xml/1/12331/G0711.PDF.

—. 2018. "Maritime and Logistics Profile of Latin America and the Caribbean." Accessed September 22, 2018. http://perfil.cepal.org/l/en/start.html.

ECSIP Consortium. 2015. "Study on the Competitiveness of the Recreational Boating Sector." Accessed September 21, 2018. https://ec.europa.eu/growth/tools-databases/vto/content/study-competitiveness-recreational-boating-sector.

EKNP (Embassy of the Kingdom of the Netherlands in Panama). 2017. "Panama Port Development Investment Opportunities in the Maritime Sector 2017." Accessed August 4, 2018. https://www.nederlandwereldwijd.nl/.../01/.../Panama+Port+Development+2017.pdf.

Gereffi, Gary, Lukas Brun, Shawn Stokes, and Andrew Guinn. 2013. "The NSPS Shipbuilding Value Chains." Accessed September 20, 2018. https://gvcc.duke.edu/wp-content/uploads/NSPS_GVC_Analysis_Jan2013_01282013.pdf.

GORTT MT (Government of the Republic of Trinidad and Tobago Ministry of Tourism). 2012. “Statistical Overview of Tourism Performance in Trinidad & Tobago.” Accessed September 22, 2018. http://tourism.gov.tt/Portals/0/Documents/Statistical%20Overview%20 Report%202010.pdf.

GORTT MTI (Government of the Republic of Trinidad and Tobago Ministry of Trade and Industry). 2008. “A Strategic Plan for the Development of the Merchant Marine Industry.” Accessed October 7, 2013. www.tradeind.gov.tt/LinkClick.aspx?fileticket...tabid=180&mid.

—. 2016. “Trinidad and Tobago’s Maritime Industry.” Accessed September 21, 2018. https://tradeind.gov.tt/commercial-maritime/.

—. 2017. “Yachting Policy of Trinidad and Tobago: 2017-2021.” Accessed September 21, 2018. https://tradeind.gov.tt/yachting-policy-trinidad-tobago/.

InvesTT. 2018. “Major Shipping Lines.” Accessed August 5, 2018. http://www.investt.co.tt/industries-and-opportunities/maritime-services/.

Mickeviciene, Rima. 2011. “Global Competition in Shipbuilding: Trends and Challenges for Europe.” In *The Economic Geography of Globalization,* edited by Piotr Pachura, 201-224. London, United Kingdom: Intech Open Limited.

Nathan Associates. 2014. “Port Rationalization Study for Trinidad and Tobago.” Accessed September 22, 2018. http://shipping.co.tt/sitepdf/Final%20Report%20Port%20Rationalization%20Study%20VMar14%20(1).pdf.

OECD (Organization for Economic Co-operation and Development). 2008. “The Interaction Between the Ship Repair, Ship Conversion and Ship Building Industries.” Accessed September 3, 2013. http://www.oecd.org/-sti/ind/42033278.pdf.

Peretomode, Victor. 2014. “The Role of the Maritime Industry and Vocational and Technical Education and Training in the Economic Development of Nigeria.” *IOSR Journal of Humanities and Social Science* 19(5): 45-50.

Preville, Claudius. 2013. “Assessment of the Opportunities for the CARIFORUM Yachting Sector in Exporting Services to the European Union (EU) under the CARIFORUM-EC EPA.” Accessed September 21, 2018. http://c-nsc.org/download/trade_in_services/February%20 2014-Yachting.pdf.

RBC (Royal Bank of Canada). 2018. “Exchange Rates.” Accessed August 4, 2018. http://www.rbcroyalbank.com/caribbean/tt/customer-service/ exchange-rates.html.

Ramnarine, Kristy. 2017. "Government moves to collect US$4 million rent from TransOcean for Rigs in TT Waters." Accessed October 14, 2018. http://www.cnc3.co.tt/news/government-moves-collect-us4-million-rent-transocean-rigs-tt-waters.

Singh, Nadaleen. 2016. "Panama Canal Challenges for PoS Port." *Trinidad and Tobago Guardian Newspaper,* May 25. Accessed August 4, 2018. http://www.guardian.co.tt/business/2016-05-25/panama-canal-challenges-pos-port.

The Maritime Post. 2018. "Top 10 Biggest Shipping Companies in the World." Accessed September 20, 2018. http://www.themaritimepost.com/top-10-biggest-shipping-companies-world/.

UNCTAD (United Nations Conference on Trade and Development). 2018. "Container Port Throughput, Annual, 2010-2017." Accessed September 22, 2018. http://unctadstat.unctad.org/wds/TableViewer/tableView.aspx.

CHAPTER FOUR

CAN DOMINICA ACHIEVE CLIMATE RESILIENT BANANA VALUE CHAIN DEVELOPMENT?

Abstract

The Commonwealth of Dominica is a mountainous Caribbean island nation, traditionally involved in the production and export of bananas. Unreciprocated preferential trade allowed the country's small-scale farmers to prosper over the 1950s to 1990s period. However, changes in the international trade environment resulted in the gradual erosion of preferences in bananas for the country. Given that the small-scale farmers in Dominica are not as competitive as large-scale producers in Latin America, several of Dominica's farmers left the industry. Thus, Dominica's banana industry has been in decline from the 1990s onwards to the present in 2018.

The country is also challenged by the multitude of hurricanes which have hit the country over the years. The recent Hurricane Maria of 2017 did significant damage to the country, destroying houses, public infrastructure and completely decimating the banana industry. Indeed, the erosion of trade preferences and climate-related stressors are significant challenges to Dominica's banana industry.

This chapter utilizes the global value chain analysis framework and explores how the trade-related and climate-related challenges may be addressed. Moreover, this chapter also explores the prospects for Dominica to achieve climate resilience and acquire more value from its banana value chain.

4.1 Introduction

Dominica, officially the Commonwealth of Dominica, is a mountainous Caribbean island nation. It is situated 1,400 miles south of Miami, at latitude 15° north and longitude 61° west, and between the island of Guadeloupe to the northwest and Martinique to the south-southeast (Invest Dominica

2013). Although Dominica is the largest Windward Caribbean island (CaRC 1997), it is still relatively small as it is only 48 km long and 24 km at its widest point. It has a maximum altitude of 1447 m, at Morne Diablotin, and receives an extremely high rainfall, in excess of 10,000 mm on the highest peaks (Malhotra et al. 2007).

Historically, the agriculture industry has been the main economic driver of the Commonwealth of Dominica. The country's agricultural industry includes the production of bananas, citrus, coconuts, cocoa, herbal oils and extracts. Traditionally, banana production has employed over one-third of the country's labour force. However, the banana sector has been challenged ever since the gradual erosion of preferences[70] to the European Union (EU) market (Tandon 2014).

In the 20th century, the Commonwealth of Dominica, as part of the African Caribbean and Pacific (ACP) countries experienced preferential access to the EU market under the former Lomé Agreements. A special protocol of the Lomé Convention assured preferential treatment of banana exports from the ACP countries to the EU market, the Banana Protocol. The Banana Protocol included a banana quota for duty-free export from the ACP countries to the EU market. Also, importation of bananas into the EU required a licence, thus raising the banana import costs. As a result of the Banana Protocol, the price of imported bananas in the EU was up to 80% higher than the world free-market price (McQueen 1997; Mlachila et al. 2010).

Following World Trade Organization (WTO) rulings that the EU's banana import regime discriminated against Latin American exporters, the EU requested a WTO waiver authorizing tariff preferences for ACP countries under the Cotonou Agreement. The EU also pledged to switch to a tariff-only system. The shift to the tariff-only regime meant that no quotas or licences would have been required for agricultural exports to the EU market. While by 2006 there was a Most Favoured Nation (MFN) tariff of €176 per

---

[70] Trade preferences can only exist where there is tariff protection. As tariff protection is progressively dismantled there is an automatic erosion of the margin of tariff preferences. The traditional ACP agricultural-trade preferences were eroded by the EU's internal process of reform of the Common Agricultural Policy (CAP), and the unilateral EU tariff reductions, for instance the "Everything but Arms" (EBA) initiative for least developed countries (LDCs) and revisions to the Generalized System of Preferences (GSP). In fact, the CAP reform directly affected the value of trade preferences as it affected the prices that ACP exporters would receive for exports to the EU market (Goodison 2007).

tonne for non-trading partner countries, and a duty-free 0.775 million-tonne quota for ACP countries, the gradual reforms to the EU's banana regime increased the competition between the Caribbean banana exporters and the more efficient Latin American producers (Mlachila et al. 2010).

Apart from trade-related challenges, the Commonwealth of Dominica is also vulnerable to climate-related stressors. In fact, the Commonwealth of Dominica was one of the Caribbean countries which were severely affected by the hurricanes of the 2017 season.[71] On the evening of September 18, 2017, Hurricane Maria, a category 5 hurricane, hit Dominica with 160-mile-per-hour winds, damaging roads, buildings, and wiping out banana crops.[72] Maria did significant damage estimated at approximately EC$2.51 billion (US$931 million). What is even more alarming is the fact that although Maria was the most intense and devastating hurricane in the nation's history, the warming of the Atlantic Ocean and the Caribbean Sea could mean that this size of disaster could be of increasing frequency (Commonwealth of Dominica 2017a).[73]

Indeed, both the erosion of trade preferences and the extreme weather conditions served as threats to the banana sector in the Commonwealth of Dominica. This raises an important question. "Are there any climate resilient banana value chain options for the Commonwealth of Dominica?" This study seeks to answer the aforementioned question. Subsequently, this study performs a global value chain analysis of the banana value chain in the Commonwealth of Dominica. Additionally, this chapter also uses the global value chain framework to identify Dominica's position in the banana global value chain and its prospects of upgrading to extract more value.

The global value chain framework is used since it has become an increasingly popular framework for analysing the changes in the global trade environment for producers of the commodity. The GVC framework considers the activities and actors in production, processing, distribution, and marketing.

---

[71] The Caribbean countries affected by the hurricanes of the 2017 season include: Anguilla, Barbuda, Dominica, Puerto Rico, St. Barts, St. Maarten/Martin and the British Virgin Islands (BVI).

[72] Dominica was also hit by Hurricane Irma. However, it was worse affected by Hurricane Maria (ACP 2018).

[73] Note: Climate change is the change in the statistical distribution of weather patterns. It can lead to more frequent and intense rainfall, floods, droughts, and storms.

This study is structured as follows. Section 4.2 provides an outline of the GVC analysis methodology. Section 4.3 will review the global value chain for bananas. Section 4.4 considers the value chain for bananas in Dominica. Section 4.5 assesses the challenges experienced in the banana industry in Dominica. Section 4.6 explores the policy response that can be used to address the trade-related, climate-related stressors, and upgrading issues. Section 4.7 concludes the chapter.

4.2 Global Value Chain Analysis Methodology

Global Value Chain Analysis (GVCA) has been used to analyse international production chains. GVCA takes a non-traditional approach to international trade research as it focuses on the examination of cross-national activities that take goods from raw materials to final products. It considers the network of activities as well as the actors that are interconnected along the value chains. This approach provides insight about the dynamics of different actors and the linkages binding them to various activities in a given production chain (Gereffi et al. 2005; Gereffi and Fernandez-Stark 2016).

GVCA can be used to investigate the power relation in which trade is embedded within the chain, the characteristics of economic governance, the share of value and costs, and the price structure, along with the key actors who dominate and "set the rules" along the chain. GVCA also emphasizes global structures by considering issues of how and by whom production and trade are governed. It encompasses the full range of activities that are required to bring a product from its conception to the final markets (Gereffi et al. 2005; Gereffi and Fernandez-Stark 2016; Danes 2017).

In the context of Dominica's banana industry, GVCA can be used to determine which countries are the global leaders in the banana trade, which companies exercise dominance, the position of Dominica in the global value chain, the constraints to banana production in Dominica, and the prospects for Dominica to upgrade along the value chain.

4.3 Global Banana Industry

The global value chain for bananas is comprised of a production/farming stage, a transportation stage, and a retail/distribution stage. The way the aforementioned stages are interlinked is reflected in Figure 4.1.

Figure 4.1: The Banana Export Value Chain

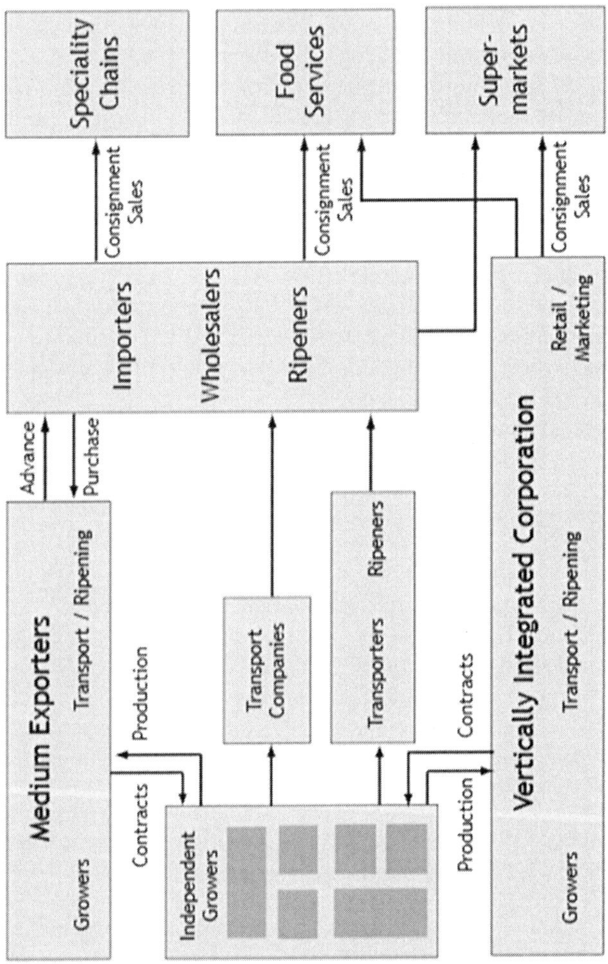

Source: Mather (2008)

In the production stage, bananas tend to be produced either on very small land holdings or on very large plantations. The majority of bananas that are traded in international markets are produced on large plantations. There is diversity between production scales both within and between banana exporting countries. For instance, in Ecuador, there are both small-scale and large-scale banana farmers. While in Costa Rica, banana cultivation is dominated by large-scale producers, but in the Windward islands of the Caribbean, banana cultivation is dominated by small-scale producers (Mather 2008).

In the transportation stage, there exist some transportation companies which facilitate the export of bananas to destination markets. For instance, shipping companies such as APL, CMA, and ZIM currently have direct shipping service routes between Latin American countries (banana exporting countries), and European countries (banana importing countries). However, the banana transportation sector is dominated by a few large multinational companies, namely Dole, Del Monte, Chiquita, Fyffes, and Noboa. The aforementioned companies are also vertically integrated, and to varying degrees are involved in the production, transportation, and distribution of bananas (Mather 2008).

In the banana distribution stage, as previously mentioned, the "big-five" multinational banana companies are also involved in banana distribution. However, a few supermarkets have significant market power and market share. For instance, in the United Kingdom (UK), Tesco has over 30% of the market sales, closely followed by Asda/Walmart and Sainsbury's with approximately 16% each, and Morrisons with a 12% market share (Banana Link 2004).[74]

The global trade in bananas can be divided into three systems (Arias et al. 2003). First, there is the Latin American banana trade, which involves equal exports mainly to North America, and Europe. The residual exports from Latin America tend to go to Russia, Asia, and New Zealand. Second, there are the Caribbean and African exports, which tend to focus on the EU market. Third, there are the Pacific exporters, of which the Philippines is the largest exporter. The Pacific banana exporters tend to target the EU, the Middle East, and the Asian markets. In general, banana exporters tend to focus on the North American, EU, and Asian markets (Mather 2008).

Table 4.1 illustrates data from World Top Exports, indicating the top 15 banana exporting countries, on the basis of trade value, in 2017.

[74] In Europe, the UK, France, Italy and Spain are the main banana importers (Banana Link 2004).

Table 4.1: Top 15 Banana Exporting Countries in 2017

Rank	Country	Trade Value	Trade Share
1	Ecuador	US$3 billion	(24.6% of total banana exports)
2	Belgium	$1.1 billion	8.5%
3	Costa Rica	$1 billion	8.4%
4	Colombia	$918.1 million	7.4%
5	Guatemala	$882.3 million	7.1%
6	Philippines	$687.4 million	5.6%
7	Netherlands	$579.9 million	4.7%
8	United States	$445 million	3.6%
9	Dominican Republic	$393.3 million	3.2%
10	Côte d'Ivoire	$350.1 million	2.8%
11	Germany	$319.5 million	2.6%
12	Cameroon	$317.8 million	2.6%
13	Honduras	$311.1 million	2.5%
14	Panama	$294.7 million	2.4%
15	Mexico	$241.7 million	2%

Source: Workman (2018a)

It can be clearly seen in Table 4.1 that Ecuador, Belgium, and Costa Rica are the top banana exporting countries. In fact, 7 countries from the Latin American region (Ecuador, Costa Rica, Colombia, Guatemala, Honduras, Panama, and Mexico) are among the top banana exporting countries in the world. The Dominican Republic is the only Caribbean country that ranks among the top 10 banana exporting countries in the world.[75]

Table 4.2 displays the top 15 banana importing countries, on the basis of trade value in 2017.

Table 4.2: Top 15 Banana Importing Countries in 2017

Rank	Country	Trade Value	Trade Share
1	United States	US$2.8 billion	(18% of total bananas imports)
2	Belgium	$1.4 billion	9.1%
3	Russia	$1.1 billion	7.4%
4	Germany	$1 billion	6.6%
5	Japan	$850.8 million	5.6%
6	Netherlands	$832 million	5.4%
7	United Kingdom	$829.3 million	5.4%
8	France	$586.7 million	3.8%
9	China	$579.5 million	3.8%
10	Italy	$523.8 million	3.4%
11	Canada	$421.7 million	2.8%
12	South Korea	$365.1 million	2.4%
13	Poland	$300 million	2%
14	Saudi Arabia	$263.8 million	1.7%
15	Argentina	$240 million	1.6%

Source: Workman (2018b)

[75] Dominica has a less than 1% market share to the EU market.

It can be clearly seen in Table 4.2 that the EU is the largest importer of bananas in the world. In fact, 6 countries from the EU (Belgium, France, Germany, Italy, Poland, and the United Kingdom) rank among the top banana importing countries. Collectively, the aforementioned EU countries comprise 35% of the banana import market. When considering individual countries, rather than economic unions, the United States (US), Belgium, and Russia emerge as the top three banana importing countries in the world. The majority of the EU banana imports are sourced from Latin American producers, with Ecuador, Costa Rica and Columbia emerging as the top suppliers.

The previously mentioned "big-five" multinational fruit companies tend to control a large share of the international banana trade.[76] They own fleet and ripening facilities, and have their own distribution networks in the importing countries, generating large economies of scale (FAO 2014).

In the 1980s, the big-five banana multinational companies traded 80% of the world's bananas (BL&FTA) 2015). They also owned large plantations in Central and South America, and other major banana-producing regions. Thus, the global banana industry was highly oligopolistic, and largely a producer driven value chain. Over the years, the multinational banana companies divested a large share of their own banana productions (FAO 2014; BL&FTA 2015). Subsequently, their dominance weakened, resulting in their market share dropping to approximately 33% of the banana export market share by the end of 2015 (BL&FTA 2015).

While the disengagement from production was partly caused by legal and operational challenges at the plantation level in host countries, the market share change also reflected the change in market power along the banana value chain. Major supermarket chains in the US and the EU have emerged as dominant players in the retail segment of the banana value chain. These retailers increasingly purchase bananas from small wholesalers or directly from banana farmers.

The shift of market power away from the multinational banana companies' brands towards retailers was facilitated by the development of direct shipping container liner services from South America to Europe. Improvements in the fuel efficiency of specialized container transport, as well as enhancements in port infrastructure resulted in the lower cost of

[76] The FAO (2014) reports that the "big-five" controlled approximately 44% of the international banana trade by 2014.

entry barriers for new buyers. The changing market conditions favoured an increase in competition (FAO 2014). Thus, the power relationships in the global banana industry seem to have shifted from a "producer-driven" value chain to a "buyer-driven" value chain (Danes 2017).

4.4 Overview of the Banana Industry in Dominica

In contrast to many other Caribbean islands, the mountainous terrain of Dominica prevented the country from being a suitable island for the large-scale cultivation of sugarcane. The topography of the island is more suitable for tree crops, hence the reason why coffee, cocoa, and bananas have been cultivated. Bananas have also been an attractive crop for cultivation in Dominica as they can be harvested throughout the year, subsequently, they can offer a more frequent paycheck than most export crops (NERA and OPM 2004). Furthermore, as each banana tree requires constant, skilled care for nine months in order to produce high quality fruit, it is labour intensive, and can produce jobs for several people (Clegg 2002).

The banana value chain in Dominica is comprised of production by the farmers, and export by the national production management companies. While, the global value chain has production, transportation and export, and retail distribution stages, Dominica operates only in the first 2 stages. Figure 4.2 provides an illustration.

Figure 4.2: Dominica Banana Value Chain

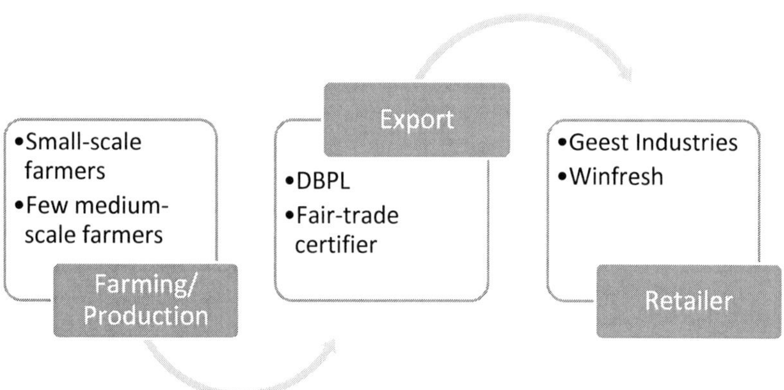

Source: Adapted from EP (2010)

In the farming stage, Dominica's banana production is undertaken by small-scale farmers. Families often engage in banana farming on steep hillsides on small land holdings typically less than one hectare (2.4 acres) (Torgerson 2010). The family typically supplies the labour for the farm, thus the labour force on each farm is significantly less than that of a Latin American banana plantation. The small land holdings, and small labour force are typically responsible for the low yield per acre, and higher per unit production costs relative to Latin American banana producers (NERA and OPM 2004).[77]

Dominica's banana industry has been in a state of continuous decline since its peak in 1988 when 72,000 tons were produced on 15,000 acres of cultivation by approximately 7,000 farmers. Although the country has experienced years in which hurricanes would wipe out the entire crop, it was the weakening of trade preferences which contributed to the country's banana output dropping to approximately 12,000 tons by less than 1,000 farmers by 2015 (Dominica NU 2015).

With regard to the transport and export stage, initially the Dominica Banana Association (DBA) purchased the bananas from the farmers. In fact, the DBA was established in 1934 to market, regulate, and control banana exports. It initially signed a contract to sell its exports to the Canada Banana Company (CBC). Later in 1959, the DBA's name was changed to the Dominica Banana Growers Association (DBGA) (Josling and Taylor 2003). Eventually, the DBGA's role was replaced by the Dominica Banana Marketing Corporation (DBMC). The DBMC bought banana yields from farmers and sold the output to Geest Industries, a multinational company which monopolized the export of bananas from the Windward Caribbean islands to the UK (McAfee 2007). The DBMC eventually found itself competing with the Windward Islands Banana Development and Exporting Company Limited (WIBDECL), the regional company which also purchased and exported bananas to multinational fruit companies. Financial woes experienced by DBMC caused the government to restructure the company and form the Dominica Banana Producers Limited (DBPL), which current performs the role of purchasing bananas from the small farmers and reselling to multinational fruit companies.

---

[77] In contrast, large Latin American banana plantations tend to range from several tens to hundreds of hectares. The plantations are also located on flat lands which have richer soil that gives higher yields. The large size allows the Latin American banana producers to enjoy economies of scale, which are not achievable by the Windward Caribbean Islands (Torgerson 2010).

Another major player in the Dominica banana industry is the registered fair-trade certifier (Klak et al. 2009). The Windward Islands Farmers Association (WINFA) became the regional organization responsible for certifying farmers in Dominica, as well as the other Windward Caribbean islands (Barker 2012).

4.4.1 History of Dominica's Banana Industry

Consideration for exporting bananas from Dominica can be traced as far as 1890 to Alford Nicholls, an agriculturalist who wrote a paper on "*The Cultivation of the Banana in Dominica*" (Clegg 2000, 2). Commercial interest in the export of bananas from the neighbouring St. Lucia in 1925 influenced the interest in the export of bananas from Dominica. The CBC negotiated supply contracts with the banana associations of Dominica, Grenada and St. Lucia in early 1934. While some exports of bananas occurred from the 1930s, it was not until a 15-year supply contract was signed between the DBA and Antilles Products Limited in December 1949 that the Dominica banana export industry fully excelled (Clegg 2000).

Like St. Lucia, St. Vincent and the Grenadines, and Grenada, the banana export industry which was established in Dominica in the 1950s, was aimed at supplying the UK market. However, the first Lomé agreement, which was signed in 1975, provided stable and high banana prices for Dominica (Greenaway and Milner 2003). In fact, the preferential prices ushered in an era of prosperity for several banana exporting ACP countries during the 1970s and 1980s.

While thriving on banana exports, the risk of monocrop dependency became evident in 1979 and 1980 when Hurricanes David and Allen devastated Dominica's banana production. Later in 1989, the country experienced hurricane damage again, this time it was due to Hurricane Hugo. Other hurricanes which wiped out the banana output in the past include Hurricane Luis in 1995, and Hurricane Lenny in 1999. Fortunately, bananas produce fruit relatively quick after replanting, allowing the resilience of Dominica.

Apart from the historical adverse weather conditions, the erosion of trade preferences has also been a great threat to the banana industry in Dominica. One aspect of the preference erosion is related to the shift towards reciprocated preferential trade agreements. In 1993, European countries deepened their integration when the Maastricht Treaty came into force, formerly establishing the European Union as an economic and political union. The Single European Market (SEM)[78] was a component of the economic union, and it allowed goods and services to freely move between EU member states. This SEM ended the 12 separate systems under which individual European countries could import bananas from ACP countries under the Lomé IV Convention (Klak et al. 2009).

The EU import regime continued to provide preferential treatment to ACP exports, but it placed an annual two-million-ton import quota for Latin American bananas. This change in trade policy coincided with the conclusion of the Uruguay Round of the General Agreement on Tariffs and Trade (GATT) negotiations which sought to multilaterally reduce trade barriers and promote more fair trade. Significant from the conclusion of the Uruguay Round was the establishment of the World Trade Organization (WTO), which had stronger trade rules than its GATT predecessor (Klak et al. 2009).

Several Latin American countries filed complaints against the Council Regulation 404/93 with the WTO in 1996. They were joined by the US since the multinational banana companies had their headquarters in the US (Klak et al. 2009). They complained that the EU's unreciprocated preferential treatment of the ACP countries under the Lomé agreements was discriminatory and not compliant with WTO rules (Greenaway and Milner 2003).[79] The WTO found that the preferential arrangement of Lomé offered the ACP countries an unfair trading advantage over other WTO members. Lomé IV, which was signed in 1990, formally came to an end in February 2000.

[78] The SEM was a common market which allowed the free movement of goods and services between member states.

[79] The WTO rules on non-discrimination – MFN and national treatment – are designed to encourage conditions for fair trade. The first article of the General Agreement on Tariffs and Trade (GATT), which governs trade in goods, requires unconditional and universal most-favoured-nation (MFN) treatment among all members. The principle of national treatment, required that the products of locals and foreigners should be treated equally (VanGrasstek 2013). If these 2 principles were applied to ACP countries trading with the EU under the Lomé agreements, then the ACP countries should have been engaging in reciprocated trade. Since the ACP countries are non-member countries of the EU, they should have been facing the same MFN tariff imposed on all non-EU member countries. Otherwise, the principle of national treatment would require that all non-EU member countries receive the same preferential access to the EU market, which the ACP countries were receiving. Therefore, the solution to the problem would be for the EU and the ACP to enter a trade agreement which provides reciprocal treatment to both parties.

Applying the principle of Special and differential (S&D) treatment,[80] the EU successfully negotiated for a waiver on the reciprocity to continue into Contonou, Lomé's successor (Greenaway and Milner 2003). As Contonou expired in 2008, the Caribbean Community (CARICOM) and the Dominican Republic agreed to an Economic Partnership Agreement (EPA) with the EU, a reciprocated preferential trade agreement.

Another aspect of the erosion of preferences is related to the dismantling of the banana protocol. The EU market for bananas started to undergo reform in 1993 with the implementation of the SEM (Mlachila et al. 2010). Prior to 1993, the EU banana regime was comprised of tariff and tariff rate quota (TRQ) elements. It combined pure tariffs, import quotas, de facto prohibitions, and provisions for preferential trade. A licence was also required for the import of bananas. Between 1993 and mid-1999, the EU introduced a banana regime which was applicable to all EU member countries. No major changes to the TRQ system were proposed, but a new method was introduced for the administering of the banana import licences (EP 2010).

The banana regime of the 1993 to 1999 period was challenged at the WTO by US and Latin American producers (EP 2010). Although the 1993-1999 banana regime was in force before the inception of the WTO, the regime became subject to new obligations of the WTO. After the WTO found the EU's banana import regime to be discriminatory, the EU pledged to eventually switch to a tariff-only system in order to be compliant with WTO rules (Mlachila et al. 2010).

From mid-1999 until 2005 the EU banana regime gradually shifted to the tariff-only system. But the shift to the tariff-only system further eroded preferences for Dominica as part of the ACP group. The removal of quota restrictions meant that more bananas could be exported from the dominant Latin American producers to the EU market, subsequently improving their relative competitiveness.

From January 2006 to 2017, further litigation in the WTO was largely aimed at making the EU's trade regime less discriminatory. This resulted in the "Geneva Agreement" of 2009, whereby the EU pledged to reduce tariffs on bananas for non-ACP MFN exporters gradually until 2017 (EP 2010).

---

[80] S&D treatment posits that countries at lower levels of economic development should not be mandated to liberalize their markets at the same pace as more advanced competitors (VanGrasstek 2013).

Indeed, the removal of quotas, and the gradual reduction of tariffs erode the trade preferences for Dominica and the banana exporting ACP group.

4.5 Challenges Experienced in the Dominican Banana Industry

Dominica's banana exports are not as competitive as exports from large-scale Latin American banana producers. The Dominican banana industry was allowed to thrive due to the preferential treatment, and preferential prices it received under the Lomé agreements. Ever since the WTO ruling in favour of the US and the Latin American complaints, and the gradual erosion of preferences and the dismantling of the banana protocol, Dominica experienced a decline in its banana exports. The decline in banana production was also influenced by the decrease in the utilization of land for banana cultivation.[81]

As can be seen in Table 4.3, Dominica's banana exports peaked at approximately 74,200 tons in 1988. However, there was a gradual decline in the country's banana exports to 57,900 tons in 1990, 33,366 tons in 1995, 27,776 tons in 1999, and 10,934 tons by 2008. Therefore, it was no surprise that there was a decline in the trade value of Dominica's banana exports as seen in Figure 4.3.

Table 4.3: Dominica's Banana Exports

Year	Exported Production (tons)
1988	74,200
1989	50,900
1990	57,900
1991	55,300
1992	59,200
1993	55,500
1994	43,047
1995	33,366
1996	39,926
1997	34,900
1998	28,642

[81] The growing demand for land for residential and commercial use in Dominica has contributed to the rapid alienation of agricultural lands to these alternative sectors.

1999	27,776
2006	<21,600
2008	10,934

Source: Campbell (2000); CARDI (2008); Barker (2012)

Figure 4.3: World Imports of Bananas from Dominica (1990-2017)[82]

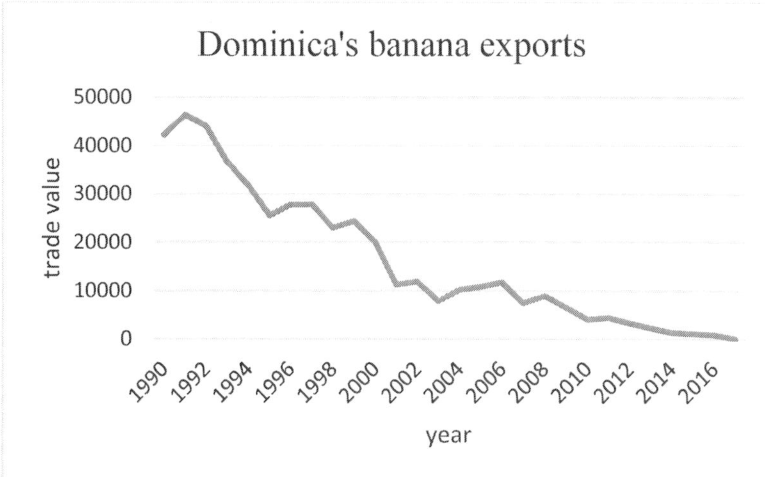

Source: WITS (2018)

There has also been a significant decline in the number of banana farmers in Dominica. This exodus of farmers from the banana industry occurred because most farmers could not afford to produce bananas without high prices and trade barriers to give them an artificial competitive edge against more efficient banana producers (Torgerson 2010).

Table 4.5: Number of Banana Farmers in Dominica

Year	No of Banana Farmers
1988	>7000
1990	>6,600
2006	<900
2007	858

Source: CARDI (2008); Barker (2012); Omeka (2014)

[82] Mirror data on the world imports of Dominica's banana had to be used to determine Dominica's banana exports.

As can be seen in Table 4.5, in 1988, when Dominican banana production peaked, there were over 7,000 farmers involved in the banana industry (Omeka 2014). There has been a decline in the number of banana farmers to over 6,600 in 1990, and a further decline to less than 900 in 2006 (CARDI 2008). Furthermore, the unattractiveness of agriculture, especially among young people has prevented the renewal of the country's banana labour force (Campbell 2000).

Even before the country experienced the erosion of trade preferences in bananas in the 1990s, it experienced difficulties in filling its 71,000 ton quota to the UK.[83] This was due to the island frequently being hit by hurricanes,[84] unsustainable farming practices, and labour productivity challenges (CaRC 1997).

Fruit quality problems have also been a major challenge in the banana industry in Dominica. In fact, one of the reasons why Dominica's banana exports to the UK market were less competitive than Latin American producers was due to the variability in its fruit quality (CaRC 1997). Moreover, Black Sigatoka,[85] a leaf-spot disease caused by the ascomycete fungus which leads to the premature ripening of the banana fruit, has been ravaging Dominica since 2011 (Jamaica Observer 2017). Black Sigatoka affects the leaves of the banana tree, which turn yellow and black then die. The associated banana fruit of Black Sigatoka infected trees is also significantly smaller and ripens very unevenly (Dominica NU 2015).

Monocrop cultivation is highly vulnerable to pests and diseases. In fact, a pest or disease which targets the monocrop can devastate the entire agricultural output. For this reason, pesticides and fungicides are often needed to support monocrop cultivation. In Dominica, farmers use Gramoxone (a chemical herbicide) to clear the land before planting, fungicides to address the Black Sigatoka disease, and chemical fertilizers to speed up the banana fruit growth rate. Blue cellophane bags are also used to assist the ripening of the fruits (Dominica NU 2015). However, the inadequate disposal of for example pesticide-impregnated plastic bags or rejected fruit, results in pollution. Black Sigatoka is able to mutate and develop resistance to

[83] The total Windward Islands quota was 294,000 mt (CaRC 1997).

[84] Since Hurricane David in 1979, the island has been hit by several hurricanes, including: Hortense in 1989, Hugo in 1989, Marilyn in 1989, Klaus in 1990, Debby in 1994, Iris in 1995, Luis in 1995, Georges in 1998, Gilbert in 2005, Dean in 2007, Matthew in 2007, Tomas in 2010, and Maria in 2017.

[85] Black Sigatoka is also referred to as black leaf streak.

fungicides, posing a problem to farmers seeking to curb their chemical use in agriculture. Growing awareness of international consumers' concerns regarding the ethics of food production and its associated trade has raised issues of "fair-trade" in food production. International consumer associations want assurances that the food is safe for consumption, and that the workers were not exploited, or health put at risk during the production process.

The drive towards higher quality standards demanded by EU consumers started to occur from the 1990s. These higher standards resulted in changes in the packing system employed by Dominica's farmers, and farmers in the other Windward Caribbean islands. The increased standard caused more of the work and costs to be transferred to the farmers. This factor was a contributory reason for the exit of some farmers from the banana industry (Klak et al. 2009). The remaining farmers in Dominica's banana industry turned to the fair-trade system (Klak et al. 2009; Torgerson 2010).[86]

4.6 Policy Response

The demand side problems in the banana export industry in Dominica resonate with dependency theory. The erosion of trade preferences, the gradual reduction of banana prices, the shift in power dominance to the large supermarket chains, and the dominance of the retailers in the distribution industry result in the small-scale farmers possessing very little power and consequently capturing the smallest share in the larger global value chain. The disparity in power reflects the structural inequity in the industry.

While many of the small-scale farmers would desire subsidies for inputs (fertilizer, agrochemicals, and boxes for packaging) and price controls to protect their incomes, it is highly unlikely that the public authorities would deploy such strategies since the implementation of export subsidies would invite new WTO disputes, and the government is too small a player in the global arena to affect global prices. However, there is scope for the small-scale farmers to earn prices slightly higher than market prices from the trade of fair-trade bananas.

4.6.1 Fair-Trade Bananas

As previously mentioned, growing consumer awareness of the ethics of food production and its trade gives rise to the concept of "fair-trade" in food

[86] The first shipment of fair-trade bananas left Dominica for the UK in the year 2000 (Barker 2012).

production. Issues such as working conditions, the wages of farm workers, and the price paid to small-scale farmers in developing countries have attracted the attention of public opinion in developed countries (Liu 2009).

Fair trade poses a challenge to the liberal view that free trade is fair. The fair-trade system offers a model of trade that disregards the equilibrium price framework that results from the intersection of supply and demand, and sets price floors for producers. It also advances the social and ecological standards that prioritize the needs of producer communities. Thus, the fair-trade system introduces measures for social protection (Torgerson 2010).

Fair-trade certification is a written guarantee by an independent certification agency that a production process of a product meets the criteria stipulated in a specific standard. Fair-trade certification can be used to differentiate products, which can be helpful to promote the product in different markets, improve its market access, and in some cases results in a higher price paid to the producer. Fair-trade certification is mainly used when the producer and the consumer are not in direct contact, which is often the case where commodities are traded in international markets (Liu 2009).

Four international non-governmental organizations (NGOs) are involved in fair trade. They include the International Fair Trade Association (IFAT), the Fair Trade Labeling Organizations International (FLO), the Network of European Worldshops (NEWS), and the European Fair Trade Association (EFTA). In the agriculture industry, the most widespread system is that of the FLO. The FLO's member organizations work with small-scale producers and farm workers to enhance their economic well-being. While the FLO fair-trade certification is voluntary, it is certainly advantageous to producers as it results in a minimum price and a price premium on certified agricultural products (Liu 2009).

It is noteworthy that while the FLO develops the standard, it does not perform the assessment for the fair-trade certification. This assessment must be undertaken by an independent organization, FLO-Cert (Liu 2009).

The FLO has developed and regularly updates a detailed standard for bananas. In order to obtain fair-trade certification for bananas, the applicant must comply with the FLO's conditions. These vary based on the type of applicant. For instance, for small-scale farmers, there are requirements for sustainable land use practices to be undertaken during banana cultivation. Whereas for plantations, there are a number of requirements related to labour-industrial relations (Liu 2009).

In Dominica, fair trade guarantees a minimum farmgate price of US$7.60 per 18.14 kg box of bananas. This guaranteed price is also a minimum price since a higher price will be paid to farmers if market prices are higher. Apart from better prices and better price stability, fair trade also guarantees farmers a long-term contract (of at least one year) in which importing companies commit to buy their bananas (Torgerson 2010).

4.6.2 Climate Related Policy

Extreme weather conditions, specifically hurricanes, have historically had disastrous outcomes for banana production in Dominica. It is noteworthy that in the banana agriculture sector, climate-related impacts affect the entire value chain in the country, from the planting of crops, through to the reaping of crop yields, affecting how much is transported and exported.

Farmers in Dominica's banana industry continue to rely upon a combination of informal (crop diversification, off-farm income) and traditional (saving, borrowing) financing. As a consequence, most of the costs imposed by weather hazards are absorbed by the farmers (Gallina and Giannozzi 2014). It is important to emphasize the role of the government, given the small size of the average farm in the country and given the vulnerability of the country's banana industry to frequent and intense weather events.

One policy measure that can be utilized by the government to address the country's banana sector's vulnerability to hurricanes and other weather-related stressors is the utilization of agriculture insurance.

The idea of agriculture insurance is not new to the Windward Caribbean islands. In fact, agriculture insurance and disaster relief funds have been considered from the 1950s to the 1980s in each Windward island. The insurance strategies were unsuccessful largely due to high claims, and a lack of separation of claims for different types of farmers (Carballo and Reis 2013).

In 1987, the Windward Island Crop Insurance Ltd. (WINCROP) was incorporated in Dominica to provide agriculture insurance to the country's banana farmers. It was later extended to banana farmers in St. Vincent and the Grenadines (SVG) in 1996, and Grenada in 2000 (Carballo and Reis 2013). The WINCROP banana insurance scheme covers the entire export crop in Dominica, Grenada, St. Lucia and SVG, and is owned by the banana marketing organizations of the four aforementioned countries.

The WINCROP insurance scheme only provides cover against a small proportion (20%) of any losses. Premiums are collected from the banana farmers in each country to help mitigate the financial risks. Verification of losses is easy as the scheme only covers one crop against two hazards (volcanic eruptions and hurricanes). WINCROP's insurance scheme does suffer from covariant risk.[87] In fact, the income WINCROP raises from premiums is a relative loss when taking into consideration the covariant risk (Benson and Clay 2003). Moreover, the downturn in the Windward Caribbean island economies in the 2000s caused a reduction in the premium income for WINCROP, particularly due to the decrease in the region's banana farmer population, and losses experienced in the banana industry (GOSL 2013).[88]

The difficulties in making affordable agriculture insurance available to small farmers in Dominica have to do with:

i) the frequent occurrence of hurricanes, which will reduce the willingness for the private sector to provide such insurance since a lot of farmers will make frequent claims especially when an extreme weather event occurs;
ii) the tendency for extreme weather events to affect a large number of farmers simultaneously, thus private sector insurance companies will be unwilling to provide such insurance since they will have to pay out to huge numbers of claims after extreme events;
iii) the insufficient quality of the information available about the agro-climate to undertake probabilistic analysis at a disaggregated level;
iv) the lack of knowledge of the public authorities on the potential benefits of agriculture insurance or commodity-price risk hedging; and
v) the lack of technical knowledge and "know-how" by the public authorities to design and administer agricultural insurance contracts (Gallina and Giannozzi 2014).

There is scope for the private-public partnership model to be used to develop an appropriate insurance scheme for farmers in Dominica to mitigate their losses against hurricanes. This model is not farfetched since it has been used by Aseguradora Agropecuaria Dominicana SA (AGRODOSA) in the

[87] Covariant risk is that which arises when many farms/households located in one area are adversely affected by a single phenomenon such as a natural disaster.
[88] In 1992, WINCROP had insured more than 30,000 farmers, but this declined to 2,380 by 2008 largely due to the general decline in the farming population.

Dominican Republic to insure rice, banana, and other crop farmers. AGRODOSA was capitalized from private and public equity but is managed on strictly commercial insurance principles. The company currently offers a banana crop insurance which covers yield shortfalls due to drought, floods, excess rain, wind and cyclone (tropical storms and hurricanes), and unknown pests and diseases. The insurance coverage is triggered when the actual yield obtained on the insured banana crop falls below the guaranteed yield determined for each country and crop season. The insured farmers receive an indemnity proportional to the percentage damage to the plant population on the insured unit, times the sum insured (Carballo and Reis 2013). Although WINCROP made payments to banana farmers in Dominica after Hurricane Maria in 2017, there is still scope to ramp up the relief effort by adopting a similar approach to the AGRODOSA model.

To build climate resilience within Dominica's banana value chain, a range of additional strategies can be deployed. Table 4.6 displays the established agricultural climate resilient strategies recognized in the literature.[89]

After countries are hit by hurricanes governments try to rebuild public infrastructure. However, the Post-Disaster Needs Assessment of Dominica concluded that

> *Hurricane Maria resulted in total damages of EC$2.51 billion (US$931 million) and losses of EC$1.03 billion (US$382 million), which amount to 226 percent of 2016 gross domestic product (GDP).* (Commonwealth of Dominica 2017, 1).

An estimated EC$3.69 billion (US$1.37 billion) is required to restore the country's public infrastructure and "build back better" (Commonwealth of Dominica 2017). The Post-Disaster Needs Assessment report goes on to note that

> *Much of the agricultural infrastructure and equipment was damaged or destroyed including buildings, ..., agricultural roads and croplands. Sector recovery will depend heavily on the reconstruction of infrastructure in order to rehabilitate the sector and reestablish the farm to market transportation network. The ability of small farmers to recover will depend heavily on their access to funding resources as they rehabilitate their properties and re-establish their crop cycles. The estimated damage to infrastructure as a result of the storm is EC$ 95.6M (US$ 35.43M).* (Commonwealth of Dominica 2017a, 4).

[89] While all the strategies identified in Table 4.6 are relevant for building climate change resilience in the banana industry, not all are relevant for building resilience against hurricanes.

Table 4.6: Categories of Agricultural Climate Resilience Investments

Category	Sub-category	Examples
Structural and Physical	Engineered and built environment	Water and pump storage, drainage systems, greenhouses, irrigation systems, warehouses and cold stores, maintenance of existing systems, e.g. upgrading of old irrigation canals, warehouse management and marketing
	Technological	Breeding of new livestock and seed varieties, ongoing purchase of new varieties, installation of early warning systems, access to weather information
	Ecosystem based	Ecological restoration, soil management techniques, replanting of mangroves, maintenance of conservation areas, e.g. riparian buffers
	Services	Credit provision, development of market and information platforms and marketing support
Social	Educational	Building farmers' awareness of good agricultural practices linked to climate resilience, extension services, technical assistance, learning and information platforms highlighting climate risks
	Informational	Early warning systems, climate and weather forecasting, information related to soils, crops and livestock species
	Behavioural	Soil and water conservation, crop switching, changing production practices, e.g. planting dates, reducing tillage, diversification, livestock management practices
Institutional	Economic	Insurance, catastrophe bonds (Cat Bonds), microfinance, disaster funds
	Laws and regulation	Standards, trade regulations or land zoning to require sustainable production, certification of seeds (e.g. drought-tolerance)
	Government policies and programmes	Sectoral sustainability plans, ecosystem-based management, forest management, financial risk management frameworks that allow for better integration of climate risk information

Source: Havemann and Gmbh (2016)

Given that such a huge amount of finance is required for the restoration of public infrastructure, it is highly unlikely that the country would be able to self-finance its restoration works. Even if only the cost of the restoration of agriculture infrastructure is considered, it would be a heavy financial burden for the government. Most likely the country would have to rely upon aid from donor agencies as well as multilateral loan financing.

Nevertheless, the Government of the Commonwealth of Dominica aspires to rebuild its country as a climate resilient nation. The government announced plans to legislate a new state-owned organization, the Climate Resilient Execution Agency for Dominica (CREAD), which will lead the country's recovery and execute projects within a climate resilient national plan over a four-year period (Commonwealth of Dominica 2017b). CREAD's primary role will be to

- coordinate all recovery action and projects;
- collate data on all recovery needs;
- identify critical gaps between Dominica's Recovery Plan, and funded projects; and
- engage with international development partners to reduce these gaps.

If CREAD achieves its objectives, it would lead to the development of a strong adaptive capacity in Dominica to climate-related stressors.

4.6.3 Functional Upgrading Strategies

Dominica operates at the lowest end of the banana value chain. As previously established, the country's farmers are typically small-scale producing unprocessed bananas for export to the EU market. The banana value chain has evolved to one that is predominantly buyer driven and dominated by supermarket chains. While it is desirable for Dominica to upgrade in the banana global value chain, it is highly unlikely that any of the small-scale producers would upgrade to a large-scale supermarket chain in a significant import market, or upgrade to a large-scale vertical company involved in the production, packaging, export, and distribution of bananas to different markets. Therefore, Dominica's small-scale banana farmers' prospects for functional upgrading in the banana value chain are limited to activities which extract more value added from the bananas.

More value added can be extracted from bananas through the agro-processing of bananas. Bananas can be processed into a variety of products, namely:

- banana puree;
- banana concentrate;
- banana powder;[90]
- banana pulp;
- banana juices (natural fruit juice and carbonated beverages);
- banana wine;
- banana beer;
- banana chips;
- banana biscuits;
- banana wafers
- banana bread, cakes, doughnuts and other pastries; and
- banana jam.

Figure 4.4 presents an illustration of various processed and unprocessed products that can be derived from bananas.

A number of by-products are derived from banana crops. They include the pseudostem, leaves, inflorescence, fruit stalk (floral stalk/rachis), rhizome and peels. Such banana by-products are often considered as waste by farmers. However, the by-products can be used as a source of raw materials for the green technology industry.

For instance, the pith of the pseudostem and the green culled banana which are removed during fruit selection and processing can be processed into edible starches. Discarded banana peels could be processed to produce pectin via acid extraction and precipitation by using alcohols or ammonium salts. Starch and pectin are used in the food industry as gelling agents, thickening agents and stabilizers (Padam et al. 2014).

Banana by-products have been found to contain compounds with nutraceutical (health) properties which have commercial value in the pharmaceutical industry. For instance, Tin et al. (2010) identified the presence of epigallocatechin and its derivatives in male banana flowers. Saravanan and Aradhya (2011) successfully isolated entisic acid, protocatechuic acid, caffeic acid, ferulic acid, and cinnamic acid from the banana pseudostem. Sterols, steryl glucosides and steryl esters have also been found in abundance in bananas (Oliveira et al. 2008). It is thus possible to use bananas as inputs for the pharmaceutical industry. Table 4.7 displays

[90] Banana powder can be used for milk shakes, cakes, biscuits, and baby foods.

the nutraceutical properties that can be derived from the banana and its by-products.

Figure 4.4: Processed and Unprocessed Products Derived from Bananas

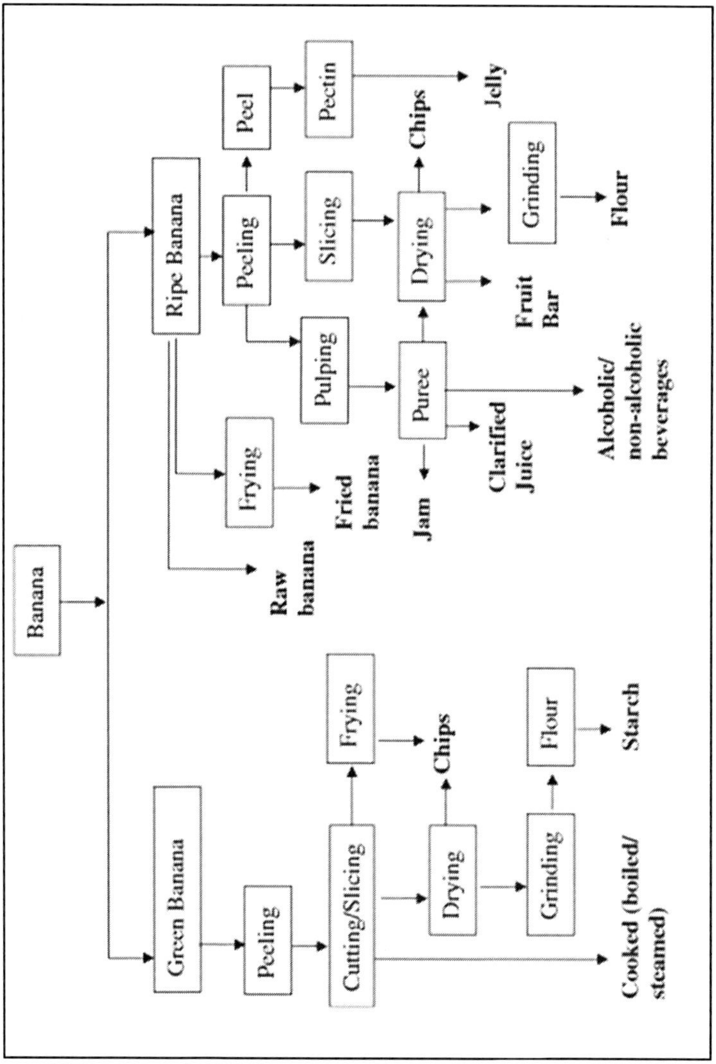

Source: Mohapatra et al. (2011)

Table 4.7: Bioactive Compounds as Potential Nutraceuticals from Banana by-products

Bioactive compounds	Banana by-products (Species/variety)
Cyanidin-3-rutinoside	Bracts (*Musa paradisiaca*)
Epigallocatechin and derivatives	Male flower (*Musa paradisiaca*)
ß-sitosterol, malic acid, succinic acid, palmatic acid, 12-hydroxystrearic acid, glycoside	Peels (*Musa acuminata* cv. Cavendish)
Campesteryl 3-β-d-glucopyranoside, stigmasteryl 3-β-d-glucopyranoside and sitosteryl 3-β-d-glucopyranoside	Petioles, leaves, floral stalk (*Musa acuminata* cv. Cavendish)
Sterols, steryl glucosides, sterol esters, tocopherols, phenolic compounds	Peels and pulp (*Musa acuminata* cv. Dwarf Cavendish)
Putrescine, spermidine, serotonin, dopamine, tyramine, spermine	Pulp (*Musa acuminata* x *Musa balbisiana*)
Entisic acid, (+)-catechin, protocatechuic acid, caffeic acid, ferulic acid, and cinnamic acid	Pseudostem (*Musa acuminata x balbisiana* cv. Nanjanagudu Rasabale)
Anthocyanins, catecholamines, tocopherols, phytosterols, ascorbic acid	Peel (*Musa acuminata* Colla AAA)

Source: Padam et al. (2014)

Banana by-products can also be used to produce natural fibres which can make composite boards, paper, textiles, and rope. The composting of banana by-products can be used to produce organic fertilizer (Padam et al. 2014).

Natural bio-ethanol can be produced from the fermentation and biochemical conversion of bananas and their by-products. For instance, banana peels are noted to be a good substrate in producing ethanol via a fermentation process (Manikandan et al. 2008), while the banana pseudostem and leaves are also a potential substrate for ethanol production through the utilization of the cellulolytic thermophilic process (Reddy et al. 2009).

There are a multitude of sub-industries that can be derived downstream from the banana industry. Therefore, there is tremendous potential for Dominica to capture more value added from its banana industry. Given the recent negative economic shock that the country would have experienced from

Hurricane Maria in 2017, the country will be unlikely to have the finances to self-develop these new industries. However, there is still potential for these industries to be developed via the utilization of foreign direct investment (FDI). The Government of the Commonwealth of Dominica could actively seek foreign investors to develop such downstream industries. Such a feat is not impossible for a Caribbean country since neighbouring Trinidad and Tobago (T&T) managed to develop its oil and gas industry, and downstream natural gas industries (ammonia, urea, and methanol) from the implementation of this model.

Given that T&T currently has a developed agro-processing industry, and that both Dominica and T&T are members of the Caribbean Community (CARICOM), the Government of the Commonwealth of Dominica can consider approaching the Government of the Republic of Trinidad and Tobago (GORTT) to obtain technical assistance in developing agro-processing in the banana industry. Partnerships can be developed between T&T agro-processing firms and potential banana processing firms in Dominica. With regard to the processing of banana by-products into non-food products, the Government of Dominica can consider engaging the respective competent firms in the EU.[91]

4.7 Conclusion

Dominica is a small Caribbean island that has traditionally relied upon its agriculture sector for economic survival. The steep and mountainous terrain of the country makes its more suitable for tree crops, one of which is the banana.

From the 1950s to the early 1990s, the country's banana export industry thrived as it enjoyed unreciprocated preferential trading arrangements in its banana exports to the EU market. However, the changing international trade environment in the 1990s has resulted in the gradual erosion of preference in the banana industry.

The country has also been challenged by being hit by several hurricanes over the years. The recent Hurricane Maria of 2017 did significant damage

[91] Dominica, as part of CARIFORUM signed the EPA in 2008. The EU agreed to provide technical assistance to CARIFORUM countries in the agreement. Therefore, it would be reasonable for Dominica to engage the EU to partner with firms to develop a downstream banana industry.

costing billions of EC dollars. Indeed, Hurricane Maria would set back the economy of Dominica.

Recognizing the potential for increased risk and uncertainty, integrating initiatives for climate and weather adaption into policies and strategies related to banana value chain development will be critical for Dominica in achieving climate resilience. There is capacity for the private-public partnership model to be used to provide a more scaled-up banana insurance based upon the AGRODOSA model used in the Dominican Republic. Agriculture insurance will not remove the risk of a hurricane occurring, but it can be used to reduce the losses incurred by farmers whenever adverse weather conditions materialize.

The proposed state-owned agency, CREAD can be used to coordinate the rebuilding effort in Dominica. Emphasis should be placed on developing climate resilient infrastructure, enhancing social systems, and building strong institutions that are well equipped to address future climate-related threats.

The preferential prices incurred in the Lomé agreements are not going to return. Therefore, the banana farmers need to look for new avenues to improve their banana incomes. Given that a multitude of products can be produced from bananas and their by-products it would be rational for the farmers to pursue functional upgrading into the agro-processing of bananas and their by-products. The government can seek out established international producers to form partnerships with a pool of the country's banana farmers. Banana farmers can be trained to process bananas into a variety of food products, and process banana by-products into different goods. Once the government creates a working enabling environment for functional upgrading into banana agro-processing and the processing of by-products, it would create new downstream industries and economic opportunities that would allow the citizens of Dominica to capture more value from their banana industry.

References

ACP (Assessment Capacities Project). 2018. "Thematic Report – 23 January 2018 – Dominica: Hurricane Irma and Maria Caribbean Response." Accessed December 19, 2018. https://reliefweb.int/report/dominica/thematic-report-23-january-2018-dominica-hurricane-irma-and-maria-caribbean-response.

Arias, Pedro, Pascal Liu, and Cora Dankers. 2003. *The World Banana Economy, 1985-2002*. Rome, Italy: Food & Agriculture Organization.

Banana Link. 2004. "Retailers." Accessed July 3, 2018. http://www.bananalink.org.uk/retailers.

Barker, David. 2012. "Caribbean Agriculture in a Period of Global Change: Vulnerabilities and Opportunities." *Caribbean Studies* 40(2): 41-61.

Benson, Charlotte, and Edward Clay. 2003. "Economic and Financial Impacts of Natural Disasters: An Assessment of Their Effects and Options for Mitigation." Accessed August 19, 2018. https://www.researchgate.net/publication/228395565_Economic_and_Financial_Impacts_of_Natural_Disasters_an_Assessment_of_Their_Effects_and_Options_for_Mitigation.

BL&FTAO (Banana Link and Fair Trade Advocacy Office). 2015. "Banana value chains in Europe and the consequences of Unfair Trading Practices." Accessed July 1, 2018. http://www.makefruitfair.org/wp-content/uploads/2015/11/banana_value_chain_research_FINAL_WEB.pdf.

Campbell, Dunstan. 2000. "Positioning Dominica's Agriculture for Sustained Economic and Social Development." Accessed July 15, 2018. http://www.open.uwi.edu/sites/default/files/bnccde/dominica/conference/papers/CampbellD.html.

Carballo, Diego Arias, and Laura dos Reis. 2013. "The Agricultural Insurance Market in the Caribbean." Accessed August 19, 2018. http://siteresources.worldbank.org/INTLAC/Resources/257803-1269390034020/EnBreve_183_Eng_Print.pdf.

CaRC (Caribbean Regional Centre). 1997. "Agriculture in Dominica." Accessed July 15, 2018. http://orton.catie.ac.cr/repdoc/A9131i/A9131i.pdf.

CARDI (Caribbean Agricultural Research and Development Institute). 2008. "Dominica: Country Highlights Report." Accessed July 15, 2018. https://www.cardi.org/wp-content/themes/default/files/Highlights/Dom-High.2008.pdf.

Clegg, Peter. 2000. "The Development of the Windward Islands Banana Export Trade: Commercial Opportunity and Colonial Necessity." Accessed July 4, 2018. http://community-languages.org.uk/SCS-Papers/olv1p4.pdf.

—. 2002. *The Caribbean Banana Trade: From Colonialism to Globalization*. London, United Kingdom: Palgrave Macmillan.

Commonwealth of Dominica. 2017a. "Post-Disaster Needs Assessment Hurricane Maria September 18, 2017." Accessed August 20, 2018.

https://resilientcaribbean.caricom.org/wp-content/uploads/2017/11/DOMINICA-EXECUTIVE-SUMMARY.pdf.

—. 2017b. "Rebuilding Dominica as a Climate Resilient Nation: the Climate Resilient Execution Agency for Dominica (CREAD)." Accessed August 20, 2018. https://resilientcaribbean.caricom.org/documents/rebuilding-dominica-as-a-climate-resilient-nation-the-climate-resilient-execution-agency-for-dominica-cread-proposal-from-the-government-of-the-commonwealth-of-dominica/.

Danes, Gabriela. 2017. "The EU's Banana Market and Value Chains: Analysis of the Commercial Practices and their Consequences on the Living Conditions of Banana Farmers and Workers in Ecuador and Colombia." Master's Thesis. Aalborg University, Denmark.

Dominica NU. 2015. "Dominica and Our Global Environment: Dominica and Bananas – An Overview." Accessed July 4, 2018. http://www.dominica.nu/Bananas.html.

EP (European Parliament). 2010. "The EU Banana Regime: Evolution and Implications of its Recent Changes." Accessed July 3, 2018. http://www.europarl.europa.eu/RegData/etudes/etudes/join/2010/433852/EXPO-INTA_ET(2010)433852_EN.pdf.

FAO (Food and Agriculture Organization). 2014. "The Changing Role of Multinational Companies in the Global Banana Trade: Market and Policy Analyses of Raw Materials, Horticulture and Tropical (RAMHOT) Products Team." Accessed July 1, 2017. http://www.fao.org/docrep/019/i3746e/i3746e.pdf.

Ferreira, Hernica. 2008. "Windward Islands Crop Insurance (1988) Ltd. (WINCROP)." Accessed July 15, 2018. argus.iica.ac.cr/.../Experiences%20of%20Small%20Farmer%20Commercial%20Insura....

Gallina, Andrea, and Sara Giannozzi. 2014. *Making Reforms Work in the Caribbean: A Collective Action Approach to Growth.* Washington DC, United States: World Bank.

Gereffi, Gary, and Karina Fernandez-Stark. 2016. *Global Value Chain Analysis: A Primer,* 2nd Edition. Durham, United Kingdom: Duke Center on Globalization, Governance & Competitiveness.

Gereffi, Gary, John Humphrey, and Timothy Sturgeon. 2005. "The Governance of Global Value Chains." *Review of International Political Economy* 12(1): 78-104.

Goodison, Paul. 2007. "The ACP Experience of Preference Erosion in the Banana and Sugar Sectors and Possible Policy Responses to Assist in Adjusting to Trade Changes." Accessed June 28, 2018.

http://cenida.una.edu.ni/relectronicos/REE71G646.pdf.

GOSL (Government of Saint Lucia). 2013. "Food and Nutrition Security Policy for Saint Lucia 2013." Accessed August 19, 2018. http://www.caribbeanelections.com/eDocs/strategy/lc_strategy/lc_food_nutrition_security_policy_2013.pdf.

Greenaway, David, and Chris Milner. 2003. "A Grim REPA?" Leverhulme Centre for Research on Globalisation Economic Policy, University of Nottingham.

Havemann, Tanja, and Clarmondial Gmbh. 2016. "Value Chain Finance for Agricultural Climate Change Resilience." Accessed August 19, 2018. https://www.clarmondial.com/wp-content/uploads/2017/04/CTA_Value_Chain.pdf.

Invest Dominica. 2013. "Location and Physical Description." Accessed June 27, 2017. http://www.investdominica.com/country-profile-of-the-commonwealth-of-dominica/location-physical-description/.

Jamaica Observer. 2017. "Dominica seeking to resume banana shipment to the UK." Accessed July 15, 2018. http://www.jamaicaobserver.com/news/Dominica-seeking-to-resume-banana-shipment-to-the-UK.

Josling, Timothy Edward, and T. Geoffrey Taylor, eds. 2003. *Banana Wars: The Anatomy of a Trade Dispute.* Oxfordshire, United Kingdom: CABI Publishing.

Klak, Thomas, James Wiley, Emma Mullaney, Swetha Peteru, Sean Regan, and Jean-Yves Merilus. 2009. "Inclusive Neoliberalism? Perspectives from Eastern Caribbean Farmers." Accessed July 4, 2018. https://www.users.miamioh.edu/klakt/index_htm_files/Inclusive_Neolib_Farmer_paper_to__PIDS.pdf.

Liu, Pascal. 2009. *Certification in the Value Chain for Fresh Fruits: The Example of the Banana Industry.* Rome: Food and Agriculture Organization of the United Nations.

McAfee, Kathy. 2007. "Banana Bust." Accessed July 4, 2017. https://nacla.org/article/banana-bust.

Malhotra, Anita, Roger S. Thorpe, Eric Hypolite, and Arlington James. 2007. "A Report on the Status of the Herpetofauna of the Commonwealth of Dominica, West Indies." *Applied Herpetology* 4(2): 177-194.

Mather, Charles. 2008. "Value Chains and Tropical Products in a Changing Global Trade Regime." Issue Paper No. 13, University of the Witwatersrand, South Africa.

McQueen, Matthew, Christine Phillips, and David Hallam. 1997. "ACPEU Trade and Aid Cooperation: Post Lomé IV." Economic Paper, No. 32, Commonwealth Secretariat, London,

https://doi.org/10.14217/9781848596320-en.
Mlachila, Montfort, Paul Cashin, and Cleary Haines. 2010. "Caribbean Bananas: The Macroeconomic Impact of Trade Preference Erosion." IMF Working Paper, Washington, DC, United States.
Mohapatra, Debabandya, Sabyasachi Mishra, Chandra Bhan Singh, and Digvir Singh Jayas. 2011. "Post-harvest Processing of Banana: Opportunities and Challenges." *Food Bioprocess Technology* 4: 327-339.
NERA (National Economic Research Associates) and OPM (Oxford Policy Management). 2004. "Addressing the Impact of Preference Erosion in Bananas on Caribbean Countries." Report Prepared for the Department for International Development, London.
Oliveira, Lúcia, Carmen S.R. Freire, Armando J.D. Silvestre, and Nereida Cordeiro. 2008. "Lipophilic Extracts from Banana Fruit Residues: A Source of Valuable Phytosterols." *Journal of Agricultural and Food Chemistry* 56(20): 9520-9524.
Omeka. 2014. "The Banana Industry in Dominica." Accessed July 15, 2018. https://questionaires.omeka.net/the-impotance-of-agriculture-in-dominica.
Padam, Birdie Scott, Hoe Seng Tin, Fook Yee Chye, and Mohd Ismail Abdullah. 2014. "Banana By-products: An Under-utilized Renewable Food Biomass with Great Potential." *Journal of Food, Science and Technology* 51(12): 3527-3545.
Quandl. 2018. "Bananas Price." Accessed July 4, 2018. https://www.quandl.com/data/ODA/PBANSOP_USD-Bananas-Price.
Tandon, Nidhi. 2014. "Strengthening Sustainable Agriculture in the Caribbean: A Guide for Project Support and Guidelines for a Policy Framework." Accessed June 27, 2018. https://competecaribbean.org/wp-content/uploads/2015/02/Strengthening_Sustainable_Agriculture_in-the-Caribbean_web.pdf.
Tin H.S., B.S. Padam, F.Y. Chye and M.I. Abdullah. 2010. "Study on the Potential of Antimicrobial Compounds from Banana/Plantain By-products Against Foodborne Pathogens." National Biotechnology Seminar, 24-26 May, 2010, Kuala Lumpur, Malaysia.
Torgerson, Anna McLoughlin. 2010. "Fair Trade Banana Production in the Windward Islands: Local Survival and Global Resistance. *Agric Hum Values* 27: 475-487.
Saravanan, K., and S.M. Aradhya. 2011. "Polyphenols of pseudostem of different banana cultivars and their antioxidant activities." *Journal of Agricultural and Food Chemistry* 59(8): 3613-3623.

Shannon, Harlan D., and Raymond P. Motha. 2015. "Managing Weather and Climate Risks to Agriculture in North America, Central America and the Caribbean." *Weather and Climate Extremes* 10: 50-56.

VanGrasstek, Craig. 2013. *The History and Future of the World Trade Organization*. Geneva: World Trade Organization.

WITS (World Integrated Trade Solution). 2018. "Trade Data – UN Comtrade." Accessed July 12, 2018. http://wits.worldbank.org.

Workman, Daniel. 2018a. "Banana Exports by Country." *World Top Exports.* Accessed July 1, 2018. http://www.worldstopexports.com/bananas-exports-country/.

—. 2018b. "Banana Imports by Country." *World Top Exports.* Accessed July 1, 2018. http://www.worldstopexports.com/bananas-imports-by-country/.

CHAPTER FIVE

A ROBUST LOCAL CONTENT POLICY FRAMEWORK FOR VALUE CREATION IN THE HYDROCARBON INDUSTRY

Abstract

Many developing countries are fortunate to be endowed with commercial reserves of hydrocarbon resources. Lacking the necessary factors of production to commercialize the hydrocarbon resources on their own, many developing countries turn to multinational firms in developed countries for technical support. However, without the correct policy framework to allow the benefits of the hydrocarbon industry to spill over to the local population, the locals will be mere spectators of their hydrocarbon industry rather than true actors.

Local content policy (LCP) is designed to increase the amount of value captured by the local population. Successful LCPs place attention on the provision of preferential treatment to both local labour and local firms to allow them to gain employment and business opportunities over the foreign counterparts. Although LCPs are contrary to the principle of "national treatment" which is enshrined in the trade liberalizing rules of the World Trade Organization (WTO), a protectionist regime is required for developing countries since their stakeholders cannot compete with those of the advanced countries.

In the Caribbean Community (CARICOM) region, both Trinidad and Tobago (T&T) and Guyana have commercial reserves of the hydrocarbon industry. T&T's industry is over one hundred years old, while Guyana's hydrocarbon revenues are expected to commence from 2020. Despite being at different stages in their industrial life cycle, a robust LCP framework is required for both countries to facilitate the capture of local value and encouragement of the spillover of hydrocarbon wealth to their people.

5.1 Introduction

Many developing countries are richly endowed with commercial reserves of hydrocarbons. Lacking sufficient financial and physical capital, the countries often rely on multinational firms to help develop their hydrocarbon extractive sector. In periods of economic windfall, the bulk of returns to the hydrocarbon extractive sector often goes to the head office of multinational companies via retained earnings, the flamboyant salaries of expats, and other forms of profit. However, governments in developing economies are increasingly becoming aware of the policy mechanisms to capture more local value and increase local participation in the extractive sector. One such policy mechanism is local content policy (LCP).

LCP may be defined as the policy framework which encourages the optimal use of in-country human resources, materials and services. LCP is a policy mechanism that is designed to allow the people of a country to capture a greater share of the benefits and wealth generated from the country's natural resources.

The development of LCPs is premised upon the fact that in developing economies where there are no laws or regulation to encourage local participation of the indigenous population in their extractive industry, very little is transferred to the indigenous population by way of employment, technology transfer, and commerce (Matthews and Lynch 2011). It is true that the indigenous population may often lack the technical capacity to perform various support functions for the extractive sector at its inception. However, since the citizens of a country are all owners of the natural resource, then they should all benefit from this resource. Therefore, there should be some mechanism to facilitate the development of the capacity of the indigenous population to allow them to reap the benefits of their extractive industry.

This is the case for many developing countries engaged in oil and gas production and export. Thus, many countries in Africa, Asia, and the Latin America and Caribbean (LAC) region develop LCPs for their oil and gas industry. LCPs are required to shift the citizens of a country from being mere spectators of their oil and gas industry to real participants in the industry.

In the hydrocarbon industry (oil and gas industry), governments use LCPs as a strategy to increase the participation of indigenous companies in the hydrocarbon value chain, improve backward and forward linkages with other industries in the host country, and create more employment opportunities for the local labour force.

Local value creation is a more important contribution of the extractive sector to the host country than its direct contribution to economic growth (Adedeji et al. 2016). For example, countries such as Botswana, Norway, and Malaysia have greatly benefited from their natural resource wealth. In fact, local value creation from the natural resource sector in the aforementioned countries ranges from 45% to 75% (UNCTAD 2006).

In the Caribbean Community (CARICOM) region, Trinidad and Tobago (T&T) currently produces and exports crude oil and natural gas. The country's hydrocarbon industry is more than 100 years old, and currently operates in the upstream, midstream, and downstream segments of both the crude oil and natural gas value chains.

Guyana, another CARICOM member state, has prospects of becoming a significant oil producer and exporter. In 2015, the ExxonMobil affiliate, Esso Exploration and Production Guyana Ltd., made a commercial find of more than 295 feet (90 metres) of high-quality oil-bearing sandstone reservoirs in the Stabroek Block, 190 kilometres (120 miles) off Guyana (ExxonMobil 2018). Since that find, several commercial discoveries have been made, resulting in the estimated total recoverable reserves in the Stabroek Block standing at more than 4 billion barrels (Montgomery 2018; OGJ editors 2018). Export of crude oil from Guyana is expected to commence as early as 2020 (ExxonMobil 2018; OGJ editors 2018).

In August 2018, the price of a barrel of West Texas Intermediate (WTI) oil was US$70. Given that daily production can be as high as 700,000 barrels per day (Montgomery 2018), daily revenues to the multinational company from oil exports can be as high as US$49 million per day.[92] The Government of Guyana is certainly going to earn significant revenue. Even if the production sharing contracts result in the take for the government being only US$30/bbl, and a modest production of 200,000 barrels per day is assumed, the resulting government revenue would be US$219 million per annum.

[92] This is based on the assumption of an oil price of US$70/bbl. It is important to note that in 2014 the price of oil collapsed due to global oversupply. As recent as February 2016, WTI prices were as low as US$30.32/bbl (US EIA 2018). If oil prices decline below US$70/bbl, less revenue will be generated. It is also important to note that this estimated revenue is not the taxation revenue that would accrue to the Government of Guyana.

This revenue represents approximately 62% of Guyana's GDP, which was US$3.5 billion in 2016 (World Bank 2017).

Indeed, the announcement of commercially viable quantities of hydrocarbons in a country generates excitement about the future developments that the new resource can bring. The indigenous population is likely to be excited at the potential for development, and the improvement of household incomes and general living standards once hydrocarbon revenues start flowing.

However, the hydrocarbon industry is very capital intensive. There is tremendous potential for multinational companies to extract the bulk of the wealth from the country's hydrocarbon sector with very little value-added trickling down to the majority of the country's people. Furthermore, there can be low participation of indigenous labour and indigenous firms in the industry due to claims that indigenous stakeholders lack the capacity to meet the industry's requirements. In the absence of a coherent LCP framework, the citizens of a country are likely to be mere spectators of their hydrocarbon industry rather than true participants.

The objectives of this chapter are to

1) review successful local content policies;
2) outline the key requirements for a successful local content policy; and
3) provide local content policy recommendations for the hydrocarbon producers in the CARICOM region.

This chapter is structured as follows. Section 5.2 elaborates on what is local content. Section 5.3 considers some case studies of countries with LCPs. Section 5.4 indicates the key characteristics that should be embodied in a LCP. Section 5.5 highlights the challenges in implementing an LCP. Section 5.6 provides recommendations which could be useful for the Governments of T&T and Guyana in the development of a robust LCP which could build their productive capacity, facilitate industrialization, and mitigate nepotism and corruption in their hydrocarbon industries. Section 5.7 concludes the chapter.

5.2.0 Defining Local Content

Local Content refers to the degree of local ownership and control by the citizens of a nation, in a specific venture. According to a World Bank publication, local content is defined as

> *The extent to which the output of the extractive industry sector generates further benefits to the economy beyond the direct contribution of its value-added, as through links to other sectors.* (Tordo et al. 2013, 13).

Local content policy (LCP) may be defined as the policy framework which encourages the optimal use of the in-country human resource, materials and services. LCP is a policy mechanism that is designed to allow the people of a country to capture a greater share of the benefits and wealth generated from the country's natural resources. It is also a subset of a broader category of policy intervention called productive development policy (PDP) which is also geared towards enhancing the productive sectors of an economy. PDPs include measures aimed at enhancing the growth of specific sectors of the economy as well as the encouragement of the development of key activities.

Local content requirements (LCRs) are specific requirements set by governments, typically upon multinational firms operating in their country, to use a minimum amount of local inputs (OECD 2016). LCRs are requirements for a given percentage of domestic value added or domestic components to be embodied in a specified final product. They are implemented to reduce the disadvantages that domestic producers face in relation to foreign companies, increase the participation of the indigenous stakeholders in specific sectors of the economic activity, create job opportunities for nationals, support economic diversification, facilitate technological knowledge and skills transfer, promote inter-sectoral linkages and reduce over-dependence on one sector by enhancing the value-creating capacity.

In the hydrocarbon industry, LCRs are either embedded in contractual agreements between governments and multinational companies, enacted legislatively by bidding requirements as part of the criteria for winning exploration and production, or downstream processing contracts, or established more indirectly by regulation and taxes which provide a more favourable environment for local suppliers.

The term "local" within "local content" can present its own set of definitional challenges. For instance, a hydrocarbon exploration and production company may be foreign-owned, but the majority of its labour force in the domestic branch may be comprised of locals (nationals). Where the national LCP agenda is primarily interested in capturing value for locals, it would seem contrary for the LCP to be focused mainly on the number of locals employed if the total financial remuneration of the local labour is a small share relative to the share held by the expats (foreign labour). Likewise, an LCP that is to be focused on capturing value through local ownership would be failing if it allowed a locally owned company to have a labour force predominantly of foreign labour.

In different jurisdictions, there are disparities in the definition of "local content". In Nigeria, while its "Petroleum Industry Content Development Act" does not explicitly use the term "local content", clause 106 of the Act defines it local content as

> *the quantum of composite value added to, or created in, the Nigerian economy by systematic development of capacity and capabilities through the deliberate utilization of Nigerian human, material resources and services in the extractives industry.* (GON 2010, 25).

In contrast, Ghana defines local content as

> *the quantum/percentage of locally produced materials, personnel, financing, goods and services rendered to the oil industry and which can be measured in monetary terms.* (GORG 2013, 27).

In Tanzania, its Local Content Policy for the Oil and Gas Industry defines local content as

> *the added value brought to the country in the activities of the oil and gas industry in the United Republic of Tanzania through the participation and development of local Tanzanians and local businesses through national labour, technology, goods, services, capital and research capability.* (URT 2014, iii), and

> *the added value brought to a host nation (and regional and local areas in that country) through the activities of the oil and gas industry.* (URT 2014, 7).

Many countries have utilized a centralist definition of local content, referring to the preferential treatment granted to their "nationals" without distinguishing between the local populations around the geographical location of the extractive industries and other nationals. However, the dangers of this approach are that if policy makers do not pay close attention to the definition of "local", the benefits of LCRs may be captured by "outsiders", thereby producing a dreaded phenomenon where economic value is not captured by the indigenous population surrounding the extractive industry.

It is clear that in the aforementioned LCPs, attention is not paid to what Warner (2007) refers to as "community content", which is

> *the strategic deployment of local participation and local capability development opportunities arising from an oil or gas project, specifically directed to strengthen the sustainability, relevance and political visibility of community investment programmes.* (Warner 2007, 5).

Warner views local content from the perspective of "community content", and regards community content programmes as a "merit good" targeted at those negatively impacted by extractive resource development whereas local content programmes are regarded as a "public good". In the Warner *(ibid.)* framework, local content programmes only exclude foreigners whereas community content excludes both foreigners and non-community members. Thus, Warner implied that community content programmes should be pursued in addition to local content policies. Community content may still be treated as part of an LCP, however additional preferential treatment should be provided to the residents of the community in which the extractive industry resides.

5.2.1 Local Content vs. Local Participation

It is noteworthy that many developing countries have passed legislation and policies to increase the local content to allow for more citizens to be employed, and provide services to the hydrocarbon industry. However, many countries have not increased citizen participation. It is noteworthy that citizens can participate through local content, but it is wrong to conclude that citizen participation automatically occurs where there is a local content policy. A similar analogy can be noted in the international trade literature where market access from preferential trade agreements does not automatically result in market penetration by the weaker trading partner (Brenton and Ozden 2009; Arkolakis 2010; Cipollina and Salvatici 2010).

Policies to enhance citizen participation involve processes that empower individuals in a community and provide them with an opportunity to influence the public decisions that affect them. The term "citizen participation" can be disaggregated into two important concepts namely; the "citizens" and their "participation". Used in the strict sense "citizen participation" provides a connotation that only the citizens of a country would be eligible to take part in decision-making. Webler (1995) argued that citizen participation should focus on enhancing the local ownership of business, increase the tendency for locals to win contracts, and other forms of interventions through increased participation by the residents of a community as opposed to all the citizens of a country. In simple terms, citizen participation involves power relations between members of a community and their leaders and the ability of that community irrespective of where it is located to take part in decisions and activities that affect them.

By another token, participation also involves citizens taking part in processes that lead to the decision or taking part in arriving at the decision itself. It is noteworthy that in practice there is a tendency for policy makers to mix the terms "local content" and "citizen participation". Public relations communication may imply that there is promotion of citizen participation through local content, which is not the case. Many times, LCP is limited to the employment of citizens, the transfer of technology, and service provision leavening out the most important aspect of citizen participation which is participation in decision-making (Nabatchi 2012).

5.3.0 Case Studies of Local Content Policy

As previously mentioned, several developing countries have utilized local content policies. Countries that have the most successful experiences include Nigeria, Ghana, and Botswana.

5.3.1 Nigeria's Local Content Policy

Nigeria is a major producer of both crude oil and natural gas. The hydrocarbon industry remains the major sector of the economy as it tends to account for approximately 75% of government revenue and 96% of the country's total export revenue (IMF 2018).

Up until the late 1980s, Nigeria's oil industry was dominated by the multinational oil companies (MOCs). In 1991, the Government of Nigeria (GON) sought to capture more value from its domestic hydrocarbon industry by nationalizing assets of the MOCs, and awarding onshore and offshore oil blocks to Nigerian entrepreneurs through competitive bidding. Today the hydrocarbon industry in Nigeria is a more balanced mix of multinational energy companies (MECs) and local companies. Oil production is still dominated by the MOCs,[93] namely Shell, but it is done through joint venture arrangements with the Nigerian National Petroleum Corporation (NNPC).

Participation of Local Oil Companies (LOCs) in the country's oil industry is facilitated through the marginal field programme (MFP), which was

[93] The major MOCs in Nigeria include: Shell, Total, ExxonMobil, Chevron, and Agip.

implemented to open up the upstream segment of the oil industry value chain to wider indigenous participation.[94] The LCRs of the MFP mandate that only LOCs are allowed to apply to operate marginal fields. Foreign participation is only allowed through a joint venture in which the LOC has at least 51% equity.

In 2000, the GON introduced the "Nigerian Content Policy" to encourage additional local content in its hydrocarbon industry. However, in 2010, the GON passed the "Petroleum Industry Content Development Act". The notable achievements of the Petroleum Industry Content Development Act were:

- the granting of priority to Nigerian operators, goods and services;
- prescribing minimum levels of local content for its citizens;
- the establishment of the Joint Qualification System (JQS) to monitor usage of local skills;[95]
- provision for the training of nationals;
- the establishment of a timeframe for deliverables to be achieved;
- the establishment of the Nigerian Content Development and Monitoring Board (NCDMB) to monitor, coordinate, and implement the provisions of the Act; and
- the establishment of the Nigerian Content Consultative Forum (NCCF) to provide the platform for information sharing.

Notable LCRs of Nigeria's LCP are the minimum Nigerian content in all projects which can be measured by the number of man-hours worked for the duration of a project, the size of participation, tonnage and volume of certain goods, the level of certification, and the percentage of spending for procurement of local goods and services. Furthermore, specific services must be exclusively awarded to indigenous service companies (Acheampong et al. 2016). These include but are not limited to:

1. procurement of pipeline systems, risers, and steel pipes;
2. three-dimensional and two-dimensional seismic data acquisition;

---

[94] This programme arose out of the 1996 Petroleum Amendment Decree (Act No. 23) (Acheampong et al. 2016).

[95] The JQS is an internet-based portal which is intended as an avenue where local skills are matched with the projects that require them. Additionally, the JQS acts as a databank for national skills. Contractors are also pre-qualified and assessed through the same portal. This allows the provision of jobs and the awarding of contracts to be based more upon merit than nepotism (Acheampong et al. 2016).

3. field development plans;
4. marine moving services; and
5. waste disposal/drainage services and industrial cleaning services.

Provision is also made in the Act for locals to own at least 50% of the equipment deployed for execution of the work in joint venture projects in order to facilitate technology transfer and prevent high-end equipment utilized in-country from being repatriated back to the country of origin after the completion of projects.

When equipment remains in the host country, it is reused multiple times. When this equipment requires maintenance, it provides employment opportunities for local support companies. Moreover, used equipment can be sold to locals, providing them with the capacity to undertake various works.

The implementation of Nigeria's LCP has allowed for the development of backward linkages in at least three industries, namely fabrication and construction, well construction and completion and control systems, and information communication technologies (ICT). With regard to forward linkages, the country has room to develop channels for the local supply of industrial output; for instance, struggles with converting locally produced petroleum into refined products. Another example is the fact that the country continues to flare its natural gas, and has not developed a downstream natural gas industry. However, there is scope for the forward linkages to be developed in time.

5.3.2 Ghana Local Content Policy

Like Nigeria, Ghana is also richly endowed with commercial reserves of crude oil. In 2007, a consortium of companies[96] in conjunction with the Ghana National Petroleum Corporation (GNPC) discovered significant oil and gas resources in the offshore Tano/Cape Three Points Basin. After the production of the first oil in the last quarter of 2010, Ghana's economy grew at a massive 14.5% in 2011 (Acheampong et al. 2016).

In Ghana, local content is governed by the Petroleum (Local content and Local Participation) Regulations of 2013. The main objectives of the

[96] The companies were comprised of Kosmos Energy Ghana, Tullow Ghana Limited, Anadarko Petroleum Corporation, Sabre Oil and Gas Holdings Limited and the E.O. Group (Kosmos Energy 2012).

country's local content legal regulations are to i) promote job creation and achieve a minimum level of local employment in the petroleum sector; ii) develop local capacities through education and skills transfer; iii) create local support industries for the petroleum sector; and iv) achieve and maintain a level of control over its petroleum sector.

The country's Petroleum (Local Content and Local Participation) Regulations introduce a number of LCRs, namely:

- preferential treatment being granted to indigenous Ghanaian firms in the granting of petroleum licences;
- preferential treatment being granted to indigenous Ghanaian firms in procurement. For instance:
    - *Where an indigenous Ghanaian company has the capacity to execute a job, that indigenous Ghanaian company shall not be disqualified exclusively on the basis that it is not the lowest financial bidder;*
    - *Where the total value of the bid of a qualified indigenous Ghanaian company does not exceed the lowest bid by more than ten percent, the contract shall be awarded to that indigenous Ghanaian company;*
    - *Where during an evaluation of bids, the bids are adjudged to be equal, the bid containing the highest level of local content shall be selected.* (GOG 2013, 10).
- a prerequisite of at least 5% equity participation in all MOCs in order for them to win any petroleum licence;
- a prerequisite for non-Ghanaian service companies to form a joint venture with a Ghanaian firm in order to qualify for any support service work in Ghana's petroleum sector;
- a requirement for non-Ghanaian companies to submit plans to the Petroleum Commission to explain the intended local content of their project before carrying out any work;[97]
- the submission of employment and training plans for local labour to the Petroleum Commission which clearly state
    - the skills that the MOC needs;
    - the skills shortage in Ghana;
    - the specific training requirements; and

[97] Note: There is a committee to review these submitted plans. If the committee is not satisfied with the plans, it has the authority to recommend rejecting the plan to the Petroleum Commission, and subsequently prevent the MOC from undertaking the corresponding project work (GORG 2013).

  - o the time frame within which the non-Ghanaian firm will provide employment opportunities for the Ghanaian workforce for each phase of the petroleum activity.
- the submission of succession plans to the Petroleum Commission which explain how employment positions that are occupied by non-Ghanaians may eventually be filled by Ghanaians in a specified time frame in order to ensure that the company would adhere to minimum local content employment levels; and
- a schedule for local content to be achieved in employment at the inception of non-Ghanaian companies' operation in Ghana's petroleum industry, within 5 years, and within 10 years.

The schedule for employment is highlighted in Table 5.1.

Table 5.1: Ghana Minimum Local Content in Goods and Services

Item	Start	5 years	10 years
Goods and Services	10%	50%	60%-90%
Recruitment and Training			
Management Staff	30%	50%-60%	70%-80%
Technical Staff	20%	50%-60%	70%-80%
Other	80%	90%	100%

Source: GORG (2013)

The Petroleum (Local Content and Local Participation) Regulations also make provision for the Petroleum Commission to engage in consultation with the National Development Planning Commission and relevant ministries to develop a policy on technology transfer. Technology transfer is also encouraged via the formation of joint ventures between the non-Ghanaian companies and Ghanaian companies.

Ghana's local content regulations also establish a Common Qualification System (CQS) which serves as the sole system for the registration and pre-qualification of local content in the country's petroleum industry.

Another important feature of Ghana's local content regulations is the introduction of penalties for entities guilty of a number of offences. In summary, the offences include:

- The submission of a plan, report or other document which knowingly makes a false statement to a public authority in Ghana. The fine ranges from *one hundred thousand penalty units and not more than two hundred and fifty thousand penalty units or to a term of imprisonment of not less than two years and not more than five years.* (GORG 2013, 23).

- A citizen who acts as a front for a non-Ghanaian company to achieve the local content requirements to deceive the Petroleum Commission.
- Deliberate failure to comply with the stipulated local content requirements.

Ghana's local content development continues to be constrained by limited access to finance, human resource capacity and technological constraints. Strong backward linkages have not yet been fully developed since local entrepreneurs still lack the knowledge and technical skill to undertake various works.

Despite these challenges, active investment in the country following its commercial oil potential in 2007 has allowed forward linkages to develop in the downstream industries of petroleum refining, storage, distribution and marketing. The Tema Oil Refinery, Bulk Oil Storage and Transportation Company, and the Ghana National Gas Company are major players in Ghana's downstream petroleum value chain (Acheampong et al. 2016).

5.3.3 Local Content in Norway

Norway's experience with local content in its petroleum industry is regarded as one of the better success stories in the world. In spite of the large level of local content, Norway does not have any local-content legislation or regulations. The term "local content" is not mentioned in any of Norway's laws. However, the legislation introduced from the 1970s to the 1990s gave preferential treatment to Norway's firms operating in its hydrocarbon industry.

> *In 1972, Norway passed the Royal Decree, requiring that all operations were obliged to source from Norwegian companies unless they were not competitive in terms of quality, service and price.* (Sachs and Maennling 2015, 8)

Newly formed Norwegian companies were given contracts even when they did not have the capacity to implement the work. Partnerships were encouraged with foreign oil companies to act as technical advisors to Norwegian companies. In addition, foreign oil companies brought their connections to global supply chains, and were encouraged to set up fully operational subsidiaries in Norway and recruit local staff. This facilitated technology transfer from the foreigners to the locals.

> *The 1985 Petroleum Act further stipulated local content provisions to be used to allocate licenses in the North Sea. As a result, Norway's licensing bidding rounds provided preferential treatment to Norwegian companies in all bidding rounds between 1974 and 1994. The licenses also included provisions requiring the transfer of skills and technologies to Norway's infant domestic petroleum industry. In 1994, Norway joined the European Economic Area, a single market with the European Union, and as a condition of membership was not allowed to continue with its preferential treatment policies. However, by that point, the backward linkages were already established, and today Norway is exporting its offshore service expertise to the rest of the world.* (Sachs and Maennling 2015, 8).

The preferential environment created in Norway allowed the country to develop backward and forward linkages to other sectors. Preferential treatment allowed local firms to create industry clusters. For instance, the shipping, ship repair, shipbuilding, and metal processing industries were all developed as complementary industries that could capitalize on the demand created by the oil and gas industry (Acheampong et al. 2016).

5.3.4 Local Content in Trinidad and Tobago

T&T has been traditionally dependent upon its energy sector. The sector which comprises crude oil production and export, natural gas extraction and export, and downstream natural gas processing and export, typically accounts for 45% of the country's GDP, and 80% of the country's total export.

The legislative sources for T&T's local content include:

- The Fiscal Incentives Act, Chapter 85:04, which grants fiscal incentives to qualified companies;
- The Foreign Investment Act, Chapter 70:07, which is used to attract foreign investment in areas deemed to be important to T&T;
- The Unemployment Levy Act Chapter 75:03, which provides a fund used to finance employment programmes in Trinidad;
- The Petroleum Production Levy and Subsidy Act Chapter 62:02, which provides a fund used to finance subsidies on petroleum products;
- The Local Content Policy Framework.

In 2004, the Government of the Republic of Trinidad and Tobago (GORTT) developed an LCP labelled the "Local Content and Participation Policy and Framework." The fourteen-page document noted that only 10% of the value of the energy industry is captured domestically, yet the document suggested no LCRs to correct the deficiency.

A better attempt to capture more value via LCP was introduced in the country in 2006 when the GORTT introduced LCRs in the production sharing contracts (PSCs) awarded in the country's hydrocarbon industry. Some of the procurement provisions included:

- an unquantified requirement for multinational energy companies to maximize their utilization of goods and services produced in T&T;
- a requirement for MECs to submit their work programmes to the Ministry of Energy and Energy Affairs (MEEA) and clearly outline the level of local content they intend to achieve;
- the unbundling of contracts to match the capabilities of domestic subcontractors;
- the advertising of contracts locally to ensure domestic suppliers get a chance to participate in tendering; and
- the placement of greater weight on local content for local contractors to allow them to win contracts over foreign competition.

With regard to capacity development, provisions were made to:

- provide preference to nationals over foreigners in employment;
- provide training for nationals so that they may eventually replace expatriates;
- the provision of training for nationals to the standards of the operator; and
- the transfer of technology to nationals in the areas of fabrication, information technology, maritime services, marketing, operational management, and business support services.

Apart from the procurement regulations, local content in T&T is also managed via the work permit process. The Work Permit Advisory Committee (WPAC) is mandated to have a representative from the MEEA to assist in the advising of the committee to ensure that locals are not denied jobs due to foreign nationals holding the employment position. The representative from the MEEA is mandated to advise the committee to ensure that a local successor eventually gains the position formally held by the expatriate (Tordo and Anouti 2013).

Despite the deficiencies in T&T's LCP framework, the country captures value from its hydrocarbon industry via:

1. the taxes paid by the hydrocarbon industry to the GORTT;
2. the employment of nationals in the hydrocarbon industry;
3. the corporate social responsibility (CSR) programmes for the MECs; and
4. the development of the platform fabrication industry in La Brea.

In T&T's offshore hydrocarbon industry, offshore platforms are used to facilitate marine oil production. Historically, such platforms were typically fabricated, and engineered in the US. Some assembly would be performed in Trinidad. However, the local content in such projects was also low, and utilized approximately only 9% of local input. In 2005, British Petroleum Trinidad and Tobago (BPTT) facilitated the creation of local content and participation in the offshore platform fabrication industry via the construction of the Cannonball platform. The project was undertaken by Trinidad Offshore Fabricators Ltd. (TOFCO), which is a joint venture between the local company Weldfab Ltd. and Chet Morrison Ltd. (Trini View 2004).[98]

TOFCO's operations are situated at La Brea Industrial Estate, one of several industrial hubs developed to create a cluster to pool industrial activities in a centralized location. An estimated 40% of local input was used in the construction of the Cannonball platform (BPTT 2015). This 40% of local input included services such as marine transportation, the employment of nationals of T&T, the purchase of goods sold by hardware stores, the rental of equipment from domestic contractors, and the subcontracting of support services such as janitorial and security.

Since then, four additional platforms: Mango, Cashima, Savonette and Serrette have been constructed for BPTT. The aforementioned projects were locally designed and utilized approximately 80% local labour (BPTT 2015).

[98] Chet Morrison Contractors is a multinational organization that provides services in construction and maintenance, to the oil and gas industry for land, offshore, and shallow-water projects. The company also provides additional services, such as transportation, inspection, maintenance, and storage solutions for clients engaging in deep-water drilling. TOFCO, the company that built the Cannonball platform in T&T is a joint venture of Chet Morrison Contractors and Weldfab Limited, a local company in T&T (Chet Morrison Contractors 2016).

Table 5.2 Completed platforms by TOFCO

Year	Client	Project	Tonnage
2004-05	BPTT	Cannonball Deck and Jacket	1800
2005-06	EOG	Oilbird Deck and Jacket	3000
2006-07	BPTT	Mango Deck and Jacket Cashima Deck and Jacket Amherstia	1900 2000 500
2007-08	BGTT BPTT EOG	Poinsettia Deck Savonnette Deck and Jacket Toucan Deck	3000 3000 2000
2009-10	BPTT	Serrette Deck and Jacket	3000
2010	BHP	Angostura Gas Bridge and Flare	700

Source: Jones (2011)

TOFCO spent significant time training its 230 employees, of which 80% are citizens of T&T, while undertaking the Cannonball project.[99] This training was beneficial to both TOFCO and their workers as these workers were also utilized on TOFCO's later projects (Jones, 2011).

The Mango platform utilized high levels of local content from Trinidad. Approximately 25% of its total engineering, procurement and construction value was spent within the country. An estimated 65% of persons responsible for the project management were nationals (Jones 2011).

The Cashima project also utilized similarly high levels of local content. The 1200-ton Cashima jacket and the 920-ton topsides were built at TOFCO's yard in La Brea Industrial Estate. BPTT reported that it saved approximately US$11 million from the designs on Cashima and Mango due to the

[99] This training varied from a few weeks to 6 months for the workers. The training was mainly in technical vocational areas such as welding and fabrication, electrical installation, plumbing, instrumentation, etc. Some training workshops were also provided in the area of safety. The training was done to provide the workers with the skills necessary to perform specific jobs on the Cannonball project.

experience gained from the design engineering for Cannonball (Jones 2011).

The Savonette platform also had high local content from Trinidad. Approximately 30% of its total engineering, procurement and construction value was spent within the country. An estimated 55% of the persons responsible for project management were citizens of T&T (Jones 2011).

In the Angostura Gas Bridge and Flare, an estimated TT $356.9 million, 55% of the project cost was captured locally. The project expenses included expenditure on local materials and service contracts, as well as direct employment opportunities (Jones 2011).

Limitations of T&T's LCRs

While the MEEA is the lead agency for the coordination of T&T's LCRs in procurement, it experiences a number of challenges to implement the LCRs. The challenges include:

- The absence of regulatory measures to ensure compliance. There is no framework to impose fines and penalties upon multinational companies that fail to comply with the LCRs. Also, there is no framework in place to address situations in which multinational companies inaccurately report on their local content companies;
- The weak institutional capacity in the MEEA for the monitoring of the implementation of the LCRs. The MEEA typically relies upon the information supplied by the multinational companies to determine the companies' level of local content. However, if the information supplied is inaccurate, the MEEA has no way of determining this.
- There is also room for improving the MEEA's reporting on the local content achievements of the energy sector. Currently, the MEEA provides an Extractive Industries Transparency Initiative (EITI) report, which outlines the taxation revenue earned by the GORTT from the energy sector. However, nothing is reported on the level of local content in the energy sector on an annual basis;
- A lack of integration of the LCP and the LCRs with the GORTT regulatory activities. For instance, since LCRs are generally aimed at increasing the amount of business activity for nationals, then other government ministries should be focused upon building industries in T&T. There is room, for perhaps the Ministry of Trade and Industry (MTI), to conduct continuous economic research about new feasible

industries in T&T. The research should also be focused on how to address production, the supply side, and demand side constraints of local companies and how to make an upward transition in the value chain. Such research should be undertaken on a continuous basis since prices, costs, technology, international demand, and market opportunities tend to change over time. There is also room for the utilization of econometric forecasting methodologies by the MTI to forecast changes in international macroeconomic developments, so that policy action will be proactive rather than reactive;

- There is room to establish formal research programmes aimed at increasing T&T's crude oil production from mature wells. This research is desperately needed since T&T's crude oil production has been in continuous production since 2006. Although the GORTT has announced plans to close down its refinery, there is still scope for small-scale contractors that previously engaged in farm-out operations to earn revenue from the production of residual oil from mature wells via secondary and tertiary recovery techniques;
- Many new service companies do not have sufficient financial capacity to purchase equipment to expand their scope of services or undertake larger jobs. They may face difficulty in acquiring the required loans to finance their operations if their business is in the early stage of its development and if they have limited experience with past projects. It is important to note that limited access to financing limits the ability of small contractors to grow and develop into larger businesses;
- The existence of a number of bilateral treaties with foreign countries, which would prohibit the discrimination of foreign suppliers on the basis of an LCP. Since LCPs are prohibited by Trade Related Investment Measures (TRIMS), then the awarding of preferential treatment to nationals under the guise of local content, may trigger World Trade Organization (WTO) disputes. Such disputes have been raised by the US against India on its "Made-in-India" and "Digital India" programmes (Tordo and Anouti 2013).

5.4 Key Elements of a Local Content Policy

Successful local content programmes are shaped by a clear understanding of the key drivers to achieve local content (IPIECA 2011). The government setting the LCP should have clear objectives about what they plan to achieve from the local content. For instance, a government objective may be to increase the employment of locals in the extractive industry, or a government may desire to increase the share of local ownership in the extractive industry. Thus, it would be useful if the objectives of an LCP are outlined upfront.

Complementary to the objectives are the national development priorities. These would vary from government to government, however, it would be sensible for a government to align its LCP to its national development priorities. For instance, the government may be seeking to diversify its economy to help minimize the effects of unexpected oil and gas price crashes on its taxation revenue inflows. Therefore, the government can design its LCP to develop backward linkages where various small and medium entrepreneurs (SMEs) may provide technical support services to the hydrocarbon extractive sector, and forward linkages where new industries are created downstream using the oil as input for further processing and production (e.g. oil refining, production of ammonia, urea, methanol, and fertilizer).

An LCP should take into consideration the existing and potential capabilities of an economy. Factor conditions favouring production should be considered. For example, the raw materials that are available and domestically produced, and the technical capacity of the country's labour force. Infrastructure should also be assessed in this analysis. For example, the availability and quality of roads, the capacity and infrastructure of ports, the reliability of a country's electricity supply, etc., are all infrastructure-based conditions that affect firms' ability to produce. Particularly important are the supply-side capabilities, and any barriers that limit local productivity. Where constraints have been identified, it is sensible to recommend policy mechanisms to address them. For instance, the hydrocarbon industry typically requires i) health and safety standards for both workers and service companies; ii) environmental standards for companies; and iii) technical and operational integrity standards, which are typically set by international hydrocarbon companies. Therefore, it would be sensible for the LCP to recommend a training framework so that both labour and SMEs may obtain the necessary training in order to operate in the hydrocarbon industry.

An LCP should be mindful of a country's current position in the global value chain. A global value chain analysis and mapping study should inform the LCP as it would identify the opportunities for local participation. Furthermore, a study should inform the LCP about the prospects for increasing local participation over time, how backward and forward linkages may be strengthened, and how local SMEs and other producers may make an upward transition in the global value chain.

A key aspect of a successful LCP is the outlining of detailed and specific LCRs. The LCRs define explicit targets or objectives for local content development. In order to ensure that locals are employed in the hydrocarbon extractive industry, there should be LCRs to provide "reasonable" preferential treatment to locals. The term "reasonable" is used since it would be outrageous for a government to mandate international firms to employ local labour in technical capacities where there is a very large skills gap. For example, it would be unreasonable for the government to mandate that a foreign hydrocarbon exploration and production company should employ a local in the capacity of a reservoir engineer when that worker has no university education in any kind of engineering.

The LCR for labour should provide preference for the employment of labour, but given that the host country to the hydrocarbon extractive industry may have skills deficiencies in its early stages, there should be a phased progression system for increasing local content. The phased progression system in Ghana's LCP outlined in Table 5.1 provides an excellent example.

There should be LCRs to facilitate the development of local capabilities in the host country to the extractive industry. This may be achieved in multiple ways.

1) One method is for the government to mandate that the international firms provide plans which clearly outline how much local labour would be used in each project, how much local input would be used in each project, a plan to allow the training of local labour, a succession plan for the employment of local labour in positions that were held by expats, and timelines to achieve such deliverables. These plans could be a precondition for the foreign firms to obtain licences for exploration and production. Furthermore, the government should have a committee to review these plans, and retain the authority to deny the awarding of licences to the foreign firm if their plan is deficient.
2) A second method is for the government to mandate that the foreign firms develop joint venture partnerships with a local firm as a precondition to obtain licences.
3) A third method is for the government to request the foreign firm to collaborate with a local university or other tertiary institution to

develop training programmes which would develop the necessary skillset required.

4) A fourth method is where the government may require that preferential treatment to be provided to local SMEs and other suppliers in the area of procurement. In fact, preferential treatment should be given to local contractors for specific jobs once there is local capacity. For example, contracts could be reserved strictly for locals in the areas of food catering, janitorial services, transportation services, events equipment rental, basic facilities maintenance, car mechanical maintenance, electrical maintenance, welding and fabrication for small jobs, air-conditioning maintenance, painting, and carpentry. It is important to note that such an LCR is only sensible where there is existing capacity. Therefore, there should be a technical vocational educational institution which provides these skills for the industry.

An LCP should encourage the development of both backward and forward linkages in the host country to the extractive industry. A prerequisite to the backward linkages is the availability of a variety of technical labour. This labour can only be continually supplied if there are technical vocational educational institutions which provide such skills. Therefore, the LCP should have an educational policy component to encourage the development of such technical vocational schools. The government can take the lead role for the development of such schools. However, it is advisable that the government collaborates with both the private sector stakeholders as well as a foreign university to develop the necessary skillset for the extractive industry.

A partnership is encouraged with a foreign university to allow the educational programmes to have credibility. Furthermore, at some point in time in the future, there is likely to be more surplus labour produced by the technical vocational institution(s) than the domestic hydrocarbon industry can absorb. As a result, the surplus labour may emigrate to other countries where employment opportunities lie. In other words, a comprehensive education policy within the LCP would allow the country to export services and earn remittances.

Community content should also form part of a successful LCP. Community content allows the residents of the community that houses the extractive industry to benefit from their natural resources. Community content can be achieved in multiple ways.

- One method is to introduce requirements that specify a percentage of the extractive company's employment to be reserved for residents of the host community. However, given that a government represents the interests of the people in an entire country rather than just a specific community, this policy is likely to be criticized.
- A better approach is for the government to use a moral suasion approach and request the international firms to give preference in employment to residents of the community that houses the extractive industry.
- A third method to achieve community content is in the area of procurement. The government could require that the multinational extractive industry companies develop a procurement process that gives a weight to the geographic location of origin of SMEs. If a higher weight is placed upon an SME originating from the community with the extractive industry, then it could improve their chances of winning contracts.

There is a tendency for nepotism and corruption to occur in the hydrocarbon industry, especially with regard to employment and the awarding of contracts. It is advisable that an LCP incorporates an element of transparency to mitigate the occurrence of nepotism and corruption. This can be implemented in a number of ways.

One method to encourage transparency and accountability in the hydrocarbon industry is for the government to implement an Extractive Industries Transparency Initiative (EITI). The EITI would allow for the reporting of the total revenues that the government received from its multinational and national stakeholders in the hydrocarbon extractive industry.

A second method to encourage transparency is for the LCP to legislate the implementation of a Digital Hydrocarbon Employment and Procurement Platform (DHEPP) for the employment of people in the extractive industry, and the awarding of contracts in the extractive industry. Given that technology is highly advanced in present times, it should be an internet-based platform. All persons seeking employment in the hydrocarbon industry should be required to create a profile whereby they submit their name, nationality, academic qualifications, and education. The system should be able to automatically develop a score for applicants based on their qualifications and experience. With regard to hiring, all firms operating in the hydrocarbon industry should be mandated to use the platform for the employment of workers. For every position, the system should automatically submit the applicants with the highest scores and the employer should be mandated to employ persons on the basis of the highest scores. The same concept would be applied to the provision of goods and services via procurement contracts. All contractors would be scored based on their qualifications, financial capacity, track record of achievements, and their geographic location of origin, while the firms seeking to procure goods and services should be mandated to award contracts on the basis of the highest contractor score. Persons (labour as well as contractors) found guilty of intentionally submitting false information to the DHEPP should be disqualified from being eligible for consideration of employment or procurement contracts for a minimum of five years.

An LCP for the hydrocarbon industry should establish a Hydrocarbon Commission which has the authority to review and monitor compliance of the stakeholders with regard to the LCRs. Strong attention should be placed on nepotism and corruption. Where employers (both national and international) have been found to be guilty of breaches, resulting in nepotism in employment and/or corruption in the awarding of contracts, the organization should be charged heavy fines. Furthermore, the individuals found guilty of such offences should be liable to face prison sentences. It is important to note that if penalties are not enshrined in an LCP to facilitate enforcement, the LCP could be nothing more than a "paper policy" with no real effect on facilitating change, and the economic development of a country.

5.5.0 Challenges to Implementing Local Content Policies

While LCPs are beneficial to domestic economies, trade liberalization rules may restrict their use. In fact, the WTO's Trade Related Investment Measures (TRIMs) discourage the use of LCPs. The WTO defines TRIMs as investment measures which can restrict and distort trade. The TRIMs agreement states that, WTO members shall not apply any measure that discriminates against or restricts the output of foreign products, as it violates WTO principles. LCRs are on the list of prohibited TRIMs (WTO 2015). The LCRs prohibited by TRIMs include: mandating a foreign company to purchase or use domestic goods (TRIMs prohibit discrimination between domestic and imported goods); limiting the amount of imported goods that a company may purchase or utilize; restricting foreign exchange necessary to import; and restricting exports (Kayizzi-Mugerwa and Anyanwu 2015).

India, in an effort to increase electricity generation from clean sources and enhance the economic development of its economy implemented LCRs in its solar industry. India's "Make in India" and "Digital India" programmes extend a capital subsidy of 20% to solar power units and electronics manufactured within special economic zones (SEZs) and 25% outside SEZs. The United States (US) raised a dispute at the WTO over the imposition of such LCRs by India's government. The WTO ruled against India with the judgement mandating that India provide "national treatment", under which imports must be treated on a par with domestically manufactured products (Kanth et al. 2015).

It is important to note that the US has also utilized LCRs and continues to offer a range of subsidies to promote its renewable energy sector at the federal, state, regional and local levels (Wald 2014; Kanth et al. 2015). State governments within US cities such as Los Angeles and Austin provide millions of dollars annually in subsidies for renewable energy programmes (Meyer 2015). There are frequent provisions mandating companies to purchase their intermediate goods and services from US companies, as a conditionality for receiving subsidies. However, such "buy local" requirements are local content requirements.

Meyer (2015) found 44 programmes in 23 states in the US that contained LCRs. For instance:

1. Kansas's Solar and Wind Manufacturing Incentive provides loans to wind or solar projects. As an eligibility criterium recipients must make a minimum investment in Kansas of US$30 million, employ at least 200 workers, and engage in activity that might include the acquisition, modernization and retooling of property (Meyer 2015).
2. California's Self Generation Incentive Programme (SGIP) which is designed to promote electricity generation from renewable sources in California, is funded by rate payers of electricity, rather than by tax payers. However, there is provision for an additional 20% incentive for the installation of eligible energy equipment manufactured in California. Thus, the programme provides a subsidy for equipment manufactured in California (Meyer 2015).
3. Minnesota's Renewable Energy Production Incentive provides payments to on-farm biogas recovery facilities in Minnesota, which are also owned by a qualified Minnesota entity. The "Made in Minnesota Solar Production Incentive" programme provides incentive payments to consumers who install photovoltaic or solar thermal systems that are certified as made in Minnesota (Meyer 2015).

It is discernible that the Doha round of multinational trade negotiations stalled due to disagreements on how to address the problems developing countries face in implementing WTO agreements. Although the Doha round focused on agriculture and services rather than hydrocarbons, it proposed the reduction of agricultural subsidies in all developed countries to 2.5% of the value of production. The developing countries in turn would have been required to open up their market to services. The US and the EU, despite being developed countries and major producers refused to reduce their agricultural subsidies. Thus, they demonstrated that they are willing to protect their inefficient producers. Eventually, the Doha negotiations were suspended in June 2006 (Amadeo 2018).

5.5.1 Problems with the Localist Approach to Local Content Policy

As previously mentioned, community content policy emphasizes preferential treatment being provided to residents of the community which accommodates the extractive industry. This approach may be problematic for a government to implement in some jurisdictions given that extractive resources are likely to be unevenly distributed in the country. Alternatively expressed, there are some geographic locations which will have deposits of the natural resource, while in other locations the natural resource is scare. There would be a propensity for investment to follow the locations which house the natural resource, and as a result, investment is also likely to be unevenly distributed.

The provision of preferential treatment to residents of the community which holds the extractive resource is likely to facilitate interregional inequity within a country. Given that specific ethnic groups may be concentrated in specific regions, the interregional inequity would be parallel to marginalization or ethnic discrimination.

An LCP which does not require companies to give first consideration to residents of the localities where the company operates may result in the unemployment and underemployment of the local population around the extractive resources. Therefore, the government needs to find a delicate balance that would encourage the employment of locals residing in the community of the extractive resource, yet at the same time the policy would also provide opportunities for non-residents of the community with the natural resource.

5.6 Recommendations for T&T and Guyana

All of the elements outlined in Section 5.4 would be useful in the development of an LCP in T&T[100] and Guyana which will facilitate the transformation of their economies to one that would have a very strong industrial base, and create opportunities for people on the basis of merit.

Both countries should have anti-nepotism and anti-corruption measures in their LCP. To illustrate the severity of the consequences of corruption, the refining industry in T&T could be examined. T&T's state-owned refinery company considered implementing the Gasoline Optimization Programme, the World Gas to Liquids project, and the Ultra-Low Sulphur Diesel project (Dhalai 2010; The Economist 2013; CNC 2017). However, as Kevin Ramnarine, the former Minister of Energy in Trinidad and Tobago notes

> *These projects had severe cost overruns and delays which contributed to refinery losses.* (CNC 3 2017, 1)

The Prime Minister of the Government of the Republic of Trinidad and Tobago also noted that there were *"allegations of fraud at state-owned Petrotrin"* (Polo 2017, 1).

More recently in 2017, news of a "fake oil" scandal in which the state-owned refinery company was defrauded millions of dollars was released (Hassanali 2017). On September 2, 2018, at 8:15pm the Prime Minister of the Government of the Republic of Trinidad and Tobago noted that no one was held accountable for the failure in the Gasoline Optimization Programme, the World Gas to Liquids project, and the Ultra-Low Sulphur Diesel project, or the recent "fake oil" incident. In the wake of the environment of project failure and corruption, the GORTT announced its intention to shut down its refining operations.[101]

Clearly a system is needed in T&T to address nepotism, corruption and gross mismanagement of the country's hydrocarbon wealth. A robust system is required rather than just laws which impose penalties since if the

[100] For T&T the imposition of LCRs which clearly state percentages for the employment of locals would be unnecessary since nationals of T&T already make up the majority of the labour force of MECs operating in the country.

[101] The GORTT decision to shut down the refinery would result in 1,700 temporary and permanent refinery workers losing their jobs in about two months (Rampersad 2018).

laws have loop holes, the entities involved in nepotism and corruption would be allowed to get away unpunished for their deeds.

For T&T, there is scope to strengthen the country's backward linkages. For instance, the development of platform fabrication capacity in T&T was as a result of specific intervention. Given that T&T intends to undertake a number of deep-water exploration and production projects within the next 5 years, support services for deep-water exploration and production companies can be a target area for the development of local input supplying capacity. Some areas where local inputs/services may be increased include: marine transportation, maritime engineering, ship repair, ship construction, bunkering, electrical installation, civil engineering and construction, mechanical engineering and machine maintenance, onshore surveying, laboratory testing, and map drawing.

In order to produce the required skills for T&T's hydrocarbon industry, graduates in technical vocational services and engineering are needed. Inexperienced workers may not have the required competence to undertake various works. Therefore, training programmes for technical vocational services and engineering students are required. T&T currently has a national On-the-Job (OJT) programme implemented by the GORTT. The multinational companies operating in T&T also currently have their own apprenticeship training programmes. Yet there is still scope to bridge the gap between theory and practice for young graduates if they are to venture into the support services industry as SMEs.

Perhaps the GORTT could amend its OJT programme to have a training component for technical graduates. Graduates could spend two years training at the job site where they are provided with the opportunity to gain practical experience. At the same time, the graduates would be mentored in business development. At the end of their specialized training programme the graduates could be made eligible for a loan to venture into one of the aforementioned support service sub-industries for the larger hydrocarbon industry as an SME. A business mentor can work alongside the SME for an additional 1-2 years to ensure that the young graduates have a viable business model.

For Guyana, imposing LCRs on the MECs which clearly states what percentage of local labour should be employed may be unreasonable at the inception of the country's hydrocarbon industry. Rather, attention should be placed on building capacity. The local labour force is unlikely to possess sufficient skillsets for the country's hydrocarbon industry. As a result, strong emphasis should be placed on technical training. The hydrocarbon industry typically has a high demand for technical vocational and engineering skills. Emphasis should thus be placed on developing these skills. Students needed to be trained in educational institutions and graduates need practical on-the-job training.

In order to achieve the skills development of the country's labour force the government can develop educational institutions specialized in technical vocational and engineering training. Furthermore, LCRs could be imposed upon MECs to provide training for local labour. In fact, there should be compulsory requirements for the MECs to submit plans to the government clearly explaining their local content, the training plan for local labour, and the succession plan for the employment of local labour in order to achieve licences.

Capacity development should also be encouraged in Guyana by mandating the development of joint venture partnerships between foreign and local firms. Even if the local firm has a small share in the joint venture, it would still be beneficial for Guyana as it allows the locals to have some degree of ownership of their hydrocarbon industry.

To prevent the exodus of equipment of physical capital after the completion of work, an LCR could be imposed for the local companies to have at least 20% equity in each piece of capital equipment. The objective of this LCR is to encourage physical capital to stay in the country and continue to be used for various works. Moreover, it would create an avenue for the development of a backward linkage as locals could be employed to undertake maintenance work on the capital.

In order to prevent the occurrence of nepotism and corruption in Guyana's hydrocarbon industry, strong systems which discourage the two ills should be enshrined in the country's LCP. The implementation of a Hydrocarbon Commission which monitors and enforces compliance of the industry's stakeholders to the country's LCRs would be beneficial to the country.

5.7 Conclusion

Many countries are blessed to be endowed with commercial reserves of hydrocarbon energy resources. However, not all are fortunate enough to initially possess all the technology, labour, and necessary factors of production to commercially develop the sector. Consequently, the governments of such countries may opt to develop the sector through foreign investors. While this option may generate revenues for the host country, much of the value is not automatically captured by the local stakeholders in the host country.

One policy framework which may be used to address the loss of value is local content policy. LCP aims to increase the participation of local stakeholders in the extractive industry. It can be used to generate employment for locals, create business opportunities for SMEs, small contractors, and other local companies, develop the local capacity of both local labour and businesses, and increase the share of ownership of local stakeholders in the extractive industry.

Successful LCPs need to impose local content requirements upon the foreign companies operating in the extractive industry. Commonly imposed LCRs include requirements to give preferential treatment to local labour in employment, preferential treatment to local companies in business and procurement, and requirements for foreign firms to help develop local capacities.

The government of a country with hydrocarbon extractive resources needs to be mindful of the capacity deficiencies in its country in order to design a proper LCP with LCRs to correct them. Where local labour lacks technical skills, emphasis should be placed on training and knowledge transfer. Where local businesses lack technical capacity and scale, joint ventures should be encouraged. Moreover, joint ventures can facilitate knowledge spillover, increase local ownership, and encourage the strengthening of backward and forward linkages.

A government considering the development of LCPs needs to be mindful that such a policy framework would be “frowned upon” by the WTO for being “discriminatory” and granting preferential treatment to nationals over foreign trading partners. However, governments have responsibility for the development of its people. Countries with development limitations cannot compete on a level playing field with advanced countries. Thus, developing countries need protectionist policies to protect their local industries and develop the capacity of their local stakeholders. Therefore, governments of developing countries should use LCPs and LCRs to catapult the development of their people in spite of trade liberalizing WTO principles. Perhaps the correct approach to avoiding WTO disputes would be to rebrand the policy and call it another attractive name other than “local content”.

T&T has an LCP, but it is largely in deficit since it imposes no LCRs, action items, or a timeframe for the achievement of deliverables. The government has stronger LCRs in the area of procurement. Despite the country's limitations in its LCP, it managed to achieve a notable success story in the area of platform fabrication. The experience of the TOFCO platform fabrication story should be replicated in other subsectors to help strengthen the country's backward and forward linkages.

Despite the positive potential of resource extraction, to generate economic activity and create opportunities for the local population, there is a tendency for unfit people in decision-making positions to mismanage a country's mineral wealth. This can be clearly seen in the petroleum and refining industry in T&T. Therefore, a strong anti-nepotism and anti-corruption framework should be embodied within a local content policy.

Guyana is poised to be a significant producer and exporter of crude oil post 2020. The experience of T&T should be taken as a lesson so the country can develop an appropriate LCP framework that would facilitate the development of its people. Emphasis should be placed on the training of local labour, developing the technical capacity and scale of local producers through joint ventures with foreign producers, and developing a strong anti-nepotism and anti-corruption framework to prevent the gross mismanagement of the country's hydrocarbon resources.

References

Acheampong, Theophilus, Marcia Ashong, and Victoria Crystal Svanikier. 2016. "An Assessment of Local-Content Policies in Oil and Gas Producing Countries." *Journal of World Energy Law and Business* 9: 282-302.

Adedeji, Abdulkabir Niran, Shaufique Fahmi Sidique, Azmawani Abd Rahman, and Siong Hook Law. 2016. "The Role of Local Content Policy in Local Value Creation in Nigeria's Oil Industry: A Structural Equation Modeling (SEM) Approach." *Resources Policy* 49: 61-73.

Amadeo, Kimberly. 2018. "Doha Round of Trade Talks: The Reason why it Failed." Accessed December 19, 2018. https://www.thebalance.com/what-is-the-doha-round-of-trade-talks-3306365.

Arkolakis, Costas. 2010. "Market Penetration Costs and the New Consumers Margin in International Trade." *Journal of Political Economy* 118(6): 1151-1199.

BPTT (British Petroleum Trinidad and Tobago). 2015. "What we do." Accessed November 5, 2015. http://www.bp.com/en_tt/trinidad-and-tobago/about-bp-in-trinidad-and-tobago/BPinTT.html.

Brenton, Paul, and Çaglar Ozden. 2009. "Trade Preferences for Apparel and the role of Rules of Origin: The Case of Africa." Accessed August 31, 2018. https://www.researchgate.net/profile/Paul_Brenton/publication/252787451_TRADE_PREFERENCES_FOR_APPAREL_AND_THE_ROLE_OF_RULES_OF_ORIGIN_-_THE_CASE_OF_AFRICA/links/02e7e5396cd8b7a875000000.pdf.

Cipollina, Maria, and Luca Salvatici. 2010. "The Trade Impact of European Union Agricultural Preferences." *Journal of Economic Policy Reform* 13(1): 87-106.

CNC 3. 2017. "Ramnarine: Imbert's Petrotrin Statement Misleading." *CNC 3,* March 8. Accessed September 2, 2018. https://www.cnc3.co.tt/press-release/ramnarine-imberts-petrotrin-statement-misleading.

Dhalai, Richardson. 2010. "Petrotrin Boss Quits." *Trinidad and Tobago Newsday,* June 5. Accessed September 2, 2018. https://archives.newsday.co.tt/2010/06/05/petrotrin-boss-quits/.

ExxonMobil. 2018. "Guyana." Accessed August 2, 2018. https://corporate.exxonmobil.com/en/company/worldwide-operations/locations/guyana#About.

GON (Government of Nigeria). 2010. "Nigerian Petroleum Industry Content Development Act." Accessed August 31, 2018. http://www.eisourcebook.org/cms/January%202016/Nigerian%20Oil%20and%20Gas%20Industry%20Content%20Development%20Act%202010.pdf.

GORG (Government of the Republic of Ghana). 2013. "Petroleum (Local-content and Local Participation) Regulations." Accessed August 31, 2018. http://www.petrocom.gov.gh/pdfs/13-Local-Content-and-Local-Participation-Regulations-L_I-2204.pdf.

Hassanali, Shaliza. 2017. "PM: Fake Oil Probe Must Be Proper One." *Trinidad and Tobago Guardian,* September 14. Accessed September 2, 2018. http://www.guardian.co.tt/news/2017-09-14/pm-fake-oil-probe-must-be-proper-one.

IMF (International Monetary Fund). 2018. "IMF Country Report No. 18/63: Nigeria." Accessed August 31, 2018. https://www.imf.org/en/Publications/CR/Issues/2018/03/07/Nigeria-2018-Article-IV-Consultation-Press-Release-Staff-Report-and-Statement-by-the-45699.

IPIECA (International Petroleum Industry Environmental Conservation Association). 2011. "Local Content Strategy: A Guidance Document for the Oil and Gas Industry." Accessed September 2, 2018. http://www.engineersagainstpoverty.org/documentdownload.axd?documentresourceid=28.

Jones, John. 2011. "Success Stories: Examining the Development of Facilities for the Fabrication of Offshore Platforms." Accessed August 31, 2016. edftt.com/wp-content/uploads/2013/11/John-Jones-N.

Kanth, Ravi, Asit Ranjan Mishra, and Utpal Bhaskar. 2015. "WTO Rules Against India in Solar Panels Dispute with the US." Accessed September 1, 2018. http://www.livemint.com/Politics/11yE8Bz6bgZZ6LhXXlB8eL/WTO-panel-rules-against-India-in-solar-dispute.html.

Kayizzi-Mugerwa, Steve, and John C. Anyanwu. 2015. "Creating Local Content for Human Development in Africa's New Natural Resource-rich Countries." Accessed September 1, 2018. https://www.afdb.org/fileadmin/uploads/afdb/Documents/Publications/Creating_local_content_for_human_development_in_Africa%E2%80%99s_new_natural_resource-rich_countries.pdf.

Kosmos Energy. 2012. "World-Class Discovery and Foundation of the Company." Accessed September 1, 2018. http://www.kosmosenergy.com/operations-ghana-jubilee-field.php.

Matthews, Peter, and Matthew Lynch. 2011. *Local Content Strategy: A Guidance Document for the Oil and Gas Industry*. London, United Kingdom: International Petroleum Industry Environmental Conservation Association (IPIECA).

Meyer, Timothy. 2015. "How Local Discrimination Can Promote Global Public Goods." *Boston University Law Review* 95: 1937-2025.

Monday, James Unam, and Claudius Jamike Agorzie. 2014. "Strengthening Technological Capacity Building of Indigenous Oil Firms: The Local Content Policy Dimension." JORIND 12(2): 1-10.

Montgomery, Ruaraidh. 2018. "Guyana Oil Reserves Now Exceed 4 Billion Barrels; Daily Estimated Production to Hit 700,000 – Wood Mack." *Oil Now, June 27.* Accessed August 2, 2018. http://oilnow.gy/featured/guyana-oil-reserves-now-exceed-4-billion-barrels-daily-estimated-production-hit-700000-wood-mack/.

Nabatchi, Tina. 2012. "A Manager's Guide to Evaluating Citizen Participation." Accessed August 31, 2018. http://unpan1.un.org/intradoc/groups/public/documents/UN-DPADM/UNPAN048340.pdf.

OECD (Organization for Economic Co-operation and Development). 2016. "Trade Policy Note." Accessed August 2, 2018. https://www.oecd.org/tad/policynotes/economic-impact-local-content-requirements.pdf.

OGJ editors. 2018. "ExxonMobil Raises Resource Estimate for Offshore Guyana." *Oil & Gas Journal,* July 23. https://www.ogj.com/articles/2018/07/exxonmobil-raises-resource-estimate-for-offshore-guyana.html.

Polo, Dareece. 2017. "Friend or Foe, No Protection from PM on "Fake Oil" Investigation." *Loop,* September 14. Accessed September 2, 2018. http://www.looptt.com/content/friend-or-foe-no-protection-pm-fake-oil-investigation.

Rampersad, Sharlene. 2018. "Petrotrin Oil Refinery Announces Shut Down, 1700 Workers to Lose Jobs." *Trinidad and Tobago Newsday*, August 28. Accessed September 2, 2018. https://newsday.co.tt/2018/08/28/no-title-19/.

Sachs, Lisa, and Nicolas Maennling. 2015. "Resource Resilience: How to Break the Commodities Cycle." Accessed September 1, 2018. http://ccsi.columbia.edu/files/2015/11/World-Politics-Review-Resource-Resilience-How-to-Break-the-Commodities-Cycle-May-26-2015.pdf.

The Economist. 2013. "State-owned Refinery Under Pressure." *The Economist,* December 17. Accessed September 2, 2018. http://country.eiu.com/article.aspx?articleid=1561349540&Country=Trinidad%20and%20Tobago&topic=Ec_1.

Tordo, Silvana, and Yahya Anouti. 2013. *Local Content in the Oil and Gas Sector: Case Studies*. Washington, United States: World Bank Publications.

Tordo, Silvana, Michael Warner, Osmel Manzano, and Yahya Anouti. 2013. *Local Content Policies in the Oil and Gas Sector.* Washington, United States: World Bank Publications.

UNCTAD (United Nations Conference on Trade and Development)/ CALAG. 2006. "Creating Local Linkages by Empowering Indigenous Entrepreneurs (Volume 1 – Nigeria)." Report on an African Oil and Gas Services Sector Survey by United Nations, New York and Geneva.

URT (United Republic of Tanzania). 2014. "Local Content Policy of Tanzania for the Oil and Gas Industry – 2014." Accessed August 31, 2018. https://www.agcc.co.uk/uploaded_files/07.05.2014local-content-policy-of-tanzania-for-oil-gas-industry.pdf.

US EIA (United States Energy Information Administration). 2018. "Petroleum and Other Liquids." Accessed August 2, 2018. https://www.eia.gov/dnav/pet/PET_PRI_SPT_S1_M.htm.

Warner, Michael. 2007. "Community Content: The Interface of Community Investment Programmes with Local Content Practices in the Oil and Gas Development Sector." Accessed August 31, 2018. http://www.odi.org/sites/odi.org.uk/files/odi-assets/publications-opinion-files/2087.pdf.

Webler, Thomas. 1995. "Right Discourse in Citizen Participation: An Evaluative Yardstick." *Technology, Risk, and Society Volume* 10: 35-86.

World Bank. 2017. "Guyana." Accessed December 10, 2017. https://data.worldbank.org/country/Guyana.

WTO (World Trade Organization). 2015. "Trade and Investment: Technical Information, Agreement on Trade Related Investment Measures." Accessed November 4, 2015a. https://www.wto.org/english/tratop_e/invest_e/invest_info_e.htm.

CHAPTER SIX

ADDRESSING CARICOM'S ENERGY INSECURITY AND PROSPECTS OF A SOLAR PHOTOVOLTAIC ENERGY INDUSTRY

Abstract

The member states of the Caribbean Community (CARICOM) are all geographically located around the equator. Thus, they all receive a steady and reliable supply of solar insolation. This creates potential for a solar energy industry in the CARICOM region. Furthermore, volatile hydrocarbon energy prices, as well as the negative effects of climate change, all serve as factors to encourage solar energy in the CARICOM region. Economic barriers such as limited access to finance for new firms, the upfront capex cost of solar systems, and the absence of financial incentives such as feed-in-tariffs are among the factors which constrain the development of the solar industry in the CARICOM region.

The global value chain for solar photovoltaic panels is comprised of segments for the production of silicon crystals, ingots, wafers, cells, and modules, and the installation of the final product. Firms in Asia, Europe, and the United States are the market leaders in each segment. However, there is scope for the CARICOM member states to capture value at the module assembly and installation stages of the global value chain.

Indeed, the benefits of the development of the solar photovoltaic industry can be linked to other goals such as job creation, reduction in greenhouse gas emissions, and a long-term improvement in competitiveness.

6.1 Introduction

The Caribbean is a chain of islands that is geographically located close to the equator. Within the Caribbean Community (CARICOM), only Trinidad and Tobago (T&T) and Guyana have commercial reserves of hydrocarbon energy resources. Thus, with the exception of T&T, the islands in the region are net importers of hydrocarbon energy resources. This has contributed to the region bearing a high energy import bill (Guardian Media 2013).

A second major energy-related threat facing the region is related to climate change. The combustion of oil-based fuels produces a high amount of anthropogenic carbon. When released into the atmosphere, it increases the greenhouse effect resulting in the rise of global temperatures, and the corresponding change in the statistical distribution of weather patterns. While the CARICOM region is not a major emitter of anthropogenic carbon and other greenhouse gases (GHGs) on an absolute basis, member states are all highly vulnerable to climate change (IPCC 2018). Thus, it would be in the best interests of all CARICOM member states if greater climate change mitigation action is taken.

Solar energy generation is recognized by the United Nations Framework Convention on Climate Change (UNFCCC),[102] as a climate change mitigation project. All CARICOM member states receive a steady supply of solar energy. The development of the solar energy industry holds tremendous potential to gradually wean the Caribbean off its dependence upon hydrocarbon energy resources. Solar technologies have been deployed in several countries of the Caribbean, but on a limited scale. More effort is needed in order to impact upon the regional energy supply.

The solar photovoltaic industry is as global as the sun. The photovoltaic value chain comprises the production of polysilicon, the manufacturing of solar modules, and the installation of the final product. This value chain is spread over many countries. Value chain analysis can thus be used to provide a holistic overview of the photovoltaic industry. The objectives of this chapter are to:

i. highlight the position for solar companies operating in the global value chain;
ii. review the Caribbean's local competitiveness factors;
iii. identify the challenges for entering and operating in the industry; and
iv. provide recommendations that can lead to the development of a solar photovoltaic industry in the CARICOM region.

[102] The UNFCCC is an international organization formed from an international treaty of 197 countries to make a collaborative effort to mitigate and adapt to climate change.

This chapter is structured as follows. Section 6.2 will provide an overview of the energy situation in the CARICOM region. Section 6.3 reviews the global value chain for the solar photovoltaic industry. Section 6.4 explores the local competitiveness factors of the CARICOM region. Section 6.5 considers the challenges facing the development of the solar photovoltaic industry in the CARICOM region. Section 6.6 examines the lessons learned from Chain, the world leader in the solar industry. Section 6.7 proposes some strategies for developing the solar photovoltaic industry in the CARICOM region. Section 6.8 concludes the chapter.

6.2 Overview of the Caribbean Energy Situation

The Caribbean region has a high dependence on hydrocarbons for its energy production. Imported diesel and fuel oil are used for electricity generation, while imported gasoline is used for motor vehicle petrol.

While petroleum fuels are of significant importance for almost all the countries in the region, there is disparity in the countries' import shares. For instance, in Aruba the petroleum import share is less than 10% of total imports. Whereas, for countries such as Guyana, Jamaica, and Monsterrat, the petroleum import share can be in excess of 20% of total imports. This is highlighted in Table 6.1. Collectively, the countries spent US$4.86 billion on petroleum imports in 2009.

Page 1 of Table 6.1: Imports of Petroleum and Products (SITC 33) in the Caribbean/CARICOM region (US$1,000)

	Aruba				Anguilla	
	SITC 33	Total	Share	SITC 33	Total	Share
2000		835229		6282	94514	7%
2001		836234		5919	77705	8%
2002		842876		6187	69893	9%
2003		846621		7240	76777	9%
2004		876172		9076	102439	9%
2005		951785		23208	174899	13%
2006		1041334		23968	247905	10%
2007		1113877		37017	271744	14%
2008		1112620				
2009	58665	1149200	5%			
2010	69863	1071034	7%			
2011	93138	1284949	7%			
2012	95969	1259804	8%			
2013	87659	1303317	7%			
2014	92903	1284149	7%			
2015	60131	1165014	5%			
2016						

	Belize			Barbados		
	SITC 33	Total	Share	SITC 33	Total	Share
2000	70177	446933	16%	127867	1155540	11%
2001	67214	519540	13%	118110	1068113	11%
2002	53483	527037	10%	58576	996558	6%
2003	60786	551638	11%	177346	1194985	15%
2004	70365	514024	14%	4986	1093754	0%
2005	89261	438584	20%	280677	1671864	17%
2006	96613	660343	15%	283371	1628555	17%
2007	98049	684342	14%	8372	1298657	1%
2008	120732	836544	14%	299609	1744263	17%
2009	96005	665095	14%	171499	1340713	13%
2010	104347	699951	15%	10767	1196224	1%
2011	131829	835542	16%	473910	1775403	27%
2012	123438	843066	15%	537126	1767767	30%
2013	125625	906091	14%	472703	1768742	27%

Page 2 of Table 6.1: Imports of Petroleum and Products (SITC 33) in the Caribbean/CARICOM region (US$1,000)

Antigua and Barbuda			The Bahamas		
SITC 33	Total	Share	SITC 33	Total	Share
52946	338187	16%	185115	2002172	9%
			282942	1927317	15%
			230181	1838254	13%
			248267	1873809	13%
			275532	1976139	14%
177538	525206	34%	492263	2566677	19%
240317	670748	36%	588552	2984310	20%
35518	573078	6%	596695	3102602	19%
			822364	3229969	25%
3594	699056	1%	541535	2698526	20%
2534	501231	1%	668774	2861948	23%
2856	471410	1%	909562	3410316	27%
2939	339512	1%	854396	3646505	23%
3528	343109	1%	709697	3365294	21%
164219	551751	30%	846888	3790366	22%
77099	465127	17%	521885	3161314	17%
74238	490525	15%			

Dominica			Dominican Republic		
SITC 33	Total	Share	SITC 33	Total	Share
12846	148167	9%			
11715	131051	9%	1092278	5496744	20%
9777	115668	8%	44747	5329771	1%
12916	127018	10%	45881	4208657	1%
14627	145138	10%	51987	4703854	1%
19902	165342	12%	68168	6804052	1%
24090	166896	14%	86531	8421973	1%
31749	195734	16%	116515	10594387	1%
33780	232375	15%	133467	12167110	1%
32681	222156	15%	1934313	12054439	16%
36301	224597	16%	2985658	15138223	20%
			3722161	18156133	21%
44134	211868	21%	3714951	17430206	21%
			4254567	17844951	24%

Page 3 of Table 6.1: Imports of Petroleum and Products (SITC 33) in the Caribbean/CARICOM region (US$1,000)

	Belize			Barbados		
	SITC 33	Total	Share	SITC 33	Total	Share
2014	131791	962112	14%	434319	1740471	25%
2015	98279	995561	10%	293601	1617853	18%
2016	81196	952494	9%	241871	1621270	15%
	Grenada			Guyana		
	SITC 33	Total	Share	SITC 33	Total	Share
2000	18458	238784	8%	121812	573427	21%
2001	16274	212149	8%	125330	586451	21%
2002	17777	198815	9%	120964	564458	21%
2003	14904	253233	6%	131894	556791	24%
2004	12766	250482	5%	174464	636086	27%
2005	21523	334034	6%	220459	778141	28%
2006	16955	298908	6%	261508	892927	29%
2007	58378	365125	16%	236688	1028778	23%
2008	67834	363304	19%	401668	1345930	30%
2009	35547	281828	13%	280822	1175349	24%
2010				405512	1451562	28%
2011				543362	1768555	31%
2012				609146	1997074	31%
2013				564986	1866255	30%
2014				559958	1783311	31%
2015				299339	2185744	14%
2016				317943	1624986	20%

	St. Lucia			Montserrat		
	SITC 33	Total	Share	SITC 33	Total	Share
2000	30212	355049	9%	2083	21609	10%
2001	27119	275828	10%	1157	19371	6%
2002	27699	314987	9%	4904	25422	19%
2003	41907	407687	10%	3995	28415	14%
2004	50874	421582	12%	5239	28724	18%
2005	61679	485766	13%	6972	29757	23%
2006	71397	592256	12%	8323	30199	28%
2007	122527	613541	20%	8168	29621	28%
2008	157959	655737	24%	12756	38048	34%
2009	74034	617089	12%	7449	29605	25%
2010	75969	646866	12%	28231	90226	31%
2011	96242	705014	14%	11506	36942	31%
2012	99648	656006	15%	13562	42075	32%
2013	375095	887550	42%	13864	41909	33%
2014	145444	642099	23%			
2015						

Page 4 of Table 6.1: Imports of Petroleum and Products (SITC 33) in the Caribbean/CARICOM region (US$1,000)

Dominica			Dominican Republic		
SITC 33	Total	Share	SITC 33	Total	Share
			3193062	17751695	18%
			2230172	17347815	13%
Jamaica			SKN		
SITC 33	Total	Share	SITC 33	Total	Share
563468	3191633	18%	13808	195731	7%
595389	3402550	17%	12326	189071	7%
608617	3543059	17%	8047	201308	4%
723248	3616832	20%	16593	199375	8%
938589	3933099	24%	15399	182681	8%
1337712	4881425	27%	17261	210241	8%
1191067	5041379	24%	17017	249531	7%
2213850	6743759	33%	16867	271670	6%
3365025	8465405	40%	22774	324786	7%
1351115	5064256	27%	10806	295754	4%
1525830	5225227	29%	9083	269822	3%
2235797	6436592	35%	6425	246620	3%
2307055	6580358	35%			
2189243	6216091	35%			
1863467	5835517	32%			
1101367	4992697	22%			
892926	4767022	19%			

Suriname			SVG		
SITC 33	Total	Share	SITC 33	Total	Share
30949	526448	6%	13373	161578	8%
72338	456561	16%	14829	186472	8%
67656	501843	13%	13456	177688	8%
97219	703864	14%	6498	201237	3%
96762	739549	13%	21896	225256	10%
171791	1049926	16%	30009	240434	12%
184137	1013149	18%	36108	271319	13%
156772	1044269	15%	48469	326688	15%
190705	1304332	15%	47232	373181	13%
208754	1390098	15%	53436	333384	16%
255968	1397500	18%	78210	379498	21%
370907	1637826	23%	98074	383477	26%
262790	1732785	15%	109079	403102	27%
482741	2308498	21%			
376660	1826728	21%			
			34127	333710	10%

Source: WITS (2018)

The high dependence on fossil fuels results in some CARICOM member states spending as much as 50% of their total export revenue on hydrocarbon fuel imports (Shirley and Kammen 2013).

Table 6.2: Installed Power Capacity in the Caribbean Region

	Total Installed Capacity (MW)	Renewable Energy Installed Capacity (MW)	Renewable Share (%)	Peak Demand for Energy (MW)	Average energy cost US$/kWh[103]
Anguilla	33	0.0005	0.002	13.99	0.16
Antigua and Barbuda	118	0.25	0.2	50	0.37
Aruba	230	35.5	15.4	125	0.28
The Bahamas	536.0	0	0		0.32
Barbados	239.1	3.5	1.4	167.5	0.28
Belize	154	82.58	53.6	84.3	0.22
Dominica	23.8	13.33	56	16.8	0.39
Dominican Republic	3,635	670	18.4	1,800	0.19
Grenada	48.59	0.68	1.4	30.2	0.30
Haiti	244	41	16.8		0.35
Jamaica	923	74.7	8.1	644.4	0.39
Montserrat	6.22	0	0	2	0.53
St. Lucia	78.4	0.1	1.2	60.3	0.34
SKN	43.0	3.2	7.4	24	0.26
SVG	58.3	5.94	10.18	21.1	0.26
Trinidad and Tobago[104]	2,289	0.01	0.0087	1,587	0.04

Source: Ochs et al. (2015); Energy Transition Initiative (2015)

The high reliance on petroleum imports has also resulted in high electricity generation costs. Countries such as Aruba, the Bahamas, and Barbados, bear an electricity generation cost of just over US$0.20/kWh. In comparison, in Monserrat the cost can be as high as US$0.43/kWh. T&T stands as the only

[103] The Average electricity generation cost for the Caribbean region in 2015 was $0.33 USD/kWh (Energy Transition Initiative 2015).

[104] The T&T data were collected from the Ministry of Energy, the Energy Transition Initiative (2015), and Ochs et al. (2015).

outlier with its low electricity generation cost of US$0.04/kWh, well below the regional average of US$0.33/kWh (Energy Transition Initiative 2015). Table 6.2 illustrates the electricity generation costs in the Caribbean region.

Although diesel and fuel oil are the predominant choice of fuels for electricity generation, a few exceptions exist. Barbados currently has infrastructure which can use natural gas for electricity generation. Belize, Haiti, and Suriname each use hydropower. Haiti, and Belize generate some of their energy from traditional biomass, particularly charcoal. Jamaica leads the region in developed wind power. Antigua and Barbuda, Aruba, Barbados, and St. Kitts and Nevis have developed their solar energy capacity.

There is also variation in the total installed electricity capacity. T&T, Jamaica, and the Bahamas, have the largest electricity generation capacity in the region. Montserrat, Dominica, and Grenada, have the lowest electricity generation capacity. Table 6.2 also highlights the electricity generation capacity of the region.

The thrust towards renewable energy sources is also influenced by the fact that the region is comprised of Small Island Developing States (SIDS) that are vulnerable to climate change (Kelman and West 2009).

Despite all the feasible renewable energy options, this chapter considers solar energy since it is technically feasible in all the Caribbean islands and has vast potential to supply the Caribbean with sufficient power to meet their energy needs. Solar energy has additional benefits, including:

- low opex costs, since most of the costs will be incurred upfront as capex;
- immunity from energy price volatility since once the capex cost is incurred, there will be no major costs incurred in the near future;
- low need for maintenance;
- the absence of noise pollution, since solar energy devices have no moving parts;
- the absence of water pollution, since there will be no "solar energy spills" to contaminate water supplies, as in the case of oil production and transportation;
- no emissions of anthropogenic carbon dioxide to contribute to the global climate change problem;
- the potential to generate electricity on site;

- the potential to generate a small income for consumers if surplus power is fed into the grid;
- the potential to diversify the energy portfolio mix; and
- the potential to ween countries off oil dependence.

Despite all the aforementioned benefits, there are numerous obstacles to the development of solar energy and other renewable energy projects in the CARICOM member states. They include misconceptions about the industry, mainly the view that solar energy would not become as competitive as crude oil within the medium term, asymmetric information, legal requirements to produce power, high upfront capex costs, intermittent supply, insufficient government incentives in some member states, difficulties for small and micro entrepreneurs (SMEs) in acquiring financing, and limited technical support personnel.

6.3 Solar Photovoltaic Global Value Chain

The Solar Industry can be categorized on the basis of technology. First, solar technologies can be passive or active (Bradford 2006). Passive solar energy technologies refer to those that do not convert solar insolation into electricity; while active technologies do convert solar insolation into electricity (Bradford 2006). Solar water heaters are an example of passive technology. Active technology is comprised of photovoltaic and solar thermal technology. Solar photovoltaic technology utilizes an array of panels made of semiconductor material to capture and convert incoming solar insolation into direct electric current (Masters 2004; Jacobson 2008). Solar thermal technology is based upon heat. It can be further subdivided into solar thermal non-electric, which is a passive technology, and solar thermal electric. Concentrated Solar Power (CSP)[105] is a form of solar thermal electric technology which uses heat for electricity generation.

While many semiconductor materials can be used for the photovoltaic effect, commercial producers of solar photovoltaic panels tend to rely upon two technology options: crystalline silicon and thin-film.

---

[105] CSP generates solar electricity by using parabolic mirrors to concentrate a large area of sunlight, onto a small area in a facility. The sunlight is used to heat a fluid, which is converted to steam and drives a steam turbine to produce electricity. CSP technology is often used in solar power plants. The Ivanpah Solar Power Facility (392 MW) and the Mojave Solar Project (354 MW), both in the United States, were the largest CSP projects in the world by the end of 2016.

Crystalline photovoltaic cells use either monocrystalline silicon, which is a single crystal technology, and/or polysilicon which uses multiple crystals as the semiconductor. Polysilicon is typically cheaper to manufacture than monocrystalline silicon, however it has traditionally been less efficient than monocrystalline silicon. Figure 6.1 illustrates the value chain for crystalline silicon photovoltaic technology (Maehlum 2018).

Figure 6.1: Crystalline Silicon Value Chain

Silica is the primary raw material used to produce silicon crystals. Silica is highly abundant in supply and is the second most common material on earth after oxygen (Cahn 2009). Approximately 90% of demand for polysilicon is derived from the solar photovoltaic industry. Production of polysilicon and monocrystalline silicon requires large processing plants which may cost up to US$1 billion to construct. A few manufacturers dominate the polysilicon production industry, namely GLC-Poly from China, Wacker-Chemie from Germany, Hemlock from the United States (US), and OCI from South Korea (Platzer 2015).

Manufacturers in the water industry melt the silicon raw materials, and then mould them into ingots. The ingots are then cut into wafers. Wafer manufacturing is a significant step, as its quality determines the efficiency of the module. The ingot and wafer industries are highly dependent upon each other; ingot firms tend to locate close to wafer firms resulting in a cluster. In fact, silicon crystal production, ingot processing and wafer manufacturing can all be considered part of the upstream segment of the value chain of the crystalline silicon photovoltaic system. It is relatively easy for crystal manufacturing companies to forward integrate into wafer manufacturing, and wafer companies to backward integrate into crystal and ingot formation. Thus, many companies have become vertically integrated. The top five manufacturers of polysilicon and wafers in 2017 were GCL-Poly (96,111 tons), Wacker-Chemie (76,000 tons), OCI (65,800 tons), Xinte Energy (30,000 tons), and the Daqo Group (18,000 tons) (Hutchins 2018).

Cell production follows the wafer-making stage. Crystalline silicon cells: monocrystalline and polysilicon (mc-Si), comprise 90% of the solar module market (Maehlum 2018). Cell manufacturers typically have proprietary designs which aspire to convert sunlight into electricity at the lowest total cost per kilowatt hour. Although many cell manufacturers still rely on extensive supply chains for components such as wafers, glass, wires, and racks, vertical integration is becoming more common (Platzer 2015). Some of the leading firms in the crystalline cell segment include Sharp, SolarPower, Kyocera, BP Solar, Hanwha Q-Cells, Mitsubishi, SolarWorld, Panasonic (Sanyo), Schott Solar and Isofoton. China has the largest photovoltaic market in the world accounting for over 50% of global installations in 2017. Many of the photovoltaic manufacturers are thus based in China.

Solar module manufacturing involves the soldering together of cells into a single unit/module that can generate the required electricity. Manufacturers also laminate the cells with special glass to protect them from weather variations. Production of solar glass is highly capital-intensive. The solar glass sub-industry is dominated by Ashai, NSG Group (Pilkington), Saint Gobain, and Guardian. Since solar glass is relatively expensive to ship, the glass manufacturers tend to locate relatively close to the module manufacturers (Platzer 2015).

The cells and module segments can be aggregated into a midstream sector. The midstream tends to be less profitable than the upstream sector. The global leaders in this segment include: Kyocera, Sharp, Yingli, Sanyo, Schuco, Solon, Schott, Conergy, REC, Solarworld, Canadian Solar and ET Solar.

Thin-film solar photovoltaic panels differ from crystalline photovoltaic panels as the former are comprised of cells which have deposits of one or several thin layers of photovoltaic material onto a substrate. Thin-film solar cells are categorized according to the semiconductor material used: cadmium telluride (CdTe), amorphous-silicon (A-Si), copper indium gallium selenide (CIGS), dye-sensitized solar cells (DSC), and organic photovoltaic cells (OPC). Thin-film solar cells tend to have an efficiency ranging between 7% and 13%, however they are typically cheaper than crystalline photovoltaic panels (Maehlum 2018). Gradual improvements in thin-film technology are closing the efficiency gap between thin-film and crystalline panels, eventually leading to PV module cost reductions (Empa 2013). The dominant firms in the thin-film solar module industry include: 3Sun Srl, Astronergy, Conergy, Kaneka, Mitsubishi, S-Energy, and SunPower. Figure 6.2 provides an illustration of the global value chain of thin-film photovoltaic modules.

Figure 6.2 Thin Film Value Chain

Amorphous silicon, a semiconductor material sometimes used in thin-film photovoltaic applications, is also used for building-integrated photovoltaics (BIPV). BIPV refer to photovoltaic systems which are integrated in buildings, replacing the glass which would have covered the building's sides. The PV material provides the dual function of acting as a skin cover and providing power requirements. Although the efficiency of amorphous silicon ranges from 4.3% to 6.3% (Green 2007), BIPV are attractive as they allow the building to self-generate electricity from sunlight immediately after the building's construction, thus reducing the building's operational costs. Leading amorphous silicon thin-film manufacturers include: Kaneka, United Solar, Mitsubishi, RWE Solar, and Bangkok Solar.

As previously mentioned, photovoltaic panels are also assessed on their energy efficiency ratings. Efficiency (expressed as a percentage) is a quantification of a solar panel's ability to convert sunlight into electricity. In practical terms, for two solar panels of the same physical size, if one has an 18% efficiency rating and the other has a 12% efficiency rating, the panel with the 18% efficiency rating will produce 50% more kilowatt hours (kWh) of electricity that the other panel under the same conditions.

Presently in 2018, the most efficient commercially available solar panels on the market have efficiency ratings as high as 22.5%, in comparison to the majority of panels which have efficiency ratings ranging from 15% to 17%. Most solar panel manufacturers engage in product differentiation and produce several solar panel models with different efficiency ratings (Energy Sage 2018).

Table 6.3 Top Solar Photovoltaic Manufacturers on the Basis of Efficiency Ratings

Solar Panel Manufacturer	Minimum Efficiency (%)	Maximum Efficiency (%)	Average Efficiency (%)
SunPower	16	22.2	19.85
Panasonic	19	21.6	20.3
LG	16.8	21.1	18.67
Hanwha Q CELLS	14.7	19.6	17.09
Solaria	18.7	19.4	19.01
Heliene Inc.	15.6	19.3	17.45
Silfab	15.3	19	17
Itek Energy	16.49	18.94	17.99
Canadian Solar	15.81	18.63	16.99
Trina Solar Energy	15	18.6	16.35
JinkoSolar	15.57	18.57	16.95
Renogy Solar	15.3	18.5	17.3
Hyundai	14.2	18.4	15.97
Mission Solar	15.98	18.36	17.21
SunSpark Technology	15.2	18.2	16.73
Axitec	15.37	17.9	16.47
CentroSolar	15.3	17.8	16.21
Grape Solar	16.21	17.64	16.75
SolarWorld	14.91	17.59	16.64
ET Solar	15.37	17.52	16.51

Source: Energy Sage (2018)

Recent research in solar photovoltaic technology has led to the development of concentrator photovoltaic (CPV) panels which have a 44% energy efficiency (Lopez 2016; Lumb et al. 2017). While the new highly efficient CPV panels are not on the market yet, it is reasonable to expect them to be commercialized in the near future.

The last stage of the value chain for both the crystalline and thin-film photovoltaic modules is the assembly and installation stage. An electrical technician must first evaluate the power requirement of the building to determine the size, voltage, efficiency, type, and amount of solar photovoltaic modules required. The electrical technician also determines the best location to maximize the incoming sunlight.

While the wafer production stage can be considered upstream and the module creation stage is considered as midstream, the module installation stage is definitely downstream. Leaders in scientific research and innovation tend to emerge as dominant players in the upstream and midstream stages of the photovoltaic value chain. Persons trained in electrical engineering, as well as photovoltaic installation can operate at the downstream segment. In fact, SMEs can have a presence in the downstream segment amid larger firms.

It is noteworthy that apart from site/building-specific photovoltaic systems, the solar industry also has utility-scale solar photovoltaic power plants. A utility-scale solar photovoltaic facility is essentially an electric power plant which generates solar electricity and feeds it into the grid. As a large capital investment is required, project developers of utility-scale solar power facilities typically arrange a power purchase agreement (PPA) with an electric utility company, guaranteeing a market for its energy for a fixed term of time.

The total cost of a utility-scale solar photovoltaic system can be categorized into three areas: the cost of modules, the cost of inverters, and the remaining system costs (other hardware, installation and soft costs). In 2015, the remaining system costs represented 60% of the total cost of utility-scale systems, while modules accounted for 30%, and inverters 10%. As the soft costs and installation costs constitute a large percentage of total costs in many countries, it indicates that there are sizeable opportunities for value creation beyond the manufacturing of the main components (IRENA 2017).

Cost reductions driven by technological advances and economies of scale in manufacturing have brought utility-scale solar photovoltaic power within reach of grid parity[106] (IFC 2015). In fact, in the first quarter of 2017, the LCOE for utility-scale solar power without subsidies fell to between 4.4 cents per kWh to 6.6 cents per kWh in the US (Fu et al. 2017).

The manufacturing of photovoltaic components has been concentrated in the manufacturing hubs in Asia. While Europe was previously the leader in such manufacturing, there has been a shift to countries such as China,[107] Malaysia, the Republic of Korea and Thailand. This has been largely driven by declining costs in these countries. Trade policies are also driving this shift in manufacturing (IRNEA 2017).[108]

In terms of installed capacity, China is the world leader with its 130 GW capacity in 2017. It is followed by the United States (US), then Japan and India. Table 6.4 highlights the installed solar capacity in various countries.

Table 6.4 Top 10 Countries on the basis of Installed Solar capacity

China	130.4 GW
United States	85.3 GW
Japan	63.3 GW
India	57.4 GW
Germany	48.4 GW
Italy	22.6 GW
United Kingdom	14.2 GW
France	12.8 GW
Australia	12.2 GW
Pakistan	10 GW

Source: Longman (2017)

[106] Grid parity occurs when an alternative energy source can generate electricity at a levelized cost of electricity (LCOE) that is less than or equal to the price of the purchasing power from the electricity grid.

[107] China is the global leader in both solar energy systems manufacturing and installation. In 2016 the country had 1.96 million people employed in the solar photovoltaic industry, up by 15% from the previous year (IRNEA 2017).

[108] In February 2013, the United States launched a dispute against India at the WTO claiming that India had discriminated against US solar imports in favour of its domestic suppliers. WTO ruled that India had broken WTO rules by requiring solar power developers to use Indian-made cells and modules. In 2016, India appealed the ruling and lost (Miles 2016; IRNEA 2017). Subsequently, India was required to implement the WTO's dispute settlement body's (DSB) recommendations by 14 December 2017. India has fully implemented the DSB recommendations, but it launched a WTO complaint against the US for subsidies in the solar industry in eight US states (Washington, California, Montana, Massachusetts, Connecticut, Michigan, Delaware and Minnesota) (Miles 2016; Kanth 2018).

6.4 Local Competitiveness Factors

The CARICOM region has a number of characteristics that favour the increased utilization of solar energy. The most relevant factors that serve as motivation for solar energy in the CARICOM region include:

- the high amount of solar energy;
- the high cost of electricity generation from diesel-based electrification; and
- the need to reduce GHG emissions as part of a global effort to advert climate change.

Annual solar irradiation in the Caribbean region ranges from 1700 to 2300 kWh/m^2 (Blechinger et al. 2015; Timmons 2017). Given that the demand for electricity is typically less than 200 kWh/d in each member state, theoretically, solar energy can meet the islands' energy needs.

Instead, a number of technological, economic, political, and social barriers have hindered the Caribbean adoption of renewable energy. The most important barriers were economic and political, with a lack of regulatory framework, a gap between policy targets and implementation, and high initial investments being cited as the most critical.

As previously mentioned, the cost of electricity generation in the Caribbean member states is high. With the exception of T&T, diesel is used for electrification in the member states. The regional average electricity cost is US$30/kWh. However, the cost of utility-scale solar photovoltaic electrification can be as low as US$0.06/kWh. Even if photovoltaic systems (inclusive of inverters and batteries) are installed to provide the energy needs for individual buildings, once the upfront capital cost is incurred, there will be little to no operational cost for the remainder of the photovoltaic systems' life, resulting in cost savings per building.

The third motivational factor for the increased utilization of solar energy in the CARICOM region is related to climate change. The combustion of hydrocarbon fuels to produce electricity releases anthropogenic carbon into the atmosphere. The increased emissions of anthropogenic carbon, as well as other GHGs into the atmosphere, increase the greenhouse effect, contribute to the warming of global temperatures, and cause a statistical change in weather patterns, hence climate change.

Since the 1990s, the international community has sought to take collective action to reduce GHG emissions. In fact, under the Kyoto Protocol of 1997, an international convention of the UNFCCC, parties agreed that a specific list of 38 developed countries should have GHG emission reduction commitments.[109] Due to the principle of shared but differentiating responsibility, developing countries were exempted from mandatory emission reduction commitments. This difference in emission reduction commitments was frowned upon by developed countries, especially since the more advanced developing countries such as China and India were major emitters but had no emission reduction commitments (Charles 2016).

After the Kyoto Protocol expired, countries collectively negotiated the Paris Agreement at the 21st Conference of the Parties (COP 21). The Paris Agreement differed from its Kyoto predecessor in its approach to emissions reduction by countries. In order to limit the global rise in temperature to below 2^0C by the end of the century, parties agreed to implement a system of nationally determined country-level emissions reduction targets. This national emission reduction system of targets, also referred to as Intended Nationally Determined Contributions (INDCs), involved all consenting countries voluntarily setting targets to reduce their GHG emissions. Since the INDCs are all voluntary, countries can set targets that they know they can achieve. Furthermore, the new INDC system would encourage emission reduction efforts by all countries rather than just a few industrialized countries (Charles 2016).

Since the CARICOM member states all have voluntary INDCs, the increased utilization of solar energy is more attractive as it would help them to decrease their GHG emissions and help advert climate change.

The aforementioned factors favour the increased utilization of solar energy in the CARICOM region. However, they are not the factors required for the production of solar photovoltaics. One of the most crucial factors for the development of a solar photovoltaic manufacturing industry is the undertaking of scientific research. Unfortunately, the CARICOM region is weak in this area. Section 6.5 reviews the challenges to the development of a solar energy manufacturing industry in the CARICOM region.

Currently there are no firms in the CARICOM region involved in the manufacturing of polysilicon, ingots or waters. While silica may be vastly

[109] The Annex I countries agreed to cut their GHG emissions by at least about 5% for the period 2008-2012 compared with 1990 levels (ENB 2012). The emissions reduction obligation is one of the reasons why there has been a strong thrust towards the development of the solar energy industry and other renewable energy sources in Europe.

available, the production of polysilicon is very energy and capital intensive and requires significant financing and technical skills. Its production is more favourable in T&T than in the other CARICOM member states as it has cheap electricity at approximately US$0.04/kWh. However, T&T does not currently have the required capital, research competence, or specialized labour to produce polysilicon. T&T faced similar hurdles before in its natural gas and downstream gas industry. The country was able to overcome its capital, labour and institutional knowledge limitations by forming partnerships with multinational corporations with the required capacity. A similar approach can be taken by the policy makers in T&T if the country ever aspires to enter the solar photovoltaic manufacturing industry. Once a polysilicon industry is created, manufacturers in the industry can easily forward integrate into ingots, and wafer segments of the larger global value chain.

The CARICOM member states currently operate only in the downstream segment of the photovoltaics value chain. The majority of the companies operating in the solar industry are involved in the assembly of entire solar photovoltaic systems in households and buildings. See Table 6.5.

Table 6.5: Some Solar Companies in the CARICOM Region

Name of Company	Location	Type of Service
Clarke Energy Associates	Barbados	Solar energy consultancy and installation company
D C Power Systems	Trinidad and Tobago	Installation and distribution PV company
Geo Green Power	UK (Headquarters), Barbados	Installation and distribution PV company
Eco Energy Inc	Barbados	Solar energy distributer, installation, supplier of related parts
E C T Solutions Ltd.	Trinidad and Tobago	Installation and distribution PV company
Solar Dynamics	Barbados (HQ), Jamaica, St. Lucia	Manufactures and distributes solar equipment

Solaris Energy Ltd.	Trinidad and Tobago (HQ), opened a plant in Barbados in 2012	Manufacturer of solar water heaters and photovoltaic systems
Solar Gray Ltd.	Trinidad and Tobago	Installation and distribution PV company
Solar Power Systems	Trinidad and Tobago	Installation and distribution PV company
Solar World Technology	Trinidad and Tobago	Installation and distribution PV company
Sun Power Ltd.	Barbados	
Synergy Resources Ltd.	Trinidad and Tobago	Installation and distribution PV company

One competitiveness factor favouring the development of the solar energy industry in the CARICOM region is the availability of labour. The University of the West Indies (UWI), and other tertiary industries in the CARICOM member states, produce graduates trained in electrical engineering. The electrical engineers as well as electrical technicians form a pool of labour that solar photovoltaic installation companies can tap into to undertake installation work. Furthermore, the skilled electrical labour can migrate between member states without any work permit since the recent CARICOM Single Market Economy (CSME) officially liberalized the labour market for university graduates.

The solar energy industry also has great potential for the creation of indirect jobs. For instance, jobs in warehousing, financial analysis, law, and market regulation will be required to support the industry. Figure 6.3 provides an illustration of the labour value chain for the solar photovoltaics industry.

Figure 6.3: Labour Value Chain for the PV Industry

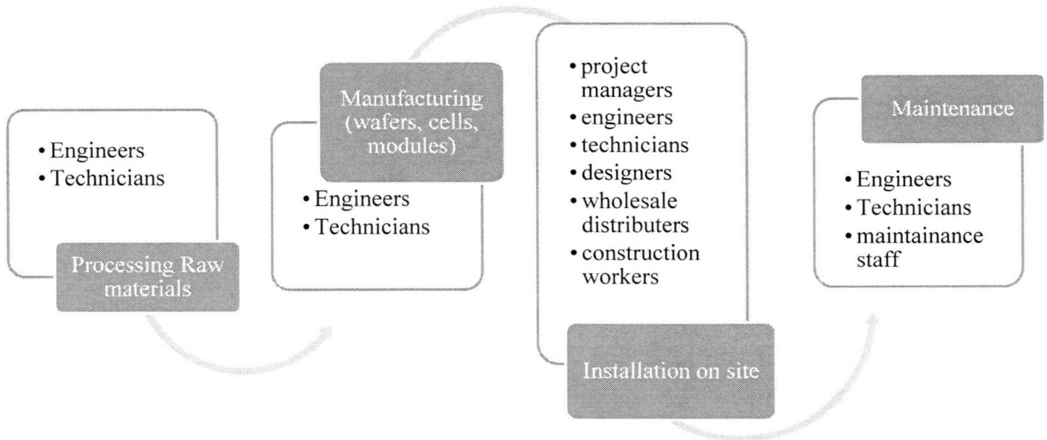

Source: IRENA (2011)

6.4.1 Strategies used in the cluster

The CARICOM region has had an uneven distribution of success in solar energy. The greatest success in the region has been achieved in Barbados in both solar water heaters and photovoltaics. Barbados' success in the solar industry was due to:

i. the actions of the early pioneers;
ii. economic, financial and regulatory support; and
iii. consumer acceptance.

In the 1970s entrepreneurs in Barbados formed Solar Dynamics, a company which supplied solar photovoltaic systems and solar water heaters (SWH) to consumers in the country. Solar Dynamics entered the value chain from the module and the assembly segments. It imported the parts required to produce modules, while some parts were produced locally. The company's engineers designed and assembled the solar photovoltaic and solar water heater systems.

Solar Dynamics achieved success in the photovoltaic and SWH industry by employing aggressive marketing strategies. The solar technologies were marketed to people struggling to bear the high electricity costs. The upfront capex cost of the solar system which was too expensive for some consumers was countered by credit unions providing loan support and allowing payback within 3 years (CDKN 2012). However, favourable government policy made the business venture a success (CDKN 2012).

In 1974 the Government of Barbados via the Fiscal Incentives Act introduced a tax exemption for the materials used to produce SWHs. Since some of the parts were also used for photovoltaic systems, the tax incentive complemented the photovoltaic industry. This resulted in a 20% cost saving in the production of solar equipment. In 1977 the Government of Barbados helped to create domestic demand for solar energy when it mandated the installation of SWH for all new government housing projects. In 1980 the Government made the full cost of an SWH installation a tax-deductible allowance for consumers up to a maximum of $1,750 USD. The policy ended in 1992 due to financial constraints but was reinstated in 1996 (CDKN 2012).

An income tax allowance, at US$5,000 per annum, was also introduced. Out of that allowance, a sum of $1,000 USD can be used for energy audits (GOB 2007). In order to make solar technology more attractive, the Government of Barbados increased import tax duties applied on gas and electric heaters.

In Barbados, both GRID-connected and standalone systems were offered by solar PV providers. However, GRID-connected systems look more attractive as energy rebates are given to independent power producers that produce surplus power for the grid (King 2011).

Customer acceptance was another important success factor for the Barbados solar industry. Jamaica attempted a solar industry in the 1970s like Barbados. However, it failed to grow to the size of the Barbados industry due to customers largely being unsatisfied with the quality of the product offered (CDKN 2012).

Public perception is an important factor in the success of the industry. Solar Dynamics attempted to replicate the Barbados model in St. Lucia. Initially the demand for the product was slow despite St. Lucia having high energy costs like Barbados. The outlook changed in a positive direction when Solar Dynamics changed their strategy and started to employ more St. Lucian citizens to execute the joint venture (CDKN 2012).

6.5 Challenges to the Development of the Solar Industry in the CARICOM Region

There are a number of barriers to the more increased adoption of solar energy in the CARICOM region.

T&T has achieved minuscule success in the photovoltaics industry largely due to

i) the cost of electrification from natural gas being very low, providing a disincentive for any large-scale electrification from solar energy;
ii) the country already having 99% grid connected electrification, thus any off-grid electrification project is likely to only be a pilot project;
iii) the absence of any strong policy framework inclusive of feed-in-tariffs and renewable energy rebates to encourage more widespread utilization; and
iv) the requirements of licences for any independent power producer (IPP) to self-generate electricity.

In summary, the barriers experienced by the wider CARICOM region include

i) Information asymmetry and misconceptions that solar energy would not be competitive against traditional diesel-based electrification.

ii) The upfront capex cost, as in the case of photovoltaic systems for buildings and households, the consumer would be required to incur the cost of the system upfront. In 2018, the cost of an 8pcs 100-watt monocrystalline photovoltaic solar panel module with a 12V battery was US$1,089 online (Amazon 2018). While US$1,000 can be easily borne by some households, others may find difficulty in raising such finances, especially since the electric utility bill for the household is likely to be less than US$100 per month.
    Furthermore, many consumers do not understand the economies of scale that will be generated from incurring a fixed, upfront capex cost for the solar photovoltaic system and bearing relatively no opex costs for the duration of the solar photovoltaic system's life. Thus, they compare the intial capex cost to their monthly utility bill costs, and find that solar photovoltaic technology is too expensive.
iii) The absence of feed-in-tariffs (FITs) in several jurisdictions.
iv) Difficulty in access to finance for new solar energy project developers.
v) The absence of a proper regulatory framework for the solar industry in several jurisdictions. There are still licence requirements for IPPs in Antigua and Barbuda, Bahamas, Dominica, Grenada, St. Kitts and Nevis, St. Vincent and the Grenadines, and T&T (NREL and OAS 2012).

6.6 Policy Lessons from China

China is currently the world leader in solar energy installation, but China does not have a comparative advantage in the production of silicon, and thus it must import silicon to facilitate any silicon crystalline solar module production. The country took on a number of supply side policies to develop their capacity, and demand side policies to stimulate domestic demand for their solar products.

In the 1950s, China's research in the solar industry was negligible. In the mid-1980s China decided to ramp up its effort in the renewable energy industry. It took a greater step into the solar industry by increasing the production of cells and modules with its focus on easy-to-follow technologies. In the 2000s, greater emphasis was focused on research.

In 2006, under its 11th 5-year plan, the government selected photovoltaics as a technology to improve national knowledge on energy technologies. The government policy was aimed at promoting high-tech manufacturing in pursuit of economic benefits. Later, under the 12th 5-year plan (2011-2015) the solar industry was included in the list of national initiatives to expand industrial activity in the country. Thus, China's thrust into the solar photovoltaic industry has been more about industrial development and achieving export competitiveness than addressing hydrocarbon price volatility or climate change (Yu 2016).

The Chinese government encouraged photovoltaic manufacturing investment through innovation funds for small technology-based firms, and by providing government backed loans with soft interest rates. China's easy access to credit gave an advantage to its local manufacturers to develop the scale for building gigawatt (GW)-scale power plants.

China experienced explosive growth in its solar industry from the mid-2000s. It managed to increase its production of cells by a factor of 23 over the 2007 to 2013 period. The country became the largest manufacturer in the solar photovoltaic market in 2007, representing approximately 29% of the global production of solar photovoltaic cells. The country also managed to reduce its module prices with mass production; from US$ 4.73/watt peak capacity (Wp) in 2007 to US$ 0.67/Wp in 2013.

In the early 2010s, as the global photovoltaic industry slowed down in lieu of the European crisis, the continuous mass production from Chinese photovoltaic system manufacturers caused an oversupply on the world market. This contributed to the weakening of prices, especially for polysilicon, ingots, and wafers.

The country also faced obstacles for imports of photovoltaic products going through trade disputes with the US and the EU. In response, some Chinese solar photovoltaic firms started to shift their production lines to Taiwan to avoid antidumping duties imposed upon Chinese solar products in the US (Yu 2016).

In terms of demand side policy, the government first sought to enhance domestic demand by implementing off-grid rural electrification programmes, namely the Brightness Programme (1996) and the Township Electrification Program (2000). Since the late 2000s, China has managed to significantly increase its on-grid solar photovoltaic installations due to a series of incentive programmes to encourage grid-connected rooftop and BIPV systems (namely the government subsidy programmes such as the "Roof top Subsidy Programme" (2009), the "Golden Sun "Demonstration Programme" (2009), and the "Solar PV Concession Programme" (2009)) and the national feed-in-tariff scheme (2011) (Yu 2016).

6.7 Strategies for Developing the Solar Industry in the CARICOM Region

Policy support is required to encourage the increased utilization of solar energy in the CARICOM region. Both supply side and demand side policies would be required. A Logic model[110] can be used to shape the policy framework for the development of the solar photovoltaic industry in the CARICOM region.

Table 6.4 presents a simplified mapping of the photovoltaic policy mechanisms and their expected outcomes.

Table 6.6: Mapping of the Photovoltaic Policy Mechanisms

Policy Objectives			
Energy Transition	Economic Growth	GHG emission reduction	
Policy Inputs	Outputs		
Supply side policy	Energy	Environment	Economic
partnerships with multinational firms	attract international investors	Reduction of GHG emissions	Social acceptance
encourage more entrepreneurs	manufacturing of PV cells, and modules		job creation
new training opportunities	better energy regulation		reduction in electricity costs improvement in the balance of trade
project finance	PV installations		multiplier effect to increase economic growth
Demand side policy	PV electricity generation		

[110] Logic models typically provide a visualized depiction of a programme in a manner that explains its key components. A logic model presents an outline of the sequence of planned actions and their expected results and changes in a single diagram (Knowlton and Phillips 2013).

FIT energy rebates consumer finance removal of licence requirements for IPPs public education			

The overall policy objective for the development of the solar photovoltaic industry should be:

1. the energy transition from an unsustainable framework which experiences "jumps" in oil prices, and causes a high energy import bill for member states;
2. the reduction in GHG emissions as part of countries' INDCs to mitigate the effects of climate change; and
3. the development of new green industries, which in turn will generate new economic growth.

Policy inputs would be required to stimulate change. The supply side policy would be essential in stimulating production at various stages of the value chain, while demand side policies can stimulate demand for the solar products that are domestically produced.

If the CARICOM member states ever seek to venture upstream in the photovoltaics value chain the first step would be for the government of the respective member state to identify an international company willing to enter a joint venture and form a new company to manufacture the modules locally.

Recall that the production of silicon crystals, ingots and wafers is dominated by a few vertically integrated firms. These firms have strong productive capacity, and have been able to achieve cost reductions to establish their competitiveness. It is unlikely that international producers which have cost advantages in Asia and Europe would be willing to establish new operations in CARICOM member states at the upstream segment where there may be cost disadvantages. Moreover, given that overcapacity in the silicon crystals, ingots and wafers segment, as well as technological improvements contributed to the decline in the price of the upstream inputs from 2009 to 2015 (INREA 2017), it would not be sensible for CARICOM member states to attempt to venture into the upstream segment of the photovoltaic value chain where prices are declining since the member states have neither the cost competitiveness, nor the research capacity to survive in the industry.

The main components of a solar system that CARICOM member states may consider manufacturing domestically are solar cells, solar modules, inverters, trackers, mounting structures and general electrical components. Such components represent over 60% of the value in the solar photovoltaic system value chain (INREA 2017).

For a country deploying solar photovoltaics, the potential to create jobs will depend on the extent to which the industry can employ domestic labour. The types of jobs that can be created for the midstream and downstream segments of the photovoltaic value chain include:

- administrative personnel;
- factory workers and technicians;
- logistics experts;
- health and safety experts;
- regulation and standardization experts;
- quality control experts;
- industrial engineers;
- marketing and sales personnel; and
- chemical engineers.

The UWI produces tertiary graduates who can perform duties in all the aforementioned fields. However, practical on-the-job training with established photovoltaic manufacturers would be required to fine-tune the local labour supply to meet the multinational companies' needs. In T&T the multinational companies in the oil, natural gas, and downstream natural gas industries operate in a similar manner when they train the local labour force to meet their specific needs.

In order to facilitate the smoother transition of tertiary graduates from the region's universities to the photovoltaic industry, specialized courses could be introduced to enhance degree programmes. For example, the UWI currently has a BSc degree in Electrical Engineering. In order to better prepare potential workers for the solar industry, courses specifically dealing with photovoltaic systems could be introduced in the Electrical Engineering Department. Additionally, an internship programme (analogous to the Caribbean-Pacific Island Mobility Scheme (CAPRIM) programme) can be introduced for the students. The students could spend 3 months in a foreign university where they would work directly under a supervisor and be allowed to develop competence in various technical areas in the solar industry.

Governments of CARICOM member states can consider incentivizing local entrepreneurs and manufacturers to enter the photovoltaic value chain especially at the assembly and installation stage. Government backed soft loans can be provided to SMEs. Tariff exemptions could also be granted to SMEs in the import of the necessary raw materials for their support services in the solar energy industry. Local companies should also be encouraged to form partnerships with more competent foreign counterparts so that there will be greater synergies and spillover effects.

Demand side policies can be used to stimulate domestic demand at the downstream installation segment of the value chain, and increased utilization can be facilitated by

i) The implementation of feed-in-tariffs.
   T&T is considering the use of feed-in-tariffs which will provide a financial remuneration to potential IPPs (Charles 2014). However, if governments are truly interested in the development of the solar industry, they need to transition from talk to action.
ii) The introduction of energy rebates.
   Barbados has considered a policy support of providing tax deductions equivalent to the cost of 50% of the cost for retrofitting households. An income tax deduction, or energy rebates can be used to incentivize households to install photovoltaic systems.
iii) The provision of solar projects finance.
   Solar Dynamics and the other early solar companies in Barbados had difficulty in attracting financing from banks. Banks did not fully understand the risks involved and were not willing to finance such projects (CDKN 2012). Even in more recent times in 2018, some financial institutions in other Caribbean islands do not fully understand the risk and are unwilling to finance solar projects. The outlook is not completely pessimistic for finance as EXIM Bank has agreed to provide a US$6.4 million loan to finance the import of solar modules to Barbados (EXIM 2012). There is scope for the governments of the member states to approach the banking sector and make arrangements for the creation of a special loan programme which would provide financing for solar projects for both project developers and consumers.
iv) The removal of the licence requirements for IPPs to generate electricity.
   There are requirements for the generation of electricity even by small-scale IPPs in Antigua and Barbuda, Bahamas, Dominica, Grenada, St. Kitts and Nevis, St. Vincent and the Grenadines, and

T&T (NREL and OAS 2012). Amendments of legislation are needed to recognize that households may generate electricity from solar sources.

v) The implementation of a public education campaign to educate the public about the cost benefits of utilizing solar electricity.
Public stakeholder consultations should be held to educate financial institutions, consumers, tertiary institutions, businesses, and all other relevant stakeholders about the benefits, costs, risk, applications and improvements in the solar industry.

The aforementioned policies should lead to the increase in solar photovoltaic installations and the expansion of solar energy output in implementing countries. In the islands facing high electricity prices, it should be expected that the increase in photovoltaic electricity supply would lead to a gradual reduction in the cost of electricity for households.

Businesses can also utilize solar technology in BIPVs. This can generate cost savings in the long run, which in turn can improve their cost competitiveness in the long run. This has significant implications. Improvements in cost competitiveness can allow private sector firms to export more goods at cheaper prices. If the demand for their products is price elastic, it would lead to a more than proportional increase in their total revenue and associated profit. It is possible for the potential increased profitability of the private sector to spill over to the wider economy via the employment of more workers, and the payment of more taxes on profits. It is well known that increases in export and investment can cause a multiplier effect to trigger a more than proportional increase in Gross Domestic Product (GDP). Therefore, it is logical to expect that any cost savings experienced by the private sector should be accompanied by an improvement in economic activity and economic growth in implementing member states.

6.8 Conclusion

The high presence of solar energy, the high cost of oil-based electrification, and the need to implement strategies to reduce GHG emissions all serve as drivers to encourage the development of solar energy in the CARICOM region. Despite these factors, the region has made limited process in its solar energy development. The greatest success in solar energy in the region has been achieved in Barbados, and this was attributed through strong government support. Subsequently, it is reasonable to expect greater headway to be made in the region if governments use their policy and legislative tools to remove economic barriers, and create an adequate enabling environment.

A lesson can be learned from China's success in the solar photovoltaic industry, which can be used to guide the overall policy framework for the CARICOM region. China's solar industry success was due to its focus on industrial development and achieving export competitiveness. Likewise, any CARICOM member state considering the development of its solar industry should be emphasizing industrial development strategies, improving productive capacity, and aspiring towards the attainment of export competitiveness.

The solar photovoltaic panel value chain is comprised of the following segments: silicon crystals, ingots, wafers, cells, modules, and installation of the final product. From the analysis of the segments in the global value chain it was revealed that the producers which are strong in scientific research are the ones that dominate the production of silicon crystals, ingots, and wafers. This occurs because research (which makes a scientific contribution to knowledge, and improves efficiency) is needed in order for producers to remain viable in these segments.

There is room for new producers in the CARICOM region to enter the value chain from the cells, modules, and installation segments. Since a producer does not have to be able to produce every component of a product in order to be competitive, it would be reasonable for new producers to import the high efficiency wafers to construct the photovoltaic panels. While it is possible for a firm to import all the intermediate products and assemble them to create the final product, from a country's perspective, it would be beneficial if at least some amount of domestic production occurs. This is justifiable since greater domestic production would create more employment opportunities and through a multiplier effect, circulate more value and wealth among the nationals. Furthermore, increased domestic production can lead to the development of clusters, which in turn will improve the ease in which the country could eventually backward integrate into more sectors of the solar photovoltaic panel global value chain.

Indeed, the development of the solar photovoltaic industry can be more attractive as it can be linked to other macroeconomic goals such as job creation, achieving energy security, reduction in GHG emissions, and long-term improvement in competitiveness.

References

Amazon. 2018. "Renogy 8pcs 100 Watt 100w Monocrystalline Photovoltaic PV Solar Panel Module 12V Battery Charging." Accessed August 11, 2018. https://www.amazon.com/Renogy-Monocrystalline-Photovoltaic-Battery-Charging/.

Blechinger, Philipp, Katharina Richter, and Ortwin Renn. 2015. "Barriers and Solutions to the Development of Renewable Energy Technologies in the Caribbean." In *Decentralized Solutions for Developing Economies*, edited by Groh, Sebastian, Jonas van der Straeten, Brian Edlefsen Lasch, and Dimitry Gershenson, 267-284. Berlin, Germany: Springer.

Bernstein, Roberta. 2006. "A Shortage Hits Solar Power." *The Wall Street Journal*, April 29. Accessed December 22, 2018. https://www.wsj.com/articles/SB114624912379938991.

Bradford, Travis. 2006. *Solar Revolution: The Economic Transformation of the Global Energy Industry.* Cambridge, MA: The MIT Press.

Cahn, R.W. 2009. "Silicon: Child and Progenitor of Revolution." In *Into The Nano Era*, edited by Howard R. Huff, 3-10. New York, United States: Springer Publishing.

CDKN (Climate and Development Knowledge Network). 2012. "Seizing the Sunshine – Barbados' Thriving Solar Water Heater Industry." Accessed December 2014. http://cdkn.org/wp-content/uploads/2012/09/Barbados-InsideStory_WEB.pdf.

Charles, Don. 2014. "From Sand to Power: An Examination of the Solar Energy Value Chain in the Caribbean." *International Journal of Green Economics* 8(1): 1-18.

—. 2016. "COP 21 and the Evolution of Climate Change Governance." *International Journal of Green Economics* 10(3-4): 287-301.

Empa. 2013. "Empa takes Thin Film Solar Cells to a New Level." Accessed April 1, 2017. http://www.empa.ch/plugin/template/empa/3/131438/---/l=2.

ENB (Earth Negotiations Bulletin). 2012. "Summary of the Doha Climate Change Conference." Accessed December 22, 2018. http://enb.iisd.org/vol12/enb12567e.html.

Energy Sage. 2018. "What are the Most Efficient Solar Panels on the Market?" Accessed August 5, 2018. https://news.energysage.com/what-are-the-most-efficient-solar-panels-on-the-market/.

Energy Transition Initiative. 2015. "Island Energy Snapshots." Accessed April 1, 2017. https://energy.gov/eere/island-energy-snapshots.

EXIM (Export-Import Bank of the United States). 2012. "Ex-Im Guarantees PNC Loan to Finance Solar Power in Barbados; Supports Small Business Jobs in Five States." Accessed April 1, 2017. http://www.exim.gov/newsandevents/releases/2012/exim-guarantees-pnc-loan-to-finance-solar-power-in-barbados-supports-small-business-jobs-in-five-states.cfm.

Fu, Ran, David Feldman, Robert Margolis, Michael Woodhouse, and Kristen Ardani. 2017. *U.S. Solar Photovoltaic System Cost Benchmark: Q1 2017*. Golden, Colorado, United States: National Renewable Energy Laboratory (NREL).

Gereffi, Gary, and Karina Fernandez-Stark. 2011. *Global Value Chain Analysis: A Primer*. Durham, England: Center on Globalization, Governance & Competitiveness (CGGC), Duke University.

Green, Martin A. 2007. "Thin-Film Solar Cells: Review of Materials, Technologies and Commercial Status." *Journal of Materials Science: Materials in Electronics* 18(1): 15-19.

GOB (Government of Barbados). 2007. "Income Tax Act." Accessed April 1, 2017. http://www.sice.oas.org/investment/NatLeg/Bar/IncomeTax_e.pdf.

Guardian Media. 2013. "Concern over Region's US$9b Fuel Import Bill." *Guardian*, Saturday, March 2. Accessed April 17, 2018. http://www.guardian.co.tt/business/2013-03-02/concern-over-region%E2%80%99s-us9b-fuel-import-bill.

Hutchins, Mark. 2018. "The Weekend Read: Polysilicon and Wafer Manufacturer Ranking." *PV Magazine* February 24. Accessed August 6, 2018. https://www.pv-magazine.com/2018/02/24/the-weekend-read-from-the-top/.

IEA (International Energy Association). 2004. "Renewable Energy Markets and Policy Trends in IEA Countries." Accessed April 1, 2017. http://s3.amazonaws.com/zanran_storage/www.iea.org/ContentPages/9895294.pdf.

IFC (International Finance Corporation). 2015. "Utility-Scale Solar Photovoltaic Power Plants: A Project Developer's Guide." Accessed August 11, 2018. https://www.ifc.org/wps/wcm/connect/f05d3e00498e0841bb6fbbe54d141794/IFC+Solar+Report_Web+_08+05.pdf?MOD=AJPERES.

IPCC (Intergovernmental Panel on Climate Change). 2018. "Global Warming of 1.5^{0}C." Accessed December 20, 2018. https://report.ipcc.ch/sr15/pdf/sr15_spm_final.pdf.

IRENA (International Renewable Energy Agency). 2011. *Renewable Energy Jobs: Status, Prospects and Policies.* Abu Dhabi: International Renewable Energy Agency.

—. 2017. *Renewable Energy Benefits Leveraging Local Capacity for Solar PV*. Abu Dhabi: International Renewable Energy Agency.

Jacobson, Mark. Z. 2008. "Review of Solutions to Global 1 Warming, Air Pollution, and Energy Security." Accessed December 12, 2018. https://pubs.rsc.org/en/content/articlehtml/2009/ee/b809990c.

Johansson, Thomas. B., Kes McCormick, Lena Neij, and Wim Turkenburg. 2004. "The Potentials of Renewable Energy: Thematic Background Paper." Accessed December 22, 2018. http://ren21.net/Portals/0/documents/irecs/renew2004/The%20Potentials%20of%20Renewable%20Energy.pdf.

Kanth, D. Ravi. 2018. "WTO: India-US Dispute Over Solar Cells, Modules Intensifies." *Livemint*, January 10. Accessed August 14, 2018. https://www.livemint.com/Politics/UNRFSuIcJ4KYvUBWfu59wL/WTO-IndiaUS-dispute-over-solar-cells-modules-intensifies.html.

Kelman, Ilan, and Jennifer J. West. 2009. "Climate Change and Small Island Developing States: A Critical Review." *Ecological and Environmental Anthropology* 5(1): 1-16.

King, Mike. 2011. "Solar Panels Bring Savings." *Nationnews*. Accessed August 14, 2018. http://www.nationnews.com/articles/view/solar-panels-bring-savings/.

Knowlton, Lisa Wyatt, and Cynthia C. Phillips. 2013. "Introducing Logic Models." In *The Logic Model Guidebook: Better Strategies for Great Results*. 2nd ed., 2-14. California, United States: SAGE Publications Inc.

Lewis, Joanna I., and Ryan H. Wiser. 2007. "Fostering a Renewable Energy Technology Industry: An International Comparison of Wind Industry Policy Support Mechanisms." *Energy Policy* 35: 1844-1857.

Longman, Nye. 2017. "Top 10 Solar Producing Countries." *Energy Digital,* May 12. Accessed August 6, 2018. https://www.energydigital.com/renewable-energy/top-10-solar-producing-countries.

Lopez, Julyssa. 2016. "Developing the Next Generation of Solar Cells." *GW Today,* August 11. Accessed August 5, 2018. https://gwtoday.gwu.edu/developing-next-generation-solar-cells.

Lumb, Matthew P., Shawn Mack, Kenneth J. Schmieder, María González, Mitchell F. Bennett, David Scheiman, Matthew Meitl, Brent Fisher, Scott Burroughs, Kyu-Tae Lee, John A. Rogers, and Robert J. Walters. 2017. "GaSb-Based Solar Cells for Full Solar Spectrum Energy Harvesting." *Advanced Energy Materials* 7(20): 1700345-1700354.

Maehlum, Mathias Aarre. 2018. "Which Solar Panel Type is Best? Mono- vs. Polycrystalline vs. Thin Film." Accessed August 6, 2018. http://energyinformative.org/best-solar-panel-monocrystalline-polycrystalline-thin-film/.

Masters, Gilbert M. 2004. *Renewable and Efficient Electric Power Systems*. New York, United States: John Wiley and Sons.

Miles, Tom. 2016. "India Loses WTO Appeal in U.S. Solar Dispute." *Reuters,* September 16. Accessed August 14, 2018. https://www.reuters.com/article/us-india-usa-solar/india-loses-wto-appeal-in-u-s-solar-dispute-idUSKCN11M1MQ.

NREL (National Renewable Energy Laboratory) and OAS (Organization of American States). 2012. "Energy Policy and Sector Analysis in the Caribbean 2010-2011: Assessing Antigua and Barbuda, the Bahamas, Dominica, Grenada, St. Kitts and Nevis, St. Lucia, St. Vincent and the Grenadines." Accessed December 22, 2018. http://www.oas.org/en/sedi/dsd/energy/doc/lccc_report.pdf.

Ochs, Alexander, Mark Konold, Katie Auth, Evan Musolino, Philip Killeen. 2015. "Caribbean Sustainable Energy Roadmap and Strategy (C-SERMS): Baseline Report and Assessment." Accessed August 5, 2018. http://www.worldwatch.org/system/files/C-SERMS_Full_PDF.pdf.

Perlack, Robert D., and William Hinds. 2003. "Evaluation of the Barbados Solar Water Heating Experience." Accessed August 5, 2018. http://solardynamicsltd.com/wp-content/uploads/2010/07/SWH-report1-2.pdf.

Platzer, Michaela D. 2015. "U.S. Solar Photovoltaic Manufacturing: Industry Trends, Global Competition, Federal Support." Accessed December 12, 2018. https://www.everycrsreport.com/files/20120530_R42509_001e9604208c2a98eb37d6c9dfd5aa9733351de8.pdf.

Sanders. 2013. "Fuel Bills – An Impending Disaster." *Trinidad Express,* Jan 4. Accessed June 14, 2018. http://www.trinidadexpress.com/commentaries/Fuel_bills_an_impending_disaster-182475151.html?m=y&smobile=y.

Shirley, Rebekah and Daniel Kammen. 2013. "Policy Development for Innovative Renewable Energy Implementation in Island Regions." *Energy Policy* 57: 244-252.

Shyu, J.Z., J.S. Wang, and C.C. Peng. 2010. *The Developmental Strategy of the Emerging Energy Industry.* Taipei, Taiwan: Hwa Tai Publishing Company.

Timmons, Liam. 2017. "Caribbean Nations Turn to Renewable Energy." *Council on Hemispheric Affairs,* July 3. Accessed August 11, 2018. http://www.coha.org/caribbean-nations-turn-to-renewable-energy/.

WITS (World Integrated Trade Solution). 2018. "Trade Data (UN Comtrade)." Accessed August 5, 2018. http://wits.worldbank.org/WITS/WITS/AdvanceQuery/RawTradeData/QueryDefinition.aspx?Page=RawTradeData.

Yu, Hyun Jin Julie. 2016. "Public Policies for the Development of Solar Photovoltaic Energy and the Impacts on Dynamics of Technology Systems and Markets." Accessed December 12, 2018. https://tel.archives-ouvertes.fr/tel-01370299/document.

CHAPTER SEVEN

AN E-COMMERCE PLATFORM FOR PROMOTING SME VALUE CHAINS IN BARBADOS, JAMAICA, AND TRINIDAD AND TOBAGO

Abstract

Electronic commerce (e-commerce) is a major opportunity for trade facilitation in countries due to its ability to connect buyers with sellers regardless of their scale. Its additional possible benefits to countries that can be actualized amongst others are the attaining of higher levels of international competitiveness, and more active participation in the global economy. The promotion of e-commerce is an even more attractive policy tool since it will allow small and micro enterprises (SMEs) to increasingly participate in regional and international trade, and reap the associated gains from trade.

Several of the Caribbean Community (CARICOM) member states desire foreign multinationals to come to their country, and engage in production which will lead to the economic progress of their economies. While this multinational based industrialization is highly probable in countries with hydrocarbon and mineral natural resources, it is not going to be the norm in countries that are hydrocarbon and mineral natural resource scare. In each member state, there are thousands of people who create their own employment opportunities with small and micro enterprises (SMEs). The SMEs do not have the scale to export large quantities on a frequent basis, however, internet-based e-commerce allows for the international trade of small parcels. Indeed, e-commerce presents an opportunity for SMEs in the CARICOM region to actively participate in and reap the benefits of international trade.

This chapter assesses the readiness of Barbados, Jamaica, and Trinidad and Tobago, three CARICOM member states, to enable their SMEs to engage in cross-border e-commerce. This chapter also explores the policy measures required to help SMEs in the aforementioned countries actively participate in cross-border e-commerce and benefit from international trade.

7.1 Introduction

The Caribbean Community (CARICOM) member states can be grouped into two categories: goods-producing and service-producing economies. The goods-producing economies include: Belize, Guyana, Suriname, and Trinidad and Tobago (T&T). The remainder can be categorized as service-producing economies. The goods-producing economies produce and export agricultural products, and in the case of T&T and eventually Guyana, hydrocarbon products.[111] In the service-producing economies, the dominant services include: tourism-based services, financial and offshore banking, culture, and entertainment services.

The region has a very narrow industrial base. While the countries do trade with each other, the intraregional trade is dominated by T&T. In fact, as can be easily seen in Table 7.1, T&T's export share ranges from 68% to 78.37% of the total intraregional exports.

While the member states do aspire to economic progress from international trade, their current regional integration process, the CARICOM Single Market Economy (CSME), has not produced its desired results.

Many of the member states agree with the Lewis "industrialization by invitation model" and are waiting for large multinational investors to come to their country, invest, and create employment opportunities for their nationals as they (the multinationals) engage in international trade. While this multinational based industrialization is highly probable in countries with hydrocarbon and mineral natural resources, it is not going to be the norm in countries that are hydrocarbon and mineral natural resource scare. In fact, the foreign direct investment (FDI) from the multinational investors tends to flow towards the economies that are rich in mineral natural resources.

[111] Guyana is expected to commence its commercial production and export of crude oil by 2020.

Table 7.1: Intraregional Export Shares to CARICOM (%)

	ATG	BHS	BLZ	BRB	DMA	GRD	GUY	JAM	SKN	SL	SUR	SVG	TT
2000	0.16	0.04	0.67	7.41	2.26	0.77	5.67	3.27	0.15	0.79	0.38	1.61	76.81
2001	0.00	0.03	0.87	6.48	1.83	0.69	5.21	3.52	0.06	0.86	0.40	1.69	78.37
2002	0.00	0.03	0.99	7.44	1.97	0.80	7.79	3.99	0.05	1.26	1.49	1.66	72.53
2003	0.00	0.05	1.30	6.38	1.85	0.69	7.16	3.50	0.04	1.25	1.45	1.33	75.00
2004	0.00	0.03	1.86	7.24	1.93	0.60	9.12	3.57	0.06	1.53	2.13	1.54	70.39
2005	0.09	0.02	0.91	4.74	0.92	0.39	4.25	1.68	0.03	0.79	1.39	0.87	83.91
2006	0.00	0.01	0.76	4.41	0.88	0.39	3.99	1.65	0.06	0.85	2.31	0.78	83.91
2007	0.10	0.02	0.75	7.58	0.98	0.53	6.57	2.06	0.08	1.25	2.78	1.06	76.24
2008	0.00	0.05	0.38	3.42	0.59	0.44	3.14	1.51	0.07	0.75	4.44	0.79	84.42
2009	0.06	0.01	0.69	5.98	1.02	0.00	6.24	3.37	0.16	1.39	6.33	1.72	73.04
2010	0.04	0.02	0.63	3.88	0.75	0.00	4.28	2.28	0.09	1.17	10.95	1.09	74.84
2011	0.04	0.03	0.93	4.44	0.00	0.00	4.72	2.27	0.11	1.03	10.50	1.14	74.79
2012	0.05	0.04	1.46	5.95	0.99	0.00	4.80	3.97	0.18	0.74	8.46	1.50	71.88
2013	0.03	0.02	1.30	3.79	0.00	0.00	2.86	1.65	0.09	0.74	6.15	1.05	82.33
2014	0.04	0.03	1.35	5.72	0.00	0.00	4.62	3.19	0.15	1.00	9.90	1.44	72.57
2015	0.05	0.13	1.99	8.30	0.00	0.00	13.24	3.11	0.29	1.84	0.00	2.49	68.56

Source: Computed from data from the World Integrated Trade Solution

In the instance where there is a strong multinational presence, the multinationals tend to employ a small percentage of the labour force. This is clearly the case in T&T, whose energy sector is dominated by multinationals, yet the energy sector only creates employment opportunities for approximately 3% of the country's labour force. The government is tasked with the responsibility of picking up the slack by generating employment opportunities resulting in a dual sector economy. Unfortunately, no CARICOM government can generate sustainable employment opportunities for all of its citizens.

In each member state, there are thousands of people who create their own employment opportunities with small businesses. In fact, most businesses in the CARICOM region can be classified as small and micro enterprises (SMEs), typically employing fewer than 25 people. These SMEs enter a variety of business ventures in the services sector ranging from food and culinary services to technical vocational services. Some SMEs also venture into goods businesses where they buy imported products and resell in the domestic market.

While many SMEs in the region do not have the scale to produce and export large quantities on a frequent basis that does not mean that they do not have the potential to produce and export. In fact, in the 2000s and the 2010s there was a proliferation of the trade of small parcels, which has been facilitated by the internet and electronic commerce (e-commerce).

The internet and e-commerce have allowed the connection of a multitude of buyers with sellers across great geographic distances. Websites such as Amazon and Ebay create an enabling environment for both large-scale and small-scale suppliers in the United States (US), providing them with real market access as buyers can directly see the products that are available, and purchase the products that they desire. Even if a potential supplier has only one product for sale, there is scope for that supplier to sell and ship the product to any customer regardless of their residential state.

Indeed, the internet and e-commerce have the potential to create market opportunities for SMEs even in the CARICOM region. The development of e-commerce would enable an excellent tool to network the SME sector, and enable the SMEs to act as a vital growth engine for their countries. Of course, the ability of the SMEs of the CARICOM member states to effectively engage in e-commerce will depend on factors of e-production, and the member states' e-readiness.

The objectives of this chapter are to

- assesses the readiness of Barbados, Jamaica, and T&T, to enable their SMEs to engage in cross-border e-commerce;
- explore the policy measures required to help SMEs in the aforementioned countries to actively participate in cross-border e-commerce and benefit from international trade.

This chapter is structured as follows. Section 7.2 explains e-commerce. Section 7.3 outlines the e-commerce value chain. Section 7.4 will assess the e-readiness of Barbados, Jamaica, and Trinidad and Tobago, three selective CARICOM member states. Section 7.5 will explore some policy recommendations which can be utilized to help SMEs in the aforementioned CARICOM member states to engage in e-commerce and actively participate in international trade. Section 7.6 concludes the chapter.

7.2 What is E-commerce?

E-commerce is more than just the buying and selling of products and services via the internet. It includes all information or services that a company may offer to its customers over the internet related to the sale of a product. This includes pre-purchase information to after sales service and support.

E-commerce is used for two major purposes. One use is to reduce transaction costs by improving efficiency in the use of time and the ease in which transactions may be conducted. The second use is as a marketing tool to grow sales and expand a firm's reach to new clients.

E-commerce can occur between three basic participant groups: businesses, governments, and consumers. Subsequently, four permutations of e-commerce models exist: i) Business to Business (B2B) where electronic transactions and commerce are occurring between businesses; ii) Business to Customer (B2C) where electronic transactions and commerce are occurring between businesses and consumers; iii) Customer to Business (C2B) which refers to reverse pricing models where the customer determines the prices of the product or services; and iv) Customer to Customer (C2C) which refers to e-commerce activities, which rely on an auction type model (Patel and Soni 2013).

Figure 7.1: E-commerce Value Chain

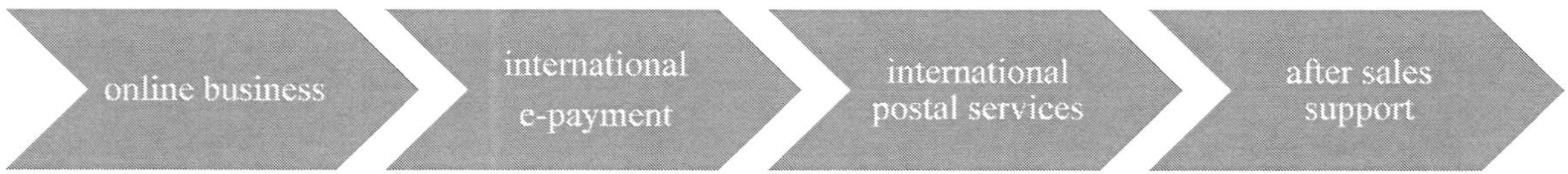

Source: ITC (2017)

E-commerce can be used to facilitate cross-border transactions regardless of the scale of the sellers and buyers. As a result, e-commerce is an excellent tool to help SMEs participate in international trade. Cross-border e-commerce is comprised of a value chain of processes that takes a product from the seller to the customer. From the perspective of an SME, the value chain may be comprised of four key areas: i) establishing an online business; ii) implementing a framework for international e-payment; iii) engaging in the international posting and delivery of products; and iv) providing after sales support.

The following section will explore the e-commerce value chain.

7.3 E-commerce Value Chain

Of particular importance in global value chains is the issue of governance, which refers to key actors within the value chain who have power to control and shape how activities are organized along the chain. Gereffi (1994) identified two types of governance structures in global value chains: producer-driven, and buyer-driven. With the growth of popularity of the internet from the mid-1990s, a third form of governance began to emerge which is oriented around the internet. This new governance structure reflects the major changes in international production and distribution that have occurred from the 1990s to the present. There has been a continuous shift in the locus of power from producers to retailers to consumers.

E-commerce and the reorientation of value chains have occurred due to enhancements in technology and improvements in computer and internet access. E-commerce has also resulted in changes in business organization, market structures, government regulations, and consumer preferences.

The Internet has transformed both buyer-driven and producer-driven chains because of two fundamental factors: i) its ability to create business opportunities regardless of the scale of the retailer, and ii) an efficient business strategy that substitutes information for inventory and ships products only when there is an effective demand for them. Thus, the internet and its complementary e-commerce have effectively led to the formation of infomediary-based value chains (Gereffi 2001).

7.3.1 Establishing an online business

In order for any individual, SME, or firm to sell a product or service via the internet, they must use an online interface. This requires the individual or firm to use a website to offer goods and/or services. The economic agent offering goods or services has three options to establish an online presence. They can: i) build a website to sell their goods and/or services; ii) utilize an e-commerce platform; and iii) use a social media website to market their goods and/or services.

If economic agents opt to use their own website for e-commerce, they can either develop the website themselves or hire a professional website developer. Even if an economic agent does not have any programming skills, they can use a What You See Is What You Get (WYSIWYG) website to build their own website from a template. If the economic agent aspires to engage in electronic transactions via their website, internet security becomes a major issue. There are thousands of hackers and other internet-based threats "surfing" the internet waiting to pounce on unsecured websites and steal customers' money and banking information. Therefore, it should be the responsibility of the seller to ensure that their website is secure against external threats. In this case, it would be advisable for the seller to procure the services of a competent individual or firm that specializes in internet security, to develop a secure interface for their electronic transactions.

If the economic agent develops their own website, they can also consider multiple languages in order to reach a wider market.[112] By another token, economic agents can consider developing their own website in such a way that it would be user friendly for various electronic media devices (such as mobile phones, tablets, and laptops).

A second option to facilitate e-commerce of SMEs is to utilize the services of an e-commerce platform. Websites such as Amazon.com and Ebay.com act as e-commerce platforms to connect millions of buyers with sellers. Any economic agent visiting such an e-commerce platform can easily see the goods and services available for sale, their prices, the sellers, popularly bought items, and reviews on the performance of these items.[113] Some advantages of utilizing an e-commerce platform include:

---

[112] If any website is built to facilitate trade between Barbados, Jamaica and T&T, the only language of relevance would be English since it is the official language of the three aforementioned countries.

[113] There tends to be a proliferation in the sale of goods rather than services on these e-commerce platforms.

- The sellers can gain access to a wide range and a large volume of customers.
- High credibility as many e-commerce platforms require the registration of sellers, and have a system for buyers to be reimbursed if their item is not received or not received in the condition that was advertised.
- Many of the popular e-commerce platforms offer a secure framework for online payment.
- Everyone on the e-commerce platform can see the prices of the products offered. Thus, in an attempt to compete, sellers can charge lower prices. This free market competition keeps prices low relative to an uncompetitive market structure.

Economic agents can also use social media websites to promote their goods and/or services. However, social media websites will be used more as a marketing tool rather than an e-commerce site since most social media websites do not have a built-in framework to support electronic transactions. Nevertheless, social media websites are excellent, especially for SMEs as they tend to be free, and have a wide range and large volume of users.

7.3.2 International e-payment

Electronic payment is a crucial stage of the e-commerce value chain. Regardless of using an economic agent's website or an e-commerce platform, both buyers and sellers would be required to set up an account linked to credit cards, debit cards, and mediators such as PayPal, in order to allow funds to transfer during transactions. SMEs looking to jump on board the e-commerce highway should use a secure framework to receive their electronic payments. Internet security for electronic payment has three basic building blocks:

- Encryption, which takes the intended information, referred to as plaintext, and applies an encryption algorithm to it, generating ciphertext which can be read only if decrypted. In essence, encryption prevents the information or message from being read by everyone without being decrypted.
- Digital signatures, refer to the digital codes that are generated and authenticated by public key encryption, and are attached to electronically transmitted documents to verify their contents and the sender's identity.

- Checksums/hash algorithms. A checksum is a small block of digital data which is used for the detecting of errors. Checksums are used to verify data integrity.

7.3.3 International Posting and Cross-border delivery

When customers purchase products from different countries, they expect them to be delivered. Unless a seller is a larger vertically integrated company with its own postal courier services, the seller will have to rely on the postal services of a third party to deliver the items. Several factors can affect the speed of delivery of a postal company. They include:

- the operational efficiency of the postal company;
- the quality of the road network and traffic in the exporting and importing countries; and
- the efficiency of the port and its customs division in clearing the products in the exporting and importing countries.

The postal company or companies selected to deliver the goods purchased through electronic transactions need to be efficient. Moreover, they would need:

- to have access to a warehouse;
- to have a system to connect products with consumers, and a system to track the movement of the parcels;
- to have secure packaging for the delivery of goods;
- to be knowledgeable about the procedure for the clearing of all categories of goods through ports and the customs division; and
- to have a reliable transportation system to deliver parcels to the customer.

The quality of the road network and traffic in the exporting and importing countries affects the speed at which goods can be transported from the vendor to the consumer. Bad roads are an obstacle to e-commerce especially if postal companies are reluctant to travel to specific geographical locations to deliver parcels. Likewise, heavy traffic can also cause delays in the delivery of parcels.

The trade rules and the Customs Division in both importing and exporting countries have a significant role to play in the international trade of products which have been purchased online. Countries may have specific rules for the export and import of products, the application of taxes and other charges.

In the importing country, the goods are typically required to pass inspection by the Customs Division before being cleared to enter the country. The Customs Division typically also has the responsibility to determine the appropriate customs duty that must be paid to clear the goods based upon the classification and the perceived value of the goods. Disputes could arise between importers and the Customs Division with regard to the classification of items, and the perceived value of items. Moreover, there is also scope for subjectivity and inconsistency in the application of customs duty.

7.3.4 Aftersales

After the product has been delivered to the customer, there is still room for after sales support. The after sales phase of the e-commerce value chain includes all the activities that occur after buyers have made their payment. After sales support includes:

- a framework for the customer to cancel orders if they change their mind before the product has been shipped;
- a dispute settlement policy for customers to contact the seller and attempt to get some form of redress if the delivered product is not in the condition that was advertised;
- a return policy for customers to return the goods to the seller in the case that the purchased product that is delivered is not in the condition that was advertised;
- a refund policy for customers to get a refund of their money if the purchased product that is delivered is not in the condition that was advertised;
- a warranty policy for customers as the purchased product should last for a period of time and should not deteriorate or malfunction immediately after use;
- a customer information confidentiality policy, where a customer's personal and banking information is not shared by the seller to any third party without the customer's authorization; and
- a framework for the customer to review and post their comments on the performance of both the product and the seller.

7.4 E-commerce and E-readiness of CARICOM

Before any country embarks upon any comprehensive e-commerce strategy or policy, it is important to assess its e-business readiness. This is the extent to which the population of a country is prepared to participate in business activities which are facilitated over the internet.

A number of factors can be used to determine the e-business readiness of countries. The main ones include:

i) Infrastructure, which refers to accessibility to communication services, their quality and reliability.
ii) Regulation, which refers to the extent to which the public authorities control the industry and encourage a fair and competitive environment.
iii) Human resources, which refer to the availability of the relevant technical personnel who can provide support to the information, communication and technology (ICT) industry.
iv) The legal framework, which covers the legal support for e-commerce transactions, the legal protection for personal information and intellectual property, and the regulatory framework to address and prosecute cybercrimes.
v) Policy framework, which refers to the government policies designed to create an enabling environment to facilitate e-commerce.

7.4.1 Infrastructure and Operators in the Market

With regard to infrastructure, satellite connections were initially the only way for Caribbean islands to access global telecommunications networks. The high cost of satellite capacity and the growing demand for bandwidth in broadband have influenced the major telecommunication providers[114] to invest in submarine fibre optic cables. As a result, submarine cable is now the most widely deployed technology in the Caribbean for international connectivity (Fonseca-Hoeve et al. 2017).

All three countries under consideration have at least two landing stations from two independent submarine cable systems. Access to multiple cables provides redundancy if one cable fails, and also increases competition, applying downward pressure on international capacity pricing. Table 7.2 provides an overview of Submarine Cable Systems available in Barbados, Jamaica, and T&T.

---

[114] There are only two significant players in the telecommunications industry in the Caribbean which own submarine cable infrastructure: Cable & Wireless and Digicel (Fonseca-Hoeve et al. 2017).

Table 7.2: Submarine Cable Systems

Country	No. of Landing Points	Submarine Cable Systems
Barbados	2	Eastern Caribbean Fiber System (ECFS) and Southern Caribbean Fiber (SCF)
Jamaica	5	ALBA-1, Cayman-Jamaica Fiber System, Colombia-Florida Subsea Fiber (CFX-1), East-West and Fibralink
Trinidad and Tobago	5	Americas-II, Eastern Caribbean Fiber System (ECFS), ECLink, Southern Caribbean Fiber (SCF), Suriname-Guyana Submarine Cable System (SG-SCS)

Source: Fonseca-Hoeve et al. (2017)

7.4.1.1 Infrastructure and Operators in Barbados

The telecommunications industry in Barbados was initially a monopoly, with Cable & Wireless (Barbados) Ltd. providing telephone services. In 2001 the Government of Barbados (GOB) and Cable & Wireless signed a memorandum of understanding to implement a phased liberalization of the country's telecommunications industry.

> *The process of liberalisation began with the mobile sector and required Cable & Wireless' issuance of the first Reference Interconnection Offer (RIO) – Mobile on August 22, 2003. This was followed by the RIO – Domestic Fixed Wireless filed January 22, 2004 and RIO – International filed July 30, 2004.* (FTC 2011, 1).

Digicel entered the Barbados telecommunications market in February 2004 providing mobile phone services. Eventually, Digicel was granted licences to provide fixed line fiber-based services, i.e. landline telephony, broadband, and television.

In 2015, a merger occurred between C&W, then trading as LIME, and Columbus Communications Inc. (CCI), then trading as FLOW, resulting in a less competitive market structure in the provision of fixed line telephone services (FTC 2017). However, the mobile phone industry remains competitive as Ozone Communications (Ozone) and Sunbeach Communications have also been granted mobile phone licences to provide these services. The internet service market is also competitive as Ace Communications, and Wi-Net Inc. also compete with the aforementioned firms in the provision of internet services. Table 7.3 provides an overview of the firms in the Barbados Telecommunications industry by market segment.

Table 7.3: Telecommunications Companies in Barbados

Internet Service Providers
Cable and Wireless (Barbados) Ltd. – Caribsurf (LIME)
Sunbeach Communications Inc.
Columbus Communications (Barbados) Ltd. trading as Flow
Ace Communications Inc.
Wi-Net Inc.
Digicel (Barbados) Ltd.
Domestic Landline
Cable and Wireless (Barbados) Limited trading as LIME
Cellular/Mobile Providers
Cable and Wireless (Barbados) Limited trading as LIME
Digicel (Barbados) Limited
Sunbeach Communications Inc.
Ozone Wireless (Barbados) Inc.

Source: Telecommunications Unit (2017)

With regard to internet subscriptions, there has been growth in the number of fixed broadband subscriptions in Barbados over the 2011 to 2017 period. Table 7.4 provides an overview of the internet statistics for Barbados.

Table 7.4: Internet Statistics for Barbados

Service	**2017**	**2016**	**2015**	**2014**	**2013**	**2012**	**2011**
Fixed Internet subscribers		0	0	0	628	885	1,258
Fixed-Broadband Internet Subscriptions	89,340	86,887	66,969	23,999	67,798	66,884	60,643
DSL subscribers		0	0	52,730	57,121	57,592	58,538
International Internet Bandwidth (Mb/s) Used	50,195	50,397	54,148	80,750	11,110	8,275	7,505
International Internet Bandwidth (Mb/s) Lit	90,500	79,032					

Source: Telecommunications Unit (2017)

7.4.1.2 Infrastructure and Operators in Jamaica

Jamaica's telecommunications industry was initially a monopoly, dominated by Cable and Wireless Jamaica (C&WJ). C&WJ was initially granted 5 exclusive licences by the Government of Jamaica (GOJ) in 1988 for the provision of telecommunications services, each for 25 years and with an option for renewal for an additional 25 years granted to the company. However, by 1999, due to widespread public dissatisfaction of the poor state of the country's telecommunications services, the government decided to liberalize the country's telecommunications industry, a task which was completed by 2003 (SMA 2005).

As Jamaica's telecommunications industry became liberalized, several firms applied for telecommunications licences. In fact, over the 2001 to 2005 period there were approximately 200 applications for licences to provide services in areas such as: international service providers (internet), domestic carriers, international voice and data transmitters, ISP cable providers, and domestic voices (Golding et al. 2012).

In 2018 there was only two primary mobile providers, FLOW (formerly LIME and CWJ), and Digicel.[115] Both Flow and Digicel offer mobile, fixed broadband and cable television services. There were approximately 121,500 broadband subscribers in Jamaica as of June 2013 (Capacity Media 2015).

7.4.1.3 Infrastructure and Operators in Trinidad and Tobago

Like many other Caribbean countries, the telecommunications industry in T&T was a monopoly. The Telecommunications Services Company in Trinidad and Tobago (TSTT) was the sole provider of telecommunications services in the country. In 2005, the regulator, the Telecommunications Authority of Trinidad and Tobago (TATT) granted licences to Digicel and Laqtel. On April 6, 2006, the wireless network of Digicel (Trinidad and Tobago) Limited was interconnected to the wireless and fixed networks of

[115] There were multiple players in Jamaica's mobile industry, but the market became a duopoly in 2011 (Capacity Media 2015). Claro had entered Jamaica's telecommunications industry in 2008 providing mobile phone services, as well as a fixed wireless and broadband service on the CDMA network in response to Digicel's entry into the El Salvador and Honduras markets. In 2011, Claro agreed to sell its Jamaica operations to Digicel, and in return Digicel agreed to sell its El Salvador and Honduras operations to American Movil (the parent company of Claro) (Golding et al. 2012).

TSTT, effectively introducing competition to end the monopolistic structure of T&T's telecommunications services industry (Sinanna et al. 2008).[116]

Presently in 2018, the TATT has authorized 11 companies to provide some form of telecommunications services in T&T. Table 7.5 provides a summary.

Table 7.5: Telecommunications Service Companies in T&T Authorized by TATT

Telephone (landline)
Columbus Communications Trinidad Limited (Flow)
TSTT
Digicel
Telephone (mobile)
TSTT-Bmobile
Digicel
Broadband Internet
Air Link Communications Limited
Flow
Digicel
Diversified Technologies Limited
Green Dot Limited
Lisa Communications Limited
Massy Communications Limited
Massy Technologies (Infocom) Trinidad Limited
Open Telecom Limited
RVR International Limited
TSTT-Blink

TSTT is the largest provider of telecommunications services to residential and commercial clients in T&T. Since the liberalization of the telecommunications industry in 2005, TSTT has expanded its business from

[116] Five companies (Digicel, Laqtel, Cingular, NatTel and Telecom Caribe) initially met the TATT's pre-qualification phase and proceeded to an auction phase to provide telecommunications services. However, only Digicel and Laqtel saw the auction through to the end (T&T Newsday 2005).

being a landline, internet and mobile provider to offering services such as voice, high speed broadband internet/data services, security and alarm monitoring services; and internet-protocol-TV (IPTV) services. In January 2014, TSTT launched a pilot project "Gigabit Community", which configures the company's network and uses fibre optic connections to allow for fibre optic access speeds of up to 1 gigabit per second (PRTT 2014).

With regard to internet subscriptions, in 2016 there were approximately 255,600 fixed internet subscriptions in T&T. This was a 9.5% reduction in the number of internet subscriptions, compared to the 279,800 recorded subscriptions in 2015. There has been a general shift from narrowband subscriptions towards broadband subscriptions over the 2012 to 2016 period. This can be clearly seen in Figure 7.2.

The number of fixed internet subscriptions can be further subdivided into residential and business categories. As can be seen in Figure 7.3, over the 2012 to 2015 period, there was strong growth in the number of residential subscriptions. However, as the economy experienced economic recession in 2016, there was a 9% decline in the number of residential subscriptions. The total business subscriptions also contracted in the recessionary period, but only by 4.1% (2015-2016).

Residential broadband subscriptions can be grouped into the following Internet speed categories: i) equal to or above 10 Mbps; ii) 2 Mbps to less than 10 Mbps; and iii) 256 kbps to less than 2 Mbps. As can be seen in Figure 7.4 there has been a general shift away from the 256 to 2 Mbps internet speed category towards faster speeds. The most popular category is internet speeds above 10 Mbps.

Figure 7.2: Fixed Narrowband and Broadband Subscriptions

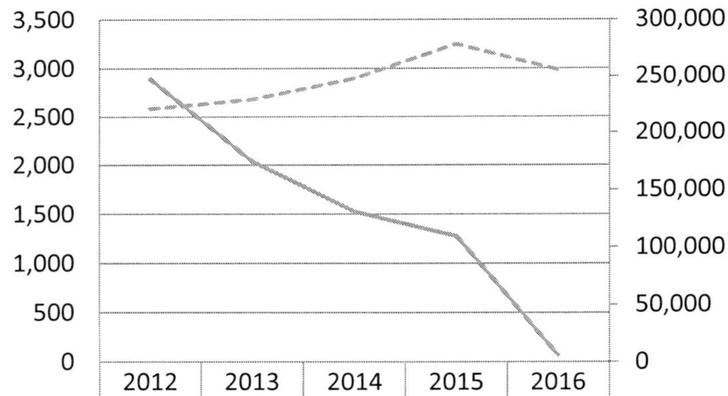

	2012	2013	2014	2015	2016
Fixed narrowband subscriptions	2,892	2,039	1,526	1,278	68
Fixed broadband subscriptions	221,300	229,600	248,100	278,500	255,600

Source: TATT (2017)

Figure 7.3: Total Residential and Business Subscriptions

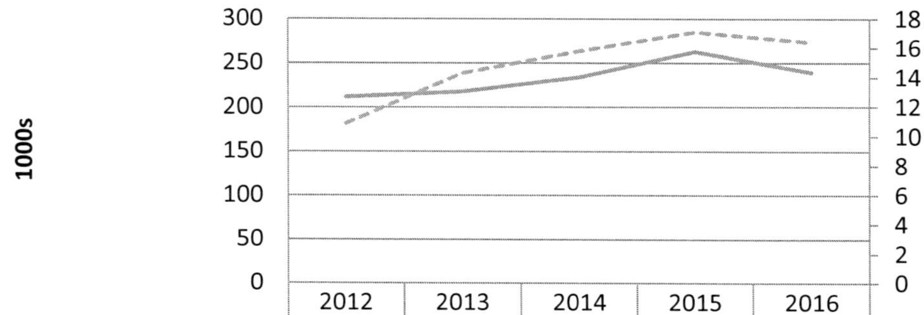

	2012	2013	2014	2015	2016
Total residential subscriptions (narrowband + broadband)	211.6	217.4	233.9	262.7	239.2
Total business subscriptions (narrowband + broadband)	10.9	14.3	15.8	17.1	16.4

Source: TATT (2017)

Figure 7.4: Number of Residential Broadband Subscriptions ('000s)

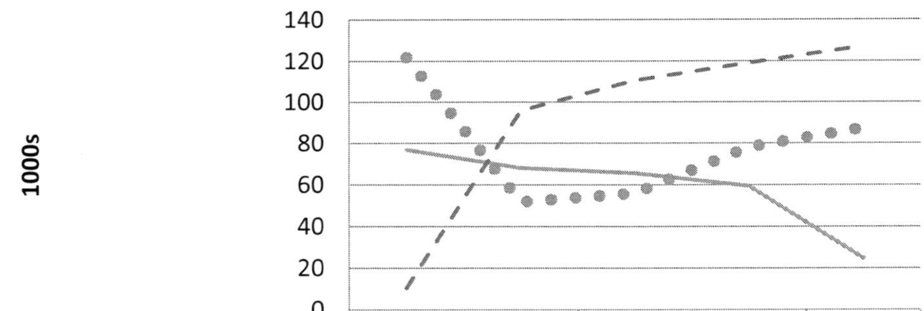

	2012	2013	2014	2015	2016
256 kbps to less than 2 Mbps	76.9	68.1	65.6	59.5	24.7
2 Mbps to less than 10 Mbps	121.8	51.8	56	78.1	87.3
Equal to or above 10 Mbps	10.5	95.9	110.5	119.1	127.1

Source: TATT (2017)

There were 239.1 thousand residential fixed broadband subscriptions,[117] and 16.5 business fixed broadband subscriptions[118] in T&T in 2016. Although some residential and business users would have more than one computer and more than one person using a computer, it is safe to assume there are at least 255,600 computer users in T&T. The TATT 2013 Digital Divide Survey revealed that 70.51% of households in T&T had access to a computer, and 44.6% of households in T&T had access to the internet in 2013 (TATT 2013).

In order to identify the possibility of a digital divide,[119] the International Telecommunications Union's (ITU) analytical tools, namely the Digital Access Index (DAI); the Digital Opportunity Index (DOI); and the ICT Development Index (IDI), can be used in this regard.[120]

Table 7.3: DAI, DOI, and IDI

	DAI	DOI	IDI
2014	0.9217	0.7194	5.5582

Source: CSTD (2018)

Although there is room for improvement in the aspect of infrastructure, T&T has:

- widespread availability of communication services, access centres and networked computers;
- the existence of effective competition among communication and information services providers;
- affordable and reliable network access;
- a reliable electricity supply for e-Business critical operations; and
- the existence of any incubator facilities/IT Parks.

---

[117] 127.1 + 87.3 + 24.7 = 239.1.

[118] 255.6 – 239.1 = 16.5.

[119] The digital divide is a gap between those that have access to computers and the internet, and those that do not.

[120] The theoretical ranges of the DAI and DOI are from 0 to 1, while the range of the IDI is from 0 to 10. For the DAI and the DOI, values closer to 1 represent no digital divide, and values closer to 0 suggest a higher digital divide. For the IDI, values closer to 10 represent no digital divide, and values closer to 0 suggest a higher digital divide.

7.4.2 Regulation

Most countries in the Caribbean were initially served by a single telecommunications company for all their telecommunications services for decades. However, the overhaul of the international trading system, more specifically the World Trade Organization (WTO) Basic Telecommunications Agreement, led to new arrangements where countries could no longer protect their service industries, telecommunications included.[121] As Barbados, Jamaica, and T&T were all signatories to the Agreement, they committed to liberalizing their telecommunications sector. Thus, they agreed to gradually open their basic telecommunications (e.g. fixed and mobile telephony, real-time data transmission, internet access, and the sale of leased-circuit capacity) sector to external competition. Moreover, they agreed to create regulatory bodies to help facilitate fair competition between companies in the telecommunications sector.

7.4.2.1 Regulation in Barbados

In Barbados, the telecommunications industry is regulated through two bodies. The first is the Minister responsible for Telecommunications, who provides the overall policy direction for the telecommunications industry, awards licences, and determines which telecommunications services will be regulated. The Telecommunications Unit residing in the Ministry responsible for Telecommunications works to help implement the work of the Minister.

The second major body is the Fair Trading Commission (FTC), which has the jurisdiction to enforce policies established by the Minister with responsibility for Telecommunications pursuant to the Telecommunications Act of 2001. The FYC also has the authority to regulate competition between telecommunications companies in Barbados, establish and administer mechanisms for the regulation of telecommunications interconnection tariffs (which in turn affect the rates for customers), and hear and arbitrate over complaints made by customers who have tried and failed to resolve their complaints with their telecommunications service provider.

---

[121] Commitments in telecommunications services were first made during the eighth round of multilateral trade negotiations (Uruguay Round: 1986-94), mostly in value-added services. In post-Uruguay Round negotiations (1994-97), WTO members negotiated specific sectors (financial services, telecommunications, and movement of natural persons) and they were able to reach agreement in basic telecommunications services.

7.4.2.2 Regulation in Jamaica

There are four entities involved in the regulation of Jamaica's telecommunications industry. They include:

i) The Office of Utilities Regulation (OUR), which was formally established by the Office of Utilities Regulation Act of 1995 as the entity with the authority to regulate Jamaica's electricity, water and sewerage, and telecommunications sectors. OUR regulates Jamaica's telecommunications sector through the guidance provided by the Telecommunications Act of 2000. As a result, the OUR mandate with regard to the telecommunications industry includes the i) receiving and processing of applications for telecommunications licences; ii) granting of telecommunications licences; and iii) encouraging of competition in the telecommunications sector.
ii) The Spectrum Management Authority (SMA), which was established pursuant to the Telecommunications Act of 2000. The SMA is the country's national regulator for the radio frequency spectrum and is an advisory body to the Minister with principal responsibility for the telecommunications sector.
iii) The Broadcasting Commission is an independent national statutory agency in Jamaica with responsibility for regulating free-to-air television, broadcast radio and subscriber television (Cable) services to ensure their operation at appropriate levels in relation to technical, programming, and service standards. Thus, the Broadcasting Commission administers the Television and Sound Broadcasting Regulations (TSBR) stipulated in the Broadcasting and Radio Re-Diffusion Act (BRRA) of 1986.
iv) The Fair Trading Commission is an independent national statutory agency in Jamaica with the mandate to implement the Fair Competition Act (FCA) of 1993 and facilitate fair competition in business in Jamaica.

7.4.2.3 Regulation in Trinidad and Tobago

The telecommunications industry in T&T was relatively unregulated until 2001 when the GORTT introduced the Telecommunications Act. The Act created scope for the liberalization of T&T's telecommunications industry by introducing a regulatory framework, to monitor and protect against abusive anti-competitive behaviour by any supplier or suppliers dominating defined telecommunication markets. The Act also established the Telecommunications Authority of Trinidad and Tobago (TATT) as the regulator of the telecommunications industry. TATT commenced operations from July 2004 after the proclamation and full passage of the Telecommunications Act of 2001 and the Telecommunications (Amendment) Act of 2004 (PRTT 2014). TATT has the authority to:

- grant telecommunications licences;
- classify telecommunications networks;
- determine the universal service obligations (USO) for telecommunications services throughout T&T;
- establish national telecommunications and broadcasting industry standards;
- regulate and manage the use of the radio frequency spectrum; and
- test and certify telecommunications and broadcasting equipment to ensure compliance with (i) international standards, and (ii) environmental health and safety standards, including electromagnetic radiation and emissions.

7.4.3 Educational and Technical Skills Potential

In economics, it is well noted that labour is required to facilitate production. Therefore, it is reasonable to expect that labour would be required to facilitate the development of the e-commerce sector. The e-commerce sector would require a number of information communication and technology (ICT) based skills, including computers and information systems managers, computer systems analysts, computer engineers, computer support specialists, database administrators, computer scientists and computer programmers. In order for individuals to acquire the technical ICT based skills, they would be required to pursue training in tertiary institutions offering ICT educational programmes. Fortunately, such training is offered in tertiary institutions in Barbados, Jamaica, and T&T, the CARICOM member states under consideration.

7.4.3.1 Educational and Technical Skills Potential in Barbados

In Barbados, the main tertiary institutions where individuals may obtain technical training in information technology are the Community College (BCC), and the University of the West Indies Cave Hill Campus. BCC provides:

- Short-term (Certificate Courses)
    - Multimedia Applications;
    - Visual Basic;

    - Computer Communications and Networking;
    - C, C++ Programming;
    - Web Page Authoring;
    - Data Warehousing; and
    - Database Management Design.
- Associate Degree in Arts/Science (Majors) in Information Technology;
- Associate Degree in Applied Science in Computer Studies; and
- Certificate in Information Technology.

The University of the West Indies (UWI) Cave Hill Campus offers BSc programmes in Computer Science, and in Information Technology, and MSc programmes in Computing Research, and Information Technology.

7.4.3.2 Educational and Technical Skills Potential in Jamaica

In Jamaica, several tertiary institutions offer certificate, associate and full degree programmes in ICT. The main institutions include the HEART College of Innovation and Technology, the INFOSERV Institute of Technology, the School of Computing and Information Technology, the University of the West Indies (Mona Campus), and the Vector Technology Institute.

The HEART College of Innovation and Technology offers:

- National Vocational Qualification of Jamaica (NVQJ)[122]
    - Multimedia Production (NVQJ Level 2)
    - Website Design (NVQJ Level 3)
    - Software Programming (NVQJ Level 3)
    - Digital Animation (NVQJ Level 3)
    - Network Administration (NVQJ Level 3)
    - System Administration (NVQJ Level 3)
    - Network Engineering (NVQJ Level 4)

The INFOSERV Institute of Technology offers certificate courses in

- CompTIA A+ certification;
- Website design;
- E-Commerce Designer webmaster; and

[122] NVQJ is a certificate of competence in a technical vocational area that is recognized island wide in Jamaica.

- Computer networking.

The University of Technology Jamaica, School of Computing and Information Technology offers:

- Certificate in Computer Studies;
- ASc in Computer Studies;
- BSc in Animation Production and Development;
- BSc in Computer Science;
- BSc in Information Technology.

The University of the West Indies, Mona Campus offers:

- BSc in Software Engineering.

The Vector Technology Institute offers:

- International Certificates
    - Cisco Certified Network Associate – CCNA;
    - Cisco Certified Network Professional – CCNP;
    - CompTIA A+ certification;
    - CompTIA Security+ certification;
    - CompTIA Network+ certification;
    - CompTIA Linux+ certification.
- Diploma and Certificate Programmes
    - ASc in Software Programming;
    - Diploma in Software Programming;
    - Diploma for Cybersecurity;
    - Webpage Design and Development (Certificate);
    - Mobile Apps Development (Certificate).
- Degree Programmes
    - BSc in Technology Management;
    - BSc in Information Communication and Technology.

7.4.3.3 Educational and Technical Skills Potential in Trinidad and Tobago

There are several tertiary educational institutions operating in T&T which provide training in ICT. For instance, the University of the West Indies (UWI), Department of Computing and Information Technology offers BSc programmes in Computer Science, Computer Science and Management,

Information Technology, and Information Technology and Management. The department also offers an MSc in Computer Science and an MSc in Data Science, along with MPhil and PhD research degrees in several research areas in computing.

The UWI's Department of Electrical and Computer Engineering offers a BSc in Electrical and Computer Engineering, an MASc in Electrical and Computer Engineering, along with MPhil and PhD research degrees in Electrical and Computer Engineering.

The University of Trinidad and Tobago (UTT) offers a diploma, a BASc, and an MSc in Computer Engineering. The National Energy Skills Centre (NESC) offers a 3-year diploma in Information Technology Network Specialization.

The School of Business and Computer Science (SBCS) offers a range of Microsoft certified courses, as well as a BSc in Computing and Information Science and an MSc in Operational Cyber Security, both from the University of Greenwich.

There is also a multitude of tertiary institutions serving as centres for the offering of degrees in ICT. Thus, since many of these tertiary institutions have been producing graduates in ICT for over 10 years, there is a pool of people in T&T that are highly trained in ICT.

7.4.4 Legislative Framework

In 1996, the United Nations Commission on International Trade Law (UNCITRAL) adopted a Model Law on Electronic Commerce (MLEC) which purports to facilitate e-commerce by providing national legal authorities with a set of internationally acceptable rules aimed at removing legal obstacles to e-commerce.

The MLEC introduced three basic principles which serve as the foundational elements of e-commerce law:

- Non-discrimination
  The principle of non-discrimination is required to ensure that a document would not be denied legal effect, validity or enforceability solely on the grounds that it is in an electronic format.

- Technological Neutrality
  The principle of technological neutrality requires that e-commerce laws are to be drafted in a general manner, such that they would not have to be redrafted every time technology changes in order for them to be applicable.
- Functional Equivalence
  The principle of functional equivalence outlines criteria which allow electronic communications to be considered equivalent to paper-based communications. For example, the concepts of "original", "copy", "signed", etc., which are applied to paper documents, are also applied to electronic documents.

Apart from the three basic principles of the MLEC, any e-commerce law should contain provisions to

- Protect consumers' rights and indicate the consumer's responsibilities. In order to achieve this:
  - Consumers[123] should be provided with clear and sufficient information regarding a good or service so that they can make a well-informed choice when purchasing goods and services.
  - Vendors[124] should be required to clearly disclose all terms and conditions of sale.
  - Vendors should be required to state all the fees, extra charges, and discounts applicable to the sale.
  - There should be a framework in place for consumers to resolve their disputes if they have any problem with a transaction with a vendor.
  - Vendors should not transmit the personal information of their customers to any third party unless they have received consent from their customer to do so.
  - All transactions between consumers and vendors should be treated as a contract.
  - There should be default rules for contract formation.
  - All vendors should be obligated to deliver on the goods or service they agreed to deliver in such contract.
  - All vendors should be mandated to promptly refund consumer payments for unauthorized transactions or for transactions in

[123] The consumer is the economic agent purchasing the good or service.
[124] The vendor is the economic agent selling the good or service.

which consumers did not receive the good or service that they paid for.
    - In instances where dispute arises, electronic documents should be admissible as evidence in court.
- Address cross-border disputes, including guidelines to determine the relevant enforcement body for the handling of cross-jurisdictional disputes relating to electronic commerce, where the trader and consumer are located in different jurisdictions. Furthermore, there should be a legal framework in place to recognize electronic documents and certificates in domestic/home countries, especially where the electronic documents and certificates originate from outside of the domestic/home countries. Note: the UNCITRAL Model Law on Electronic Signatures states that electronic certificates issued outside a domestic/home country shall have the same legal effects as domestic certificates.
- Protect user privacy, and address cyber-piracy, infringement of copyright, trademark infringement and computer hacking. As a result, the appropriate law should address online security, privacy, computer misuse, and consumer protection, and provide measures for the protection of electronic records, signatures and transactions.

The CARICOM member states considered in this chapter have all considered drafting and implementing e-commerce legislation. The following subsections provide a summary.

7.4.4.1 Legislative Framework in Barbados

In Barbados, in 2001, the GOB passed the Electronics Transaction Act, which provides the legal basis to regulate electronic financial transactions in the country. The Act establishes a legal framework for the conducting of e-commerce and the processing of electronic transactions in Barbados. Additionally, the Act provides regulations to address concerns over privacy, security, and contract enforcement. More specifically, the Act makes provision for:

- the recognition of electronic records;
- the recognition of electronic signatures;
- the retention of electronic records;
- the formation and validation of contracts;
- the recognition of parties in electronic transactions, contracts, and records;
- the regulations for encryption;

- the restrictions for the disclosure of information;
- the liability of intermediaries;
- establishing procedures to address unlawful and defamatory information;
- the liabilities of parties; and
- the penalties of parties.

While the Act is ambitious, it does not state the rights and responsibilities of consumers and vendors, and makes no mention of any framework to address cross-border disputes.

7.4.4.2 Legislative Framework in Jamaica

In 2006 the GOJ passed the Electronic Transactions Act, which provided the legal framework for secured electronic commerce. The Electronic Transactions Act sets out the legal framework by which e-commerce is governed in Jamaica. More specifically, it allows for:

- the recognition of electronic records;
- the legal recognition of electronic signatures;
- the recognition of electronic contracts.

In 2013, the Bank of Jamaica (BOJ) introduced the Guidelines for Electronic Retail Payment Services as a regulatory framework for electronic payments. The Guidelines established:

- the authorization requirements by the BOJ;
- the standards which must be observed by electronic retail payment service providers;
- the minimum financial capital requirements for electronic retail payment service providers;
- the operational requirements for electronic retail payment service providers;
- the requirement for electronic retail payment service providers to establish a framework that:
    - protects the privacy of consumers' information;
    - facilitates secure electronic transactions; and
    - contains appropriate dispute resolution mechanisms; and
- the requirement for electronic retail payment service providers to comply with the BOJ's anti-money laundering (AML) and counter financing of terrorism (CFT) requirements.

7.4.4.3 Legislative Framework in Trinidad and Tobago

In T&T, the government has drafted the Electronic Transactions Act and the Data Protection Act, to govern electronic transactions and data protection respectively. The Electronic Transactions Act makes provision for:

- the legal recognition of electronic transactions;
- the formation and validity of contracts for electronic transactions;
- the recognition of electronic signatures;
- the recognition of electronic authentication service providers;
- the liabilities of intermediaries and telecommunication services providers;
- the rights of consumers and the need for consumer protection;
- the prohibiting of the transmission of false and misleading information; and
- the establishment of penalties for parties.

The Data Protection Act makes provision for:

- the establishing of an Information Commissioner;
- the establishing of the powers of the Information Commissioner and its office;
- the protection of personal data by public bodies;
- the protection of personal data by the private sector;
- the cross-border disclosure of personal information;
- the prohibiting of the transmission of false and misleading information;
- the violation of whistle-blowing provisions;
- establishing what practices would serve as an offence;
- the penalties of parties committing offences; and
- the jurisdiction of the court.
-

However, there is the need for a Cybercrime Act, which prohibits and criminalizes cybercrime.

7.4.5 Policy Framework

Lack of preparedness, awareness, and the need for training may constrain the widespread adoption of e-commerce in many countries. To this end, a government may play a pivotal role in developing local capacity and creating an enabling environment to encourage e-commerce in its country.

The following subsections outline the e-commerce policies considered in Barbados, Jamaica, and T&T.

7.4.5.1 Policy Framework in Barbados

In Barbados, the government has recognized that electronic commerce is rapidly becoming the principal means by which transactions are conducted and changing the manner in which businesses and consumers interact. To this end, the Government of Barbados intends to develop a national e-commerce strategy which rests on the following four pillars:

- firstly, the reliance on the Electronics Transactions Act of 2001 as the legislative framework to regulate and govern electronic transactions in Barbados;
- secondly, the enhancement of Barbados' telecommunications sector so that low cost high speed internet and other telecommunications services would be readily available to consumers and potential vendors;
- thirdly, the development of an adequate banking framework to facilitate e-commerce; and
- fourthly, the adoption of e-commerce services by the government (MIIDCSBD 2018).

In 2006 the Government of Barbados also developed the "Draft E-Government Strategy." The policy focused on advocating how the government may integrate e-commerce and ICT into its routine administrative systems.

7.4.5.2 Policy Framework in Jamaica

In Jamaica, in 2003 the government developed an e-commerce policy labelled the "Electronic Transactions Policy" to create an enabling environment for e-commerce transactions (MCSTJ 2003). The Policy advocated for:

- the electronic marketplace in Jamaica to be predictable with well-established e-commerce legislation;
- the establishment of technology neutral regulations to govern Jamaica's e-commerce;
- the development of sufficient infrastructure in Jamaica to facilitate the use of e-commerce by all user groups;

- the public sector to take the lead in the utilization and development of e-commerce in the country; and
- the establishment of principles to protect the privacy and personal information of consumers.

In 2014, the GOJ also developed a National Strategy for Information and Communication Technology (ICT) which incorporates a policy framework for electronic transactions (UWI Mona 2014). In fact, the National ICT Strategy was based on the following principles:

- the e-commerce environment would be predictable with a well-established legal and economic framework;
- the e-commerce environment would be accessible to all potential user groups;
- the public sector would take a lead role in utilizing e-commerce to encourage its greater use in the country; and
- priority should be given to ensure security in e-commerce transactions and protect the privacy of consumers' personal information.

7.4.5.3 Policy Framework in Trinidad and Tobago

With regard to the policy framework, the GORTT considered the e-commerce agenda in earlier years, producing various reports, namely:

- the National e-Commerce Secretariat (NeCS) Committee report (2003);
- Fast Forward (2003-2008);
- the Policy Framework for e-Business in Trinidad and Tobago (2008);
- SmarTT (2014-2018);
- Fast Forward II (Draft 2017); and
- the National E-Commerce Strategy (2017-2021).

The National e-Commerce Secretariat (NeCS) Committee report was prepared by the named committee, with the mandate to examine T&T's digital environment and recommend a strategy for the country to capture the benefits from e-commerce. The report made a number of notable comments.

1. At that time (2003), the report highlighted that there was very little hope for the advancement of the e-commerce agenda in T&T without drastic improvements in the telecommunications infrastructure.

Furthermore, there was a strong recommendation for the improvement of the cost and bandwidth of the telecommunications infrastructure in T&T.

2. The NeCS report recognised that SMEs form the employment backbone of T&T's economy and face unique challenges with respect to access to the resources and expertise of e-commerce. Thus, the report recommended that government should play a pro-active role in helping the SMEs by providing "incubator" assistance where practical.
3. The report recommended that the government should use internet-based technology and transform itself into an "e-government", where several of its administrative services are offered online.
4. The report also recommended that the GORTT establish "Community Access Centers", in order to address the digital divide and ensure that all people residing in the country could have access to computers and the internet.
5. The report advocated for the clarification of market place rules, which will ensure that the rules which govern commercial transactions in cyberspace would be clear and available to all market participants.

There has been significant advancement in the telecommunications sector in T&T from 2003 to the present in 2018. Indeed, there has been improvement in the cost and bandwidth of telecommunications in the country over the period. Thus, internet speeds are relatively fast, cheap, and reliable.

Fast Forward (2003-2008) constituted a national connectivity roadmap which sought to integrate technology throughout communities, businesses and government in T&T. During the term of Fast Forward, the notable achievements were

- the establishment of TATT in 2004;
- increasing the competition in T&T's telecommunications industry;
- the removal of all duties and taxes on computers and computing equipment;
- the creation of TTconnect, an e-government portal;
- the equipping of all public libraries and secondary schools with computers and high speed access to the internet by 2007; and
- the incorporation of information technology into the secondary school systems (CSTD 2018).

After the Fast Forward (2003-2008) term expired, the country continued to achieve notable policy induced progress in the ICT sector. This includes:

- In 2009 a single online government portal was established as part of the thrust to establish an integrated channel for government service delivery.
- In 2011, another online government portal, TTBizLink was created for businesses. TTBizLink allowed individuals and companies to apply for various permits and licences, register businesses, and conduct other trade-related activities via a single online window.
- In 2009, iGovTT, the national ICT company (formerly the National ICT Centre), was established. iGovTT was given the responsibility for implementing ICT initiatives, programmes and projects in the country.

SmarTT (2014-2018) was a national ICT plan for T&T. The policy document asserted that it was focusing on development in 5 thematic areas: Theme #1: Innovation and Human Capital Development; Theme #2: Access and Digital Inclusion; Theme #3: e-Business and ICT Sector Development; Theme #4: Infrastructure Development; and Theme #5: e-Government.

In the aforementioned thematic areas, progress has been made under Theme #4: Infrastructure Development. SmarTT sought to provide

> *a future-proof broadband infrastructure capable of delivering access speeds of 10 Mbps and above to the population by 2018.* (CSTD 2018, 7).

Clearly, as can be seen in Figure 7.3, this goal was achieved as there was an increase in fixed broadband subscriptions for speeds greater than 10 Mbps. Additionally, in April 2013, T&T established its first Internet Exchange Point (IXP), which allowed for:

- the reduction in the average per-bit delivery cost of an Internet Service Provider's (ISP's) service;
- reduced latency for local traffic;
- improved download speeds for locally hosted content;
- improved fault tolerance in the local network;
- higher local bandwidth; and
- improved security for local data transfers.

However, mere "lip service" was paid to Theme #1: Innovation and Human Capital Development; Theme #2: Access and Digital Inclusion; Theme #3:

e-business and ICT Sector Development; and Theme #5: e-Government, as there was an implementation deficit.

Fast Forward II is the GORTT ICT plan for the 2017 to 2021 period. The plan aspires to enhance ICT development in T&T, by focusing on:

- improving connectivity;
- increasing human capacity;
- enhancing public service delivery;
- fostering economic development; and
- advancing environmental and societal benefit.

Under Fast Forward II, in order to improve connectivity, there are currently plans for iGovTT to pursue a public private partnership (ppp) for a wired National Broadband Backbone (NBB) which will accommodate increases in traffic at speeds of 10 Mbps and above. Once implemented, the backbone will improve broadband access and transmission. Moreover, the country is seeking to install a Root Server which would:

i) solve Domain Name Server (DNS) queries faster;
ii) reduce latency; and
iii) result in savings in transit costs for ISPs as DNS queries can be done locally.

The National E-Commerce Strategy (2017-2021) focuses mainly on the development of an e-commerce framework in T&T. The policy document outlines notable goals:

- the development of a comprehensive and effective regulatory environment for e-commerce; and
- the implementation of an Electronic Funds Transfer (EFT) Framework.

7.5 Challenges to the Extensive Use of E-commerce

Many reports often cite factors related to technological e-readiness such as access to computers, cheap and reliable access to the internet, the availability of technical human resources, and the existence of an adequate legal framework as the main impediments towards the widespread use of e-commerce in developing countries (Lawrence and Usman 2010; White et al. 2014; El-fitouri 2015).

T&T's National E-Commerce Strategy (2017-2021) highlights that the main factors that prevented the proliferation of e-commerce in the country include

- *Uncoordinated and unsustained efforts by the public sector entities responsible for promoting e-commerce.*
- *Lack of implementation of the legal framework to encourage and protect businesses and consumers using e-commerce.*
- *Lack of awareness of the benefits to businesses and consumers regarding e-commerce.* (GORTT MTI 2017, 6-7).

However, the main impediments to the more widespread use of e-commerce in Barbados, Jamaica, and T&T include:

1. The limited technical and financial capacity for SMEs to develop their own e-commerce website
   As previously mentioned, SMEs can either develop a website for themselves or hire a professional website developer. In the case of the former, if the SME lacks programming skills, they can easily use a WYSIWYG editor to build their website. However, a secure system within the website is needed to facilitate electronic transactions. This would require extensive knowledge about programming and encryption, skills that would be acquired from a Computer Science degree. It is highly unlikely that the average SME in Barbados, Jamaica, and T&T would have the knowledge and skill to create a secure system within their website for electronic transactions. As a result, they would need to hire a competent professional. This carries a cost, which some very small-scale SMEs would not be able to cover from their business finances.
2. The absence of any centralized e-commerce platform which connects buyers with sellers (both large scale and small scale) in the countries (Barbados, Jamaica, and T&T)
   In contrast to the United States where there are several websites that act as a platform to connect buyers with sellers, there is a scarcity of such platforms in the Caribbean. Recently, the Inter-American Development Bank (IDB) created Connect Americas, the first social network for businesses in the Americas. Connect Americas seeks to act as a platform that would bridge the suppliers, especially SMEs, with buyers in the Americas. Presently in 2018, Connect Americas reported that it had a total of 130,000 registered companies, of which 144 were in T&T, 111 were in Jamaica, and 49 were in Barbados. While Connect Americas is a commendable and bold step in the right direction, many consumers in the three CARICOM member states

under study are not aware of the website and its potential. Additionally, the website is not as user-friendly as Amazon and Ebay, two US-based online platforms.

3. The scepticism of consumers in buying products online from local SMEs
   Presently a few companies in Barbados, Jamaica, and T&T provide consumers with an option to pay for goods and services online. For instance, Flow customers can pay their internet, cable, and telephone bills online. While consumers have confidence in the security systems of the larger businesses, some consumers may have doubts about the security and privacy systems on the websites of SMEs. Moreover, consumers need to be assured that when they pay for a good or service on the website of an SME, they (the consumer) will not be robbed. Due to security and privacy doubts, many consumers may be reluctant to engage in electronic transactions on the websites of SMEs.
4. The inefficiencies in the local postal companies in delivering parcel mail
   A local postal courier company would be needed to deliver packages that are purchased locally and online. For instance, assume that a consumer in Point Fortin in South West Trinidad purchases an item via the internet from a supplier in Port of Spain, North West Trinidad. In such a case the supplier would be required to post the item locally to the consumer. If the selected postal courier company is inefficient in sorting and delivering items, there could be long delays before the consumer receives the purchased item. Even in the alternate scenario of cross-border transactions, an efficient postal courier company would be required to deliver mail in a timely fashion. Moreover, if the workers in the postal company steal, use, or tamper with the purchased products(s), this will destroy the confidence of both the consumer and the vendor in the integrity of the postal courier company. As a result, the consumer and the vendor would become reluctant to use the postal courier company to deliver parcels, which thus may hinder the development of domestic e-commerce activity.
5. Taxes on Online Purchases
   In 2016, the GORTT introduced a tax on online purchases.

6. Currency differences in the three countries (Barbados, Jamaica, and T&T)
   It is reasonable to expect cross-border transactions between three countries to be conducted in one common currency. However, Barbados, Jamaica, and T&T each have a different currency. Given that each of the aforementioned member states has a strong sovereignty stance, it is highly unlikely that a currency union will form between them. Furthermore, consumers and vendors may face difficulties in converting the currencies since domestic banks may be reluctant to convert a neighbouring CARICOM member state currency into the domestic currency. For example, banks in Barbados and Jamaica may be unwilling to convert the Trinidad and Tobago dollar (TTD) into their domestic currency. Rigidity in currency conversion could limit cross-border electronic transactions between the three countries.

7.6 Recommendations

Despite the challenges to e-commerce, domestic e-commerce as well as cross-border e-commerce can become a reality provided that the right enabling environment is provided. In this regard, there is a role for the government to use policy to help develop its domestic and regional cross-border e-commerce.

Development of an E-Commerce Platform

One of the challenges to the more widespread adoption of e-commerce is the limited ability of SMEs to develop a secure website that can facilitate electronic transactions. This problem can be addressed if the government takes the lead role and commissions a team of website developers to create a secure website that can serve as an e-commerce platform for the SMEs in their country. The e-commerce platform should:

- contain a system for vendors and consumers to register and create an account at any point in time for free;
- allow the suppliers to advertise their goods and/or service to a wide pool of buyers;
- allow consumers to compare the prices of different vendors;
- allow anyone visiting the website to easily see the products available for sale without having to register on the website;

- allow vendors and consumers to link a bank account or credit card account to their personal account on the e-commerce platform in order to facilitate electronic transactions;
- allow electronic transactions between venders and consumers;
- allow all transactions to be conducted in one common currency, perhaps the United States dollar (USD);
- allow the domestic currency to be converted to USD to facilitate transactions;
- allow consumers and vendors to link their account on the e-commerce platform to their PayPal account;
- allow for the sale of small quantities as well as large quantities of items;
- allow for shipping to any legitimate address in any of the three countries (Barbados, Jamaica, and T&T) in order to facilitate cross-border trade;
- allow consumers to track and trace the delivery of their goods;
- contain a secure system that is resistant to computer hacks and external internet-based threats;
- contain a consumer protection policy, which includes:
  - a refund policy if the item delivered is not in the condition that was advertised;
  - a refund policy if the consumer did not receive the item, and the vendor cannot produce evidence that the item was posted;
  - a warrantee policy;
  - a policy which prohibits vendors from transmitting the personal information of consumers to third parties without the consumer's consent.
- contain provisions for the consumer to cancel orders and receive a full reimbursement of their funds if they cancel the order before the product has been posted;
- contain a framework for consumers to resolve their disputes with vendors;
- contain a framework for consumers to evaluate vendors and the products purchased;
- contain a framework to protect vendors by the preventing of orders going through to the vendor without the consumer making full payment for the goods;
- contain a framework to assess the credibility of customers, and remove customers that develop a reputation for cancelling payments after orders have gone through to the vendor; and

- be very user friendly so that anyone would be able to use the platform without any special training.
-

In order for the e-commerce platform to attract the participation of a large pool of consumers and vendors, perhaps at its inception the government could consider persuading its SMEs registered with various public authorities (e.g. the Ministry of Industry, International Business, Commerce and Small Business Development in Barbados, the Ministry of Commerce, Science and Technology in Jamaica, and the Ministry of Trade and Industry in T&T) to sign up to the e-commerce platform. Although the respective Ministries should try to promote and encourage SMEs to sign up to the e-commerce platform throughout the year, an excellent opportunity to attract new SMEs would be during the business, commerce, and trade conferences which are held on an annual basis in each aforementioned member state.

Policy Needed to Improve the Postal Service Delivery and the Financial Viability of the USO Provider

Globally, the profitability of traditional mail is in decline for postal courier companies with the Universal Service Obligation (USO). The USO mandate for the national postal company requires that it must provide postal services to all citizens and areas in the country regardless of whether or not it is economical to do so. This is also the case for Barbados, Jamaica, and T&T. In fact, due to the lack of profitability in meeting the USO mandate, the national postal companies in each of the aforementioned countries, all receive subventions from their respective government.

In Barbados, the Barbados Postal Service (BPS), is the national postal courier with the USO. In an annex to the 2018-19 Estimates of Revenue and Expenditure, the GOB announced that the BPS was facing a B$7.1 million loss for the corresponding financial year, despite being allocated $29.7 million in subventions to cover its expenditure (Labs 2018). The BPS revenues have been in decline due to the decreasing volume of traditional letter mail, and the increase in competition from private postal courier companies.

In 2006, the BPS sought to improve its operational efficiency with the introduction of a new postal code service. The GOB also intends to improve the BPS operational efficiency and financial viability via the Postal Modernization Programme.

Any plan to improve the financial viability and operational efficiency of the BPS should seek to reduce unnecessary costs, and generate more revenue from the provision of new services. Given that the BPS has the USO, the increasing of tariffs will not be an option.

In Jamaica, the Post and Telecommunications Department (PTD) is responsible for meeting the country's USO. In 2000, the GOJ established the Postal Corporation of Jamaica (PCOJ) with the mandate of modernizing the PTD. However, an audit conducted by AGD Jamaica (2014) revealed that the PCOJ has been slow in delivering on this modernization of the operations of the PTD. Furthermore, the competition from private mail service providers has contributed to a continuous decline in mail volumes and revenue, making it more financially difficult to fulfill its USO and provide public postal services.

AGD Jamaica (2018) found that the PTD's ability to restrict its costs was limited since its labour bill was approximately 70% of its total operational expenditure. The retrenchment of labour to cut costs would significantly reduce the PTD's ability to meet its USO, and deliver mail in a timely manner.

There was also a disparity in the amount of mail handled and the per-unit costs of handling mail between the postal offices and the contracted postal agents. Figure 7.5 provides a summary.

Figure 7.5: The Per-unit Costs, and the Average Mail Volume of Post Offices and Postal Agents in Jamaica

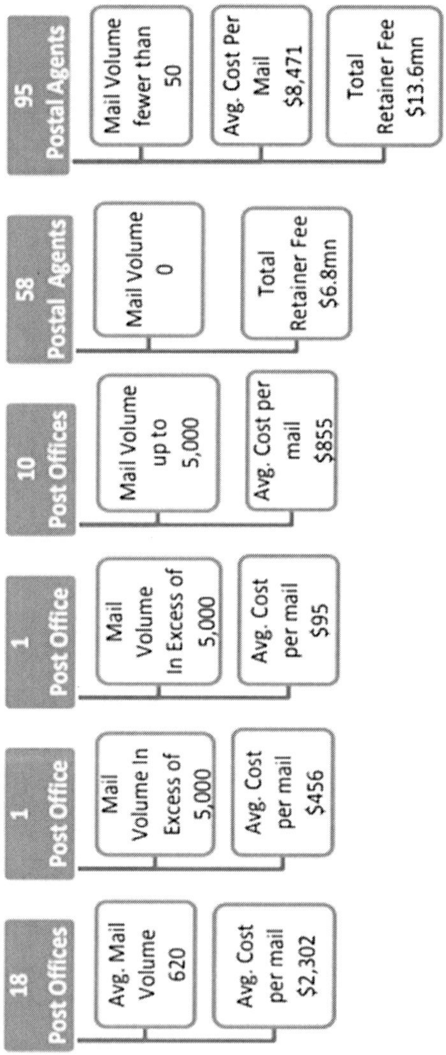

Source: AGD Jamaica (2018)

In order to improve the PTD's financial viability, AGD Jamaica (2018) recommended that:

i. The PTD should review its business model. It would be logical for the PTD to terminate its contractual arrangements with postal agents that handle little or no mail. In fact, the PTD terminated 15 of these arrangements over the 2012 to 2017 period. However, Figure 7.5 highlights that there are approximately 58 postal agents which handle no mail. Thus, there is still scope to terminate more contractual arrangements to reduce retainer fees and reduce overall costs.

ii. There should be an increased use of technology to improve operational costs.

iii. There should be increasing revenue generation from existing services. For instance, since the PTD already facilitates cross-border trade, revenue could be increased if greater effort was placed on increasing the volume of cross-border trade.

iv. New services should be introduced to help improve revenue generation.

In T&T, the Trinidad and Tobago Postal Corporation (TTPost) is the national, state-owned postal company that is responsible for the delivery of GORTT's Universal Service Obligation (USO) to provide high quality postal services, accessible throughout Trinidad and Tobago, at affordable prices.[125] The USO mandate for TTPost has profound implications, since some of TTPost's services are not profitable.[126] Furthermore, the proliferation of private postal courier companies in T&T has resulted in T&T gradually experiencing a decline in its mail volume, and a decline in its revenue.[127] The profitability challenge, as well as operational inefficiencies, has caused TTPost to no longer operate a "day plus one"

[125] TTPost has the lowest rates in T&T for the delivery of parcel mail purchased through e-commerce. Its rates start at US$5.50 for the first pound and US$2.50 for every additional pound (TTPost 2016).

[126] The author is aware of this information since he was employed in the Ministry of Public Utilities in Trinidad and Tobago in the capacity of Senior Economic Policy Analyst over the 2010 to 2013 period. The monitoring of the postal sector was part of the author's responsibilities.

[127] The private postal companies do not have a USO mandate. Thus, they operate only profitable postal services. The USO forces TTPost to continue to provide postal services on unprofitable routes. Furthermore, the affordability requirement of the USO prevents the Regulatory Industries Commission (RIC) from raising TTPost's tariffs to high rates.

delivery. A postal code system was introduced by TTPost in 2012, yet its delivery time is still in excess of a "day plus one".

Like the BPS, and the PTD, TTPost is reliant upon government subventions in order to remain in operation. In fact, TTPost received TT$40 million in subventions from the GORTT in the 2012/2013 fiscal year (Singh 2014).

TTPost's challenge has an element of feedback causality. Its annual losses and the reluctance of the GORTT to increase its subventions constrain its ability to increase its service provision as it would require increased expenditure on the acquisition of additional vehicles, the renting of more facilities to act as delivery and distribution centres, and the hiring of more distribution personnel. Yet the delays in TTPost's delivery system continue to erode its customers' confidence, motivating customers to utilize the postal services of private sector postal couriers, resulting in less revenue and higher losses for TTPost. In fact, any attempt to cut costs by reducing staff and closing down distribution centres would lengthen the average delivery time for TTPost.

In order to improve the delivery time of TTPost the organization would need to increase the number of its distribution centres and hire more delivery personnel. Given that a cost is attached to such an investment, TTPost's financial viability can be improved if:

- the GORTT vests the properties of the former Government Post into TTPost;[128]
- TTPost ceases its operation of unprofitable non-core services;[129]

[128] When the Government Post was restricted to forming TTPost in 1999, the properties of the Government Post were supposed to be vested into TTPost. This never occurred. As a result, TTPost must pay rent for several properties to act as distribution centres. If the properties are vested in TTPost, this would reduce TTPost's annual rent bill, thus improving its financial viability.

[129] TTPost's core operations are the delivery of letter, express, and parcel mail to fulfil its USO. The company also operates a series of non-core operations such as bill payment, and stationery stores, to help generate revenue with the intention of helping to subsidize the cost of its core operations. However, both core and non-core operations are unprofitable for TTPost. Therefore, non-core operations add to TTPost's financial loss.

- proper cost accounting is implemented in TTPost, and unnecessary services are terminated;[130] and
- TTPost refrains from cross subsiding activities/projects with government subventions.[131]

Need to Remove the Online Tax

In 2016, the GORTT introduced a levy of 7% on online purchases of goods and services through the internet. While this move was done to help increase the revenue collected by the GORTT, it was an additional cost imposed on the consumer.[132] Additionally, given that so many consumer goods are imported in T&T, an online tax decreases the purchasing power of consumers in T&T.

Since Barbados, Jamaica, and T&T are all part of the CSME, the imposition of an online tax on any imports from any CSME member state would be a violation of the duty-free tariff-free treatment that all members of the common market are supposed to benefit from.

7.7 Conclusion

Many producers in the Caribbean region are SMEs. Many of the SMEs do not have the scale to produce and export large quantities on a frequent basis. However, that does not mean they are ineligible to participate in international trade. In fact, there is scope for any economic agent to participate in e-commerce regardless of their size. Thus, e-commerce presents an opportunity for SMEs in the Caribbean region to expand their market access, earn more revenue, and reap the benefits from trade.

An assessment of the e-readiness of Barbados, Jamaica, and T&T reveals that the countries are very ready for e-commerce. In each of the aforementioned countries, there is a competitive telecommunications market, and affordable access to the internet for all residents. There are a

---

[130] TTPost aggregates the administrative and operational costs of its core activities with those of its non-core activities. Proper cost accounting would highlight exactly which core and non-core operations are unprofitable.

[131] In simplistic terms, if government subventions were received to implement project "X", then they should only be used to finance project "X", not project/activity "Y".

[132] A better mechanism for the GORTT to collect revenue was to focus on the implementation of better revenue collection mechanisms in the private sector in T&T that are supposed to pay taxes but do not do so.

variety of tertiary educational institutions which provide training for people in the area of information technology. The governments of all the aforementioned country also recognize the importance of e-commerce to their country's development, and have attempted to use legal and policy tools to create an adequate enabling environment to encourage e-commerce.

Despite the favourable outlook based on basic e-readiness factors, there is room for improvement in the use of e-commerce in each country. The major policy recommendation to encourage proliferation in each country would be for the public authorities to develop a robust e-commerce online platform. Such a platform should be able to link buyers with vendors, facilitate electronic transactions, while protecting the rights and interests of consumers.

Supporting recommendations would be the implementation of measures to improve the operational efficiency and financial viability of the USO postal courier companies, and removing tariff barriers which attempt to distort cross-border trade.

References

AGD (Auditor General's Department) Jamaica. 2018. "Performance Audit Report Delivery of Public Postal Service in Jamaica." Accessed November 23, 2018. https://auditorgeneral.gov.jm/wp-content/uploads/2018/04/Peformance-Audit-Delivery-of-Postal-Service.pdf.

CSTD (United Nations Commission on Science and Technology for Development). 2018. "Report on Progress made in the Implementation of the Outcomes of the World Summit on the Information Society (WSIS)." Accessed October 11, 2018. https://unctad.org/Sections/un_cstd/docs/cstd_wsis10_trinidad_and_tobago_en.pdf.

El-fitouri, Mohamed Othman. 2015. "E-Commerce in Developing Countries: A Case Study on the Factors Affecting E-commerce Adoption in Libyan Companies." *Int. Journal of Engineering Research and Applications* 1(1): 102-115.

Fonseca-Hoeve, Bionda, Michele Marius, Shernon Osepa, Jane Coffin, and Michael Kende. 2017. "Unleashing the Internet in the Caribbean Removing Barriers to Connectivity and Stimulating Better Access in the Region." Accessed October 23, 2018. https://unctad.org/meetings/en/Contribution/dtl_eWeek2017c06-isoc_en.pdf.

FTC (Fair Trading Commission). 2011. "Telecom Regulation over the Past Decade." Accessed October 26, 2018. https://www.ftc.gov.bb/index.php?option=com_content&task=view&id=211.

—. 2017. "Cable & Wireless (Barbados) Limited Standard of Service 2018-2020." Accessed October 26, 2018. https://www.ftc.gov.bb/library/sos/2017-09-26_commission_decision_sos_candwbl.pdf.

Gereffi, Gary. 1994. "The Organization of Buyer Driven Global Commodity Chains: How US Retailers Shape Overseas Production Networks." In *Commodity Chains and Global Capitalism*, edited by Gary Gereffi and Miguel Korzeniewicz, 95-122. Westport: United States: Praeger Publishers.

Gereffi, Gary. 2001. "Beyond the Producer-driven/Buyer-driven Dichotomy, the Evolution of Global Value Chains in the Internet Era." *IDS Bulletin* 32(3): 30-40.

Golding, Paul, Vanesa Tennant, and Terry-Ann Virtue. 2012. "Telecommunications in Jamaica: Monopoly to Liberalized Competition to Monopoly (2000-2011)." Accessed October 12, 2018. http://www.globdev.org/files/Shanghai%20Proceedings/18%20PAPER%20Telecommunications%20in%20Jamaica%20Sept%202.pdf.

GORTT MTI (Government of the Republic of Trinidad and Tobago Ministry of Trade and Industry). 2017. "National E-Commerce Strategy (2017-2021)." Accessed August 1, 2018. http://www.forwardmultimedia.com/pdf/MIT-e-Commerce-Strategy-2017-2021.pdf.

ITC (International Trade Centre). 2017. "New Pathways to E-commerce: A Global MSME Competitiveness Survey." Accessed November 5, 2018. http://www.intracen.org/publication/New-Pathways-to-E-commerce/.

Labs, Luova. 2018. "In the Red." *Barbados Today,* February 9. Accessed November 23. https://barbadostoday.bb/2018/02/09/in-the-red-4/.

Lawrence, Japhet E., and Usman A. Tar. 2010. "Barriers to E-commerce in Developing Countries." *Information, Society and Justice* 3(1): 23-35.

MCSTJ (Ministry of Commerce, Science & Technology, Jamaica). 2003. "Electronic Transactions Policy." Accessed November 6, 2018. http://unpan1.un.org/intradoc/groups/public/documents/caricad/unpan009914.pdf.

MIIDCSBD (Ministry of Industry, International Business, Commerce and Small Business Development). 2018. "The Opening of an E-Commerce Seminar On 'How to Obtain Your E-Business Drive?'." Accessed November 6, 2018. http://www.commerce.gov.bb/index.php/list-all/

130-the-opening-of-an-ecommerce-seminar-on-how-to-obtain-your-e-business-drive.
Patel, Trushar, and Premal Soni. 2013. "E-commerce in Developing Countries." *Oriental Journal of Computer Science & Technology* 6(3): 357-361.
PRTT (Parliament of the Republic of Trinidad and Tobago). 2014. "Twenty-third Report of the Joint Select Committee Appointed to inquire into and report on Government Ministries, Statutory Authorities and State Enterprises (Group 2): On an inquiry into the Administration and Operations of the Telecommunications Services of Trinidad and Tobago (TSTT)." Accessed October 9, 2018. http://www.ttparliament.org/reports/p10-20150529-s5-J-GMSASE-R23-TSTT.pdf.
Sinanan, Avory, Robert C. Atkinson, and Donald Bowles. 2008. "Reference No: 4/7/06/04: In the Matter of an Arbitration Telecommunications Authority of Trinidad and Tobago Section 82 of the Telecommunications Act 2001 between Digicel (Trinidad and Tobago) Limited Complainant and Telecommunications Services of Trinidad and Tobago Limited Respondent." Accessed October 9, 2018. https://tatt.org.tt/Portals/0/Documents/Dispute%20Decision%20No.%202.pdf.
Singh, Nadaleen. 2014. "TTpost: Managing our Subventions." *Trinidad Guardian Newspaper*, August 21. Accessed October 23, 2018. http://www.guardian.co.tt/article-6.2.386732.7fee49fe73.
SMA (Spectrum Management Authority). 2005. "Telecommunications in Jamaica and the Caribbean Present Scenario and Perspectives." Accessed October 23, 2018. https://www.sma.gov.jm/sites/default/files/Telecommunications_in_Jamaica_and_the_Caribbean.pdf.
TATT (Telecommunications Authority of Trinidad and Tobago). 2013. "The Digital Divide Survey Trinidad and Tobago, 2013." Accessed October 11, 2018. https://tatt.org.tt/Portals/0/documents/Digital%20Divide%20Survey2013_FINAL%2017-01-2014-reduced.pdf.
—. 2017. "Annual Report 2016." Accessed October 9, 2018. https://tatt.org.tt/DesktopModules/Bring2mind/DMX/Download.aspx?Command=Core_Download&EntryId=983&PortalId=0&TabId=222.
Telecommunications Unit. 2017. "ICT Statistics for Barbados 2017." Accessed October 26, 2018. http://www.telecoms.gov.bb/website/index.php?option=com_content&view=article&id=25&Itemid=127.

T&T Newsday (Trinidad and Tobago Newsday). 2005. "Digicel, Laqtel end TSTT Monopoly." *T&T Newsday*, June 24. Accessed October 9, 2018. https://archives.newsday.co.tt/2005/06/24/digicel-laqtel-end-tstt-monopoly/.

T&T Guardian (Trinidad and Tobago Guardian). 2016. "Online Purchases Get 7% Tax." Accessed October 18, 2018. https://www.guardian.co.tt/news/online-purchases-get-7-tax-6.2.352784.75ea24b8c9.

TTPost (Trinidad and Tobago Postal Corporation). 2016. "Ecommerce Services – Hummingbird Express Online Shopping Service." Accessed November 18, 2018. http://ttpost.net/index.php/ecommerce-services-hummingbird-express-online-shopping-service/.

TSTT (Telecommunications Services of Trinidad and Tobago Limited). 2018. "Corporate History." Accessed October 9, 2018. http://www.tstt.co.tt/corporate-history.

UWI (University of the West Indies) Mona. 2014. "Electronic Transactions Policy: Jamaica." Accessed November 08, 2018. https://www.mona.uwi.edu/cop/groups/eduexchange-impact-liberalisation-telecommunication-jamaica/electronic-transactions-policy.

White, Gareth R.T., Ademola Afolayan, and Eoin Plant. 2014. "Chapter 2: Challenges to the Adoption of E-commerce Technology for Supply Chain Management in a Developing Economy: A Focus on Nigerian SMEs." In *E-commerce Platform Acceptance,* 23-39. New York City, United States: Springer Publishing.

CHAPTER EIGHT

GENERAL CONCLUSION

8.1 Book Summary

It is true that it is not necessary for a country to produce every part of a product in order to engage in trade. In fact, it is possible for countries to specialize in the production of a few intermediate stages in the global value chain for a final product. However, a global value chain analysis of an industry reveals an entire network of activities which is feasible for a country and its producers to participate in. Moreover, the analysis reveals the potential for upgrading and how a country and its stakeholders may capture more value from an industry.

The fragmentation of production stages has profound implications for the Caribbean Community (CARICOM) region. Each segment of the global value chain in each of the region's industries, presents different opportunities for creating backward and forward linkages. Moreover, the prospects for upgrading are dependent on the regional stakeholders' present position, their supply side constraints, international trade barriers, and factor endowments. Nevertheless, governments can help stakeholders capture more value from global value chains if they use their policy tools to create the right enabling environment.

Chapter Two of this book applied the global value chain analysis framework to the agriculture sector in Trinidad and Tobago (T&T). An important finding was T&T's lack of comparative advantage in primary agriculture. The Government of the Republic of Trinidad and Tobago (GORTT) may continue its current approach and provide various incentives to farmers to stimulate primary agricultural production. Such primary agriculture should be focused to help safeguard an amount of domestic production so that farmers can earn an income, and the country's food import bill could be partially reduced. The government should focus its agricultural trade strategy on areas in which the country has a comparative advantage. These areas include the ammonia, urea, and fertilizer industries, and the agro-processing industry.

T&T has multiple training programmes in primary agriculture and agro-processing. It would be commendable for small-scale farmers to functionally upgrade into agro-processing. The same praiseworthy accomplishment would be generated if more SMEs are able to export their products. To this end, the GORTT can consider utilizing an agency such as the Trinidad and Tobago Agribusiness Association (TTABA) to provide mentorship and technical support to SMEs in agro-processing and export.

Product upgrading to increase the output of the ammonia, urea, and fertilizer industries should be attractive to the GORTT since it provides a better netback than the export of liquefied natural gas (LNG). Several of the country's natural gas supply contracts were scheduled to expire over the 2013 to 2018 period. In renegotiating new natural gas supply contracts, the government must find the delicate balance between capturing the best value for natural gas for the people of T&T and remaining competitive enough to retain its existing multinational investment.

Chapter Three performed a global value chain analysis of T&T's maritime sector. The Ministry of Trade and Industry (MTI) identified port operations, ship repair, leisure marine (yachting) and marine services as key sub-industries of the country's maritime sector. Notable challenges in the country's maritime sector include operational inefficiency at the ports, the inefficiency of the customs division and immigration division, labour inefficiencies, declining yacht arrivals, piracy and illegal trade in the Gulf of Paria.

If the GORTT wants the maritime sector and its sub-industries to make sustainable contributions to the economy of T&T, it needs to take policy action to address these challenges. Labour productivity should have a high priority since it affects the speed and ease in which containers are cleared at the port. Chapter Three recommended that labour should be hired on the basis of qualifications and competence rather than seniority. Additionally, labour should be compensated based on the achievement of deliverables rather than being allocated a fixed monthly salary that is completely detached from productivity. If the government is unable to improve labour productivity, then it should make a bold move and privatize the port. It is noteworthy that privatization will not be a popular idea among trade unions as it may result in the loss of jobs. However, if the government cannot properly manage business it should stay out of business and focus on policy, legislation, and regulation.

Disputes between importers and the Customs Division tend to occur on the classification and value of items as they affect the amount of customs duty that must be paid for clearance. This can be resolved by the reform of the customs clearance system to one that has fewer classifications and charges a lower and more homogenous customs duty for goods. The operational efficiency of the Customs Division can also be improved by the greater use of the Automated System for Customs Data – ASYCUDA World (AW).

The Immigration Division has an important role to play in the extension of time for yachting tourists. The government can consider improving the provision of immigration services by the reopening of the Immigration and Customs office in Chaguaramas. Also, the government can simplify the entry process by utilizing one simple entry form to collect the information from the yachting tourist rather than multiple forms.

The occurrence of piracy and trade of illegal goods in the Gulf of Paria is partially linked to the insecurity of T&T's coastal boarder. This can be addressed by increasing the patrols of the coast guard. The GORTT has expressed its intention to purchase new offshore patrol vessels from Australia. When they arrive, they will enable the coast guard to engage in patrols and secure the country's maritime borders.

There is room for greater collaboration with the private sector to strengthen the country's maritime sector. The collaboration could result in more maritime events which can attract more yachting tourists. By another token, collaboration with foreign private sector firms can bring the required FDI for product and process upgrades in the ship repair sector.

Chapter Four analysed the banana value chain of the Commonwealth of Dominica, and explored how it may build climate resilience in its banana industry. The country is small and has a predominant mountain terrain that favours tree crop cultivation. Historically, the country relied on banana exports to the European Union (EU) market under the Lomé and Contonou agreements. However, multilateral trade liberalization and the formation of the World Trade Organization (WTO) eventually led to the erosion of its banana trade preferences. The country's banana industry is also challenged by its frequent impacts by hurricanes. In fact, as recent as 2017, the country was hit by Hurricanes Irma and Maria, which completely devastated the banana harvest. Definitely, there is a need for a climate resilient strategy.

The farmers in Dominica are small scale and occupy the primary production stage of the banana global value chain. Since the output of Dominica's individual farmers is small relative to the large-scale producers in Latin America, they (Dominica's farmers) tend to be price takers and have little to no market power. The true power in the banana global value chain resides with the retailers and the large supermarket chains. Although the value chain is predominantly buyer-driven, there is hope for the remaining farmers to earn a living from the prices offered through fair trade bananas.

Agriculture insurance has been used to help mitigate the loss of banana farmers. The Windward Island Crop Insurance Ltd. (WINCROP), the sole agency providing agriculture insurance in the Eastern Caribbean, only provides coverage against 20% of any losses. There is a purview for the private-public partnership model to be used to develop a more scaled-up banana insurance for the farmers.

As part of a climate resilience strategy, the Government of Dominica has announced its intention to establish the Climate Resilient Execution Agency for Dominica (CREAD), an organization with the mandate of coordinating the country's climate resilience projects over a four-year period. Some excellent climate resilience projects for consideration would be the installation of early warning systems, ecological restoration, and capacity building for better soil management practices.

The global value chain analysis revealed that a lot of products can be produced from bananas and banana by-products. As a result, Chapter Four recommends that Dominica should take steps towards functional upgrading into the agro-processing of bananas, and the processing of banana products. Partnerships should be sought with established agro-processers to help build domestic capacity, facilitate knowledge spill-over, and allow for the greater capture of value from the banana value chain for the citizens of Dominica.

Chapter Five highlights the key elements of a local content policy (LCP) that is required to capture value for the citizens in a hydrocarbon exporting economy. Successful and effective LCPs should have local content requirements (LCRs) for the employment of local labour, the awarding of contracts to local contractors, the utilization of domestically produced inputs, and the utilization of local services. These LCRs help to develop the capacity of the locals through the learning-by-doing process.

Both T&T and Guyana have commercial reserves of hydrocarbons. T&T's hydrocarbon industry is mature, and thus, it currently has an LCP. But the absence of local content requirements (LCRs) in T&T's LCP undermines its effectiveness in the capturing of value for nationals. Recognizing the deficiency, the GORTT attempted to correct the problem in 2006 by introducing LCRs in its procurement provisions for production haring contracts (PSCs). While this was a step in the right direction, more work needs to be done to strengthen the country's overall LCP.

It is noteworthy that T&T captures value from its hydrocarbon industry from the energy taxes earned by the government, the employment of nationals in the hydrocarbon industry, and the corporate social responsibility (CSRs) programmes implemented by the multinational energy companies (MECs). Notwithstanding, T&T's greatest success in local content can be seen in its platform fabrication experience with Trinidad Offshore Fabricators Ltd. (TOFCO) in La Brea. Certainly, the TOFCO experience clearly demonstrates how international partnerships can be used to build domestic capacities.

Trade Related Investment Measures (TRIMs) stand out as a significant obstacle for the implementation of LCPs and LCRs. The WTO's TRIMs agreement prohibits WTO members from applying measures that discriminate against or restrict the output of foreign products in favour of local products. However, the United States (US), a country that was eager to raise a dispute at the WTO against India for its "Make in India" and "Digital India" programmes, operates preferential treatment and "buy local" requirements in several of its states. Assuredly, there is a double standard in the scrutinizing of preferential treatment. In fact, it is the double standards in trade liberalization that caused the Doha multilateral round of trade negotiations to stall.

All trading partners are not equal. Developing countries are faced with a myriad of challenges that constrain their economic growth and development. Therefore, developing countries should be allowed to operate LCPs and LCRs to help develop their domestic capacity. Perhaps developing countries should implement LCPs and LCRs with some other name, rather than "local content" as practised in the US in order to avoid WTO disputes.

Guyana is mobilizing to become a major hydrocarbon producer and exporter from 2020. A robust LCP would effectively allow the country to develop backward and forward linkages between its hydrocarbon sector and non-hydrocarbon sector. Moreover, an effective LCP would allow the national stakeholders in the industry to be true participants rather than spectators.

In Chapter Six, the energy insecurity of the CARICOM member states is given attention. The region tends to be a net importer and consumer of crude oil, and oil-based fuels for its energy consumption needs. But oil prices are volatile, often resulting in unexpected increases and the corresponding increase in the energy import bills of the member states. Withal, the combustion of oil-based fuels releases a high amount of anthropogenic carbon, contributing to a global temperature rise via the greenhouse effect, and causing climate change. As SIDS, the region is highly vulnerable to climate change. Thus, it would be in the region's best interest if there is increased global action to limit global temperature rise and mitigate the effect of climate change.

Solar energy is recognized as a climate change mitigation project by the United Nations Framework Convention on Climate Change (UNFCCC). Presently, there are multiple firms implementing solar photovoltaic system installations in the CARICOM region. An analysis of the solar photovoltaic value chain reveals that this is just one segment of the entire chain. There are segments for the production of silicon crystals, ingots, wafers, cells, and modules before the final installation segment. Globally, it is the countries that are strong in research that tend to dominate the upstream segments of the solar photovoltaic system value chain. Unless there is strong collaboration between CARICOM stakeholders and international partners in research, CARICOM's producers are best suited to enter the solar photovoltaic system value chain from the cells, modules, and final installation segments. These segments represent a lucrative business since solar cells, solar modules, inverters, trackers, mounting structures, general electrical components, and final installation represent over 60% of the value in the solar photovoltaic system value chain.

There are a number of barriers which hinder the natural free market development of the solar energy industry in the CARICOM region. The upfront capex cost, information asymmetry, the lack of understanding by consumers about potential cost savings that would be generated through the economies of scale, and the licence requirements for independent power producers (IPPs), are some of the barriers towards solar energy development across the region.

Therefore, government policy is needed to foster a better enabling environment for solar energy. Policy incentives such as the use of feed-in-tariffs (FITs), the introduction of energy rebates, the removal of licence requirements for solar energy IPPs, as well as public education campaigns can stimulate the domestic demand for solar photovoltaic systems. From the supply side, the regional governments interested in the development of the solar photovoltaic industry can consider encouraging private sector stakeholders to develop their productive capacity, and work towards the gradual achievement of export competitiveness. Such a demand and supply framework can un-pause the development of the regional solar energy industry while generating commercial and employment opportunities.

Finally, Chapter Seven presents the last case study, and it explores the prospects of unlocking the electronic commerce (e-commerce) highway to create increased commercial opportunities for SMEs in three selective CARICOM member states, Barbados, Jamaica, and T&T. The development towards better cross-border trade opportunities should be of interest to the regional governments since they all have a large number of SMEs. Furthermore, the SMEs are also part of the pool of voters that put the politicians in office.

Regional cross border e-commerce is proposed since the SMEs are likely to lack the scale to export large quantities on a frequent basis, but are likely to be able to produce small quantities based on the customer's requirements. Assuredly, the internet and e-commerce create mobility that can trade liberalize even the smallest of producers.

Government policy is required to make e-commerce a reality. One policy recommendation is for the government to provide greater support to the local postal service companies to help them improve their postal service delivery. This is also justified since the local postal service companies are financially strained from carrying the Universal Service Obligation (USO) in the face of declining traditional letter mail volumes, which eventually results in the governments providing them (the local postal companies) with subventions to stay in operation. In fact, increased parcel mail from e-commerce can improve the financial viability of the local postal companies.

The other major policy recommendation is for the governments to create an e-commerce platform to facilitate e-commerce within the region. Of course, the created platform should protect the information of consumers and sellers, provide a secure window to facilitate transactions, and have strong policies to protect the interests of both consumers and sellers.

Once implemented properly, the e-commerce platform as well as the more efficient local postal couriers can help with trade facilitation for the SMEs.

8.2 Future Work

Future research can investigate the role played by services in CARICOM's value chains, explore the patterns of specialization, highlight the gains from specialization, and identify the trade barriers that need to be removed in order to allow SMEs to benefit from trade services.

CARICOM's services industry is multi-faceted and includes the music industry, the festivals industry, the offshore medical education industry, the finance and banking industry, and the tourism industry. The development and the export readiness of the services industries are highly differentiated across member states, and across sub-industries. Some services industries are well established in member states. For example, Barbados and T&T have well established carnival industries. Other services industries are in an embryonic stage with a limited regulation and legal framework. For example, in the offshore medical education industry, several private sector investors tend to open new offshore medical universities (OMUs) in Caribbean countries with little to no domestic regulation.

It is justifiable for the regional governments to encourage the development of services industries since they draw on the creativity of local artists, cultural entrepreneurs, and SMEs, and generate sustainable employment opportunities.

There is tremendous talent held by SMEs in the region's music industry. But the music industry faces unique challenges such as copyright and intellectual property issues, difficulties in royalty collection for new market entrants, and rigidities in market access to developed country markets for new artists. From an institutional perspective, there is limited collection and availability of data on services and the economic rent earned by various stakeholders within domestic value chains.

The region's festivals industry ties economic commerce to the unique caribbean identity. Indeed, Barbados' Cropover Festival, the Reggae Sunsplash and Sumfest in Jamaica, Santo Domingo's Festival de Merengue,[133] St. Kitts' Music Festival, St. Lucia's Jazz Festival, and T&T's Carnival are all manifestations of the region's rich cultural heritage. These festivals cause a significant increase in visitor arrivals, airlifts, and hotel and

[133] Santo Domingo is the capital of the Dominican Republic. While the Dominican Republic is not a CARICOM member state it is part of the Caribbean Forum of the African, Caribbean and Pacific Group of States (CARIFORUM) bloc.

other accomodation facilities' occupancy rates. This in turn is accompanied by a positive multiplier effect which increases the commercial opportunities for the local transportation, chartered tours, clothing, food, and beverage sub-industries. Unfortunately, the negative publicity generated when tourists fall victim to various crimes during and around the festival period threatens to undermine the growth in tourist arrivals.

In the offshore medical education industry, the OMUs provide a series of economic benefits to the host economies, including: i) expenditures by students and faculty as they spend on accommodation, travel, personal expenses and other consumer goods and services; ii) the corporate and student taxes paid by the medical universities and their enrolled students; iii) the income tax paid by the local faculty staff in the medical universities; and iv) the tariffs charged upon imported products. But there is still a leakage of value in the OMU industry as there is a tendency for the universities to hire foreigners as faculty staff, the international medical graduates (IMGs) emigrate back to North America for their clinical internships, and there is a general absence of health services support provided by the OMUs to the communities in the host countries.

The banking sector in the region is relatively well developed. However, increased scrutiny in the financial sector by international financial regulators and authorities threatens to undermine and weaken the region's banking sector. Moreover, the loss in correspondent banking relationships threatens the potential of SMEs to reap the benefits from cross-border interregional trade.

The tourism industry, which is a significant revenue earner for many CARICOM economies, is faced with increasing competition. Also, there is a dearth of market research conducted about the tourism value chain, constraining the policy makers' ability to keep updated about changes in tastes and preferences which impact demand. What is even more troublesome is that if there is no proper framework for market research to inform policy, SMES could be left specializing in low value-added segments while producers in other countries are transitioning into the higher value-added segments.

It is against this backdrop that unique solutions need to be crafted to address the supply side bottlenecks, and the institutional deficiencies, in order to allow SMEs and other small-scale producers to capture greater value from global value chains.